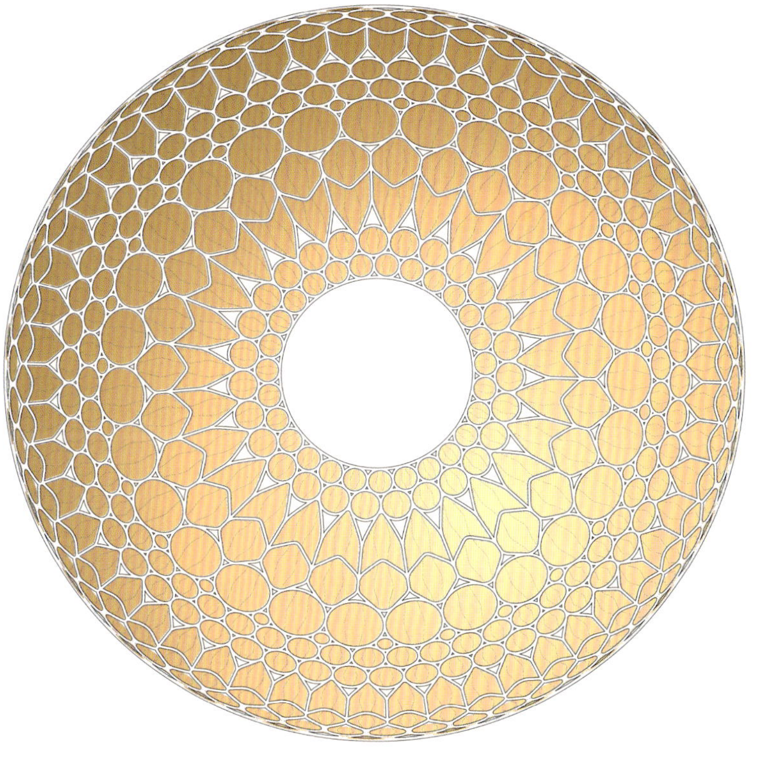

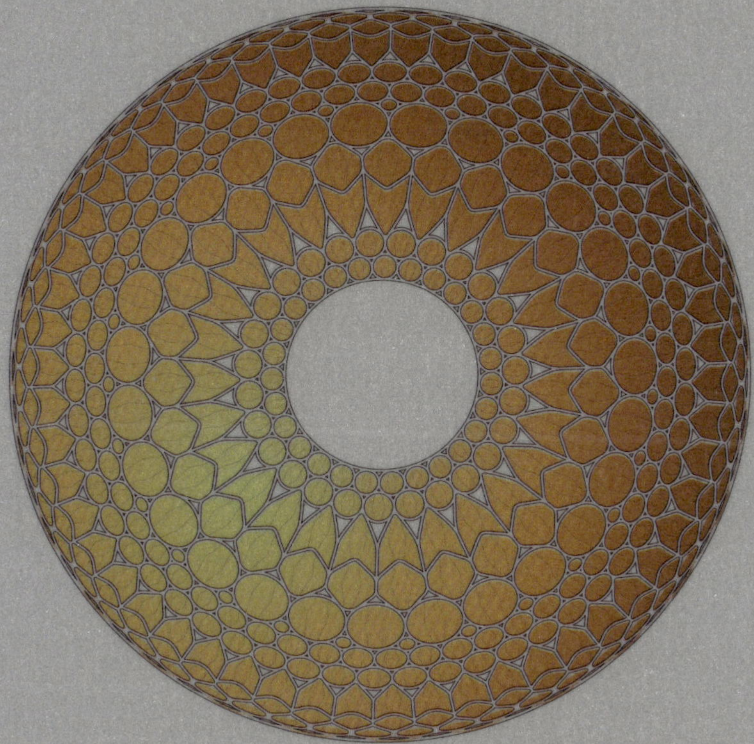

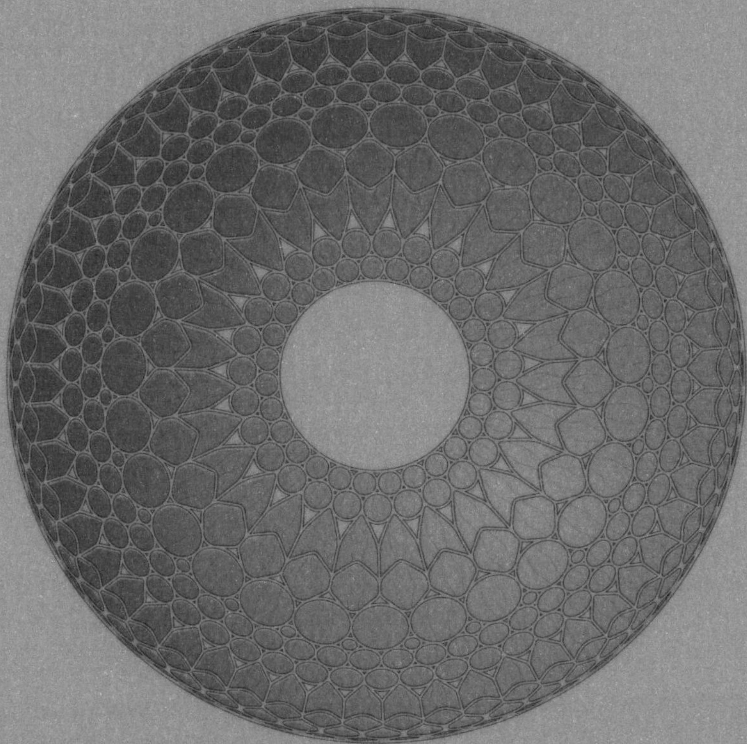

AL WASL PLAZA

DUBAI EXPO 2020

ORO Editions
Publishers of Architecture, Art, and Design
Gordon Goff: Publisher

www.oroeditions.com
info@oroeditions.com

Published by ORO Editions

Project Manager: Jake Anderson

10 9 8 7 6 5 4 3 2 1 First Edition

ISBN: 978-1-954081-83-3

Color Separations and Printing: ORO Group Ltd.
Printed in Spain.

ORO Editions makes a continuous effort to minimize the overall carbon footprint of its publications. As part of this goal, ORO Editions, in association with Global ReLeaf, arranges to plant trees to replace those used in the manufacturing of the paper produced for its books. Global ReLeaf is an international campaign run by American Forests, one of the world's oldest nonprofit conservation organizations. Global ReLeaf is American Forests' education and action program that helps individuals, organizations, agencies, and corporations improve the local and global environment by planting and caring for trees.

In Memory of Eric Tomich, FAIA

EXPO 2020 DUBAI UAE

A S G G ADRIAN SMITH + GORDON GILL ARCHITECTURE

ORO EDITIONS

TABLE OF CONTENTS

H.E. REEM AL HASHIMI

MINISTER OF STATE AND MANAGING DIRECTOR FOR THE DUBAI WORLD EXPO 2020

FOREWORD

It has been five years in its making, since the Expo 2020 Dubai Client team invited, and ultimately engaged, Adrian Smith + Gordon Gill Architecture to create an architecture that celebrates and defines the heart and soul of Expo 2020 Dubai.

The result is Al Wasl Plaza: a project that has re-written the definition of what public space can be and has brought to the World an experiential architecture that defines not only the 2020 Expo but also the Legacy heart of the District 2020 neighborhood. Framed by two hotels and three office buildings, the central park and trellis structure came to life and opened to the World on September 30th, 2021.

This project embodies the highest of sustainable principles and defines them from a cultural, social, environmental, and economic perspective. Its legacy vision ensures that this project will live on forever as the gift of the Expo to the people of Dubai and the Emirates.

This book delves into the design and making of Al Wasl Plaza from the definition of the design brief and the hopes and wishes of the Client, to the vision and concept of the Architectural team. The book highlights the depth of investigation, the innovations, and the details that were involved in the design and execution of the project. It celebrates the team aspect of the project that brought together a cadre of talent from around globe to deliver the world's largest immersive projection experience.

It was a pleasure to be an integral part of this journey and it has been my great reward to experience the realization of this most amazing space. A wonder for Dubai and gift to the people of the world.

Ahmed Al Khatib
Chief Development and Delivery Officer
Real Estate and Delivery
Bureau Expo Dubai 2020

AL WASL PLAZA
MOBILITY

OPPORTUNITY
SUSTAINABILITY

AL WASL PLAZA: A WORLD CLASS DESTINATION

Al Wasl is the historical name for what is now Dubai. The Arabic phrase translates to connection in English and symbolizes Dubai's goal of bringing people together for Expo 2020 as well as the plaza's physical location at the center of the Expo 2020 district. The project is historic. It represents much more than a place. Al Wasl is a physical and spiritual representation of the history, culture, dynamic present, and ambitious future of Dubai. It embodies the Expo 2020 theme Connecting Minds, Creating the Future, serving as a platform for gathering, idea exchange, and entertainment.

World Expos have always been an opportunity to recognize and accelerate the growth of the host city, the country and even the greater region. They mark a moment in time, when the organizing government is ready to make significant investment in the city's design and infrastructure to be showcased for millions of international visitors. Inserted in dynamic cultures; expos are developed to attract visitors and local development to the area. They provide an opportunity to expand previous city planning and incorporate innovative models of development to serve the needs of current and future populations. They attract global talent and can extend the host's leadership, influence, and recognition globally.

Expo 2020 is in Dubai South City, an emerging 145 sq. km. master planned city "based on the happiness of the individual"; a location where the expo is poised to spur further innovation and success. The master plan forms three petals that stem from Al Wasl, which represent the three Expo 2020 subthemes of Mobility, Opportunity, and Sustainability. The Al Wasl site, at the heart of the expo, was an opportunity to connect, anchor, and frame the overall expo experience at its core.

In the original master plan, developed in early 2015 by the global architectural and planning firm HOK, the central Al Wasl parcel was surrounded by two- and three-story buildings. In late 2015, Expo 2020 Dubai invited several world-renowned architects to envision the site. Some of the competition entries were tall, sculptural objects proposed to visually anchor the site in response to the ring of lower buildings. These significantly scaled designs intended to amaze and attract the visitor's attention yet were lacking a higher goal: a legacy vision. A sculptural object may showcase innovation and draw visitors but does not necessarily create a enduring community and gathering space for both expo visitors and legacy residents. A grander embodiment of the spirit of the theme, Connecting Minds, Creating the Future, was possible.

Around the same time, Adrian Smith + Gordon Gill Architecture (AS+GG) was hired by Expo 2020 to design District 2020, the post-event legacy master plan. In addition to the central space, the streets of the original 1,000-plus acre expo event master plan are lined with vibrant, but temporary, country pavilions. One of the most important attributes of this expo is the United Arab Emirates and the Expo leadership's commitment to post-event legacy to sustain a lively, livable district after the six-month event. AS+GG's charge was to convert the event master plan into a vibrant mixed-use community - a local ecosystem - with all necessary community functions. It was during the legacy design development that AS+GG's architects and urban planners identified the central space as an opportunity for public gathering. Not only should this be a lively public square, but it had the potential to increase value within the district and act as a central anchor for the master plan while also inspiring and entertaining Expo 2020 visitors and legacy residents alike.

AS+GG's concept for Al Wasl Plaza is to define the identity of a district with a public space. A node designed as a pedestrian friendly, lushly planted sunken garden covered by a monumental trellis shade structure and incorporating technology to create a full 360-degree visual and audio immersive experience. This concept was well received by the Expo leadership team. In late 2016, AS+GG was awarded the contract to implement this vision for Al Wasl along with the five surrounding, mid-rise structures.

Public plazas are important in fostering interaction between people and their communities. They have anchored ancient towns and modern cities for centuries around the globe. The public plaza was also an important space in traditional UAE communities. In the fast-paced development of Dubai, there has been a decline in defined public outdoor urban spaces as centers due to the modernization and widespread adoption of air conditioning. The design for Al Wasl Plaza is bringing back this typology and repositioned it into the contemporary urban public realm in Dubai.

Dubai is a modern, vibrant city in every way. It is a global leader in business and commerce and is culturally diverse, attracting talent from around the world. AS+GG recognized the opportunity to insert a public space surrounded by beautiful buildings that can bring joy to visitors and residents. In Dubai, due to its hot desert climate, interactive, public life occurs primarily in indoor spaces, such as shopping malls, throughout the city. The architectural team knew that this was a challenge to create a space for gathering outdoors and proceeded to envision a new type of outdoor public space not currently found in Dubai or the world; a bold vision that enhances the natural environment with technology.

Reinventing the typology of the urban public space had the potential to unite the Expo 2020 Dubai district. The intent for Al Wasl Plaza was to create an "Urban Room"; a "Room for Living" to serve as a platform for celebrations and human interaction during the expo and legacy phases. Because of its unique trellis shade structure, visitors can take advantage of the site and enjoy it on even the hottest days of the year. Priority was placed on creating a sustainable legacy; to minimize the impact on natural resources and maximize environmental comfort while limiting the carbon footprint. The methodology and typology of this new form of urban public space, sets a precedent that will influence the future of planning in the region. This ideological shift is a gift to the legacy and future of those who will work, play, and live in the district for generations after the expo. Al Wasl Plaza will serve as a reference for future urban development promoting social interaction in technologically advanced public space.

This book highlights the inspiration and innovation employed by AS+GG in the design of Al Wasl Plaza. The project includes the garden, the trellis, three office buildings, and two hotel buildings, all of which serve to define the center of Expo 2020. The book focuses on the inspiration and conception of the project with architectural studies, sketches, and models that show the process that led to the final iconic form. The book introduces each of the parcels including the garden, trellis, offices, hotels, the Leadership Pavilion, and the Arrivals Plaza. Each chapter illustrates the design process, architectural details, and the development of the technical systems. The final section summarizes the construction process, sustainability achievements, and looks to the future to reveal the District 2020 Legacy Master Plan concept designed by AS+GG.

Al Wasl Plaza was built to welcome the world to Expo 2020 and will remain for the enjoyment of generations to come. This is the story of how it was created.

1851

LONDON

The Great Exhibition was the first world's fair and was held in the iconic Crystal Palace. It showcased inventions of the Industrial Revolution.

1889

PARIS

The Eiffel Tower served as the entrance arch to the 1889 world's fair, which was the fourth held in Paris.

1958

BRUSSELS

The Atomium is a giant model representing atoms of a cell that opened with a call for world peace and economic progress.

1962

SEATTLE

The Space Needle, a 185-metre-high spire with a revolving restaurant at the top, remains a fixture o the city's skyline in Seattle

2010

SHANGHAI

The theme, Better City, Better Life signified Shanghai's new status in the 21st century as the next great world city.

2015

MILAN

Innovations in food technologies showcased the right to healthy, secure, and sufficient food for the world's inhabitants.

2021

DUBAI

Connecting Minds, Creating the Future aims to create a better world and a lasting legacy that benefits future generations explored through the sub themes opportunity, mobility, and sustainability. It is the first world expo to be held in the Middle East and the largest event ever held in the Arab world. Al Wasl Plaza is the heart of the master plan and the first immersive experience of its kind.

INSPIRATION

Adrian Smith + Gordon Gill Architecture's inspiration for Al Wasl Plaza was driven by a deep understanding of environment and culture. The goal was to develop an engaging central space for the longevity of the legacy District 2020, while also functioning as a central recognizable symbol for Expo 2020 Dubai. This required an architecture that had utility and beauty; an insertion of a new typology of a technologically rich public garden that did not yet exist in Dubai. The centrality of Al Wasl Plaza in the Expo 2020 master plan presented an opportunity to create an urban room; a space that is enveloped all at once by vibrant commerce, natural landscape, and shade. The room evoked a sense of arrival, wonder and awe. The idea was to create a timeless, welcoming, engaging, active, flexible, and memorable public space for generations to enjoy.

To achieve this concept, the circular site required definition. The adjacent buildings were increased in height to a larger presence on the public garden. To maximize shade, surround the park and increase value, buildings were sloped into the plaza increasing their occupiable area towards the top. Stepping also maximized garden views, increased privacy, self-shaded the buildings and the public realm below. The room was enriched with a lush landscape of native trees, understory planting and water features; a refreshing oasis offered as a respite in a thriving urban environment.

To make the park more comfortable and to extend its use thought the year, shade was introduced in the form of a large trellis designed based on the historic ring that defines the Expo 2020 logo. The shade structure and its beautiful, veiled surface would come to life when bathed by the sunlight resulting in a dynamic experience of an ever-changing composition of dappled light and shade below. As the grand enclosure, the trellis serves as both a symbolic inspirational and performative architectural feature enhancing the use of Al Wasl Plaza. Art would enrich the experience of the central space. The shading surface awakens at night as a canvas or screen for night-time projections, extending the use of the trellis structure. The trellis enhances occupant comfort and provides a technology platform for state-of-the-art performances.

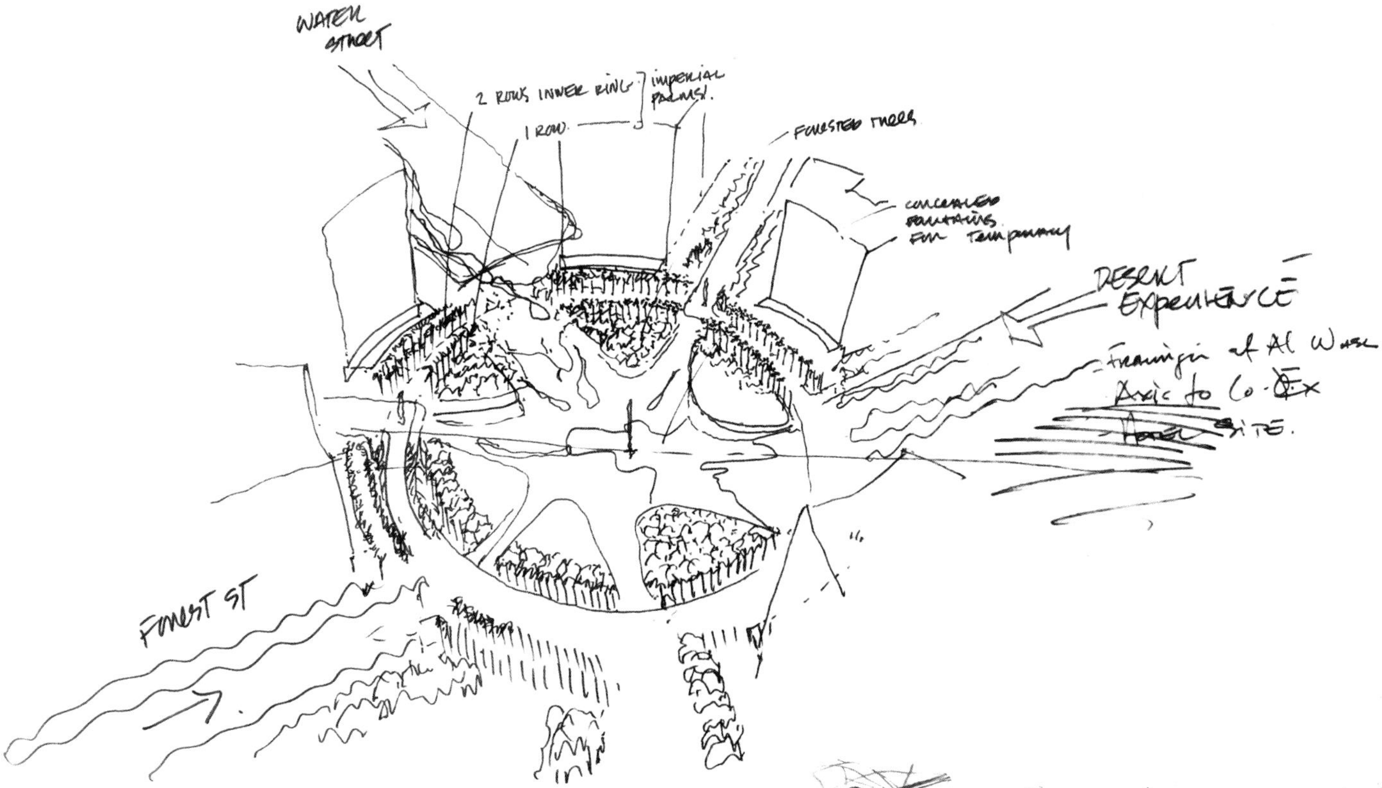

THE CONCEPTION OF AL WASL AS A GARDEN EXPERIENCE

A garden is historically associated with respite, peace, and joyful encounters with nature in a controlled environment. At a small scale, it brings family together at the heart of the house. At the larger scale, it is the place of encounter, relaxation, and community engagement, complementing the busy accelerated urban life. In desert climates, it also provides the benefits of enhancing thermal comfort, bringing flora and fauna to close proximity, and protecting its users from the harsh environment. This understanding of the garden, as a defined space to enrich personal and community life, was the inspiration for it's use at the center of expo event and of the District 2020. Expo 2020 represents a short period of time. The new district, on the other hand, benefits from an enduring asset to extend its legacy and provide identity for its future users. A garden has a timeless ability to enhance the human experience. Urban and architectural design will always find innovative ways to address human needs. Nature, however, will always be central to humankind's well-being. It will always be recognized as a critical public asset.

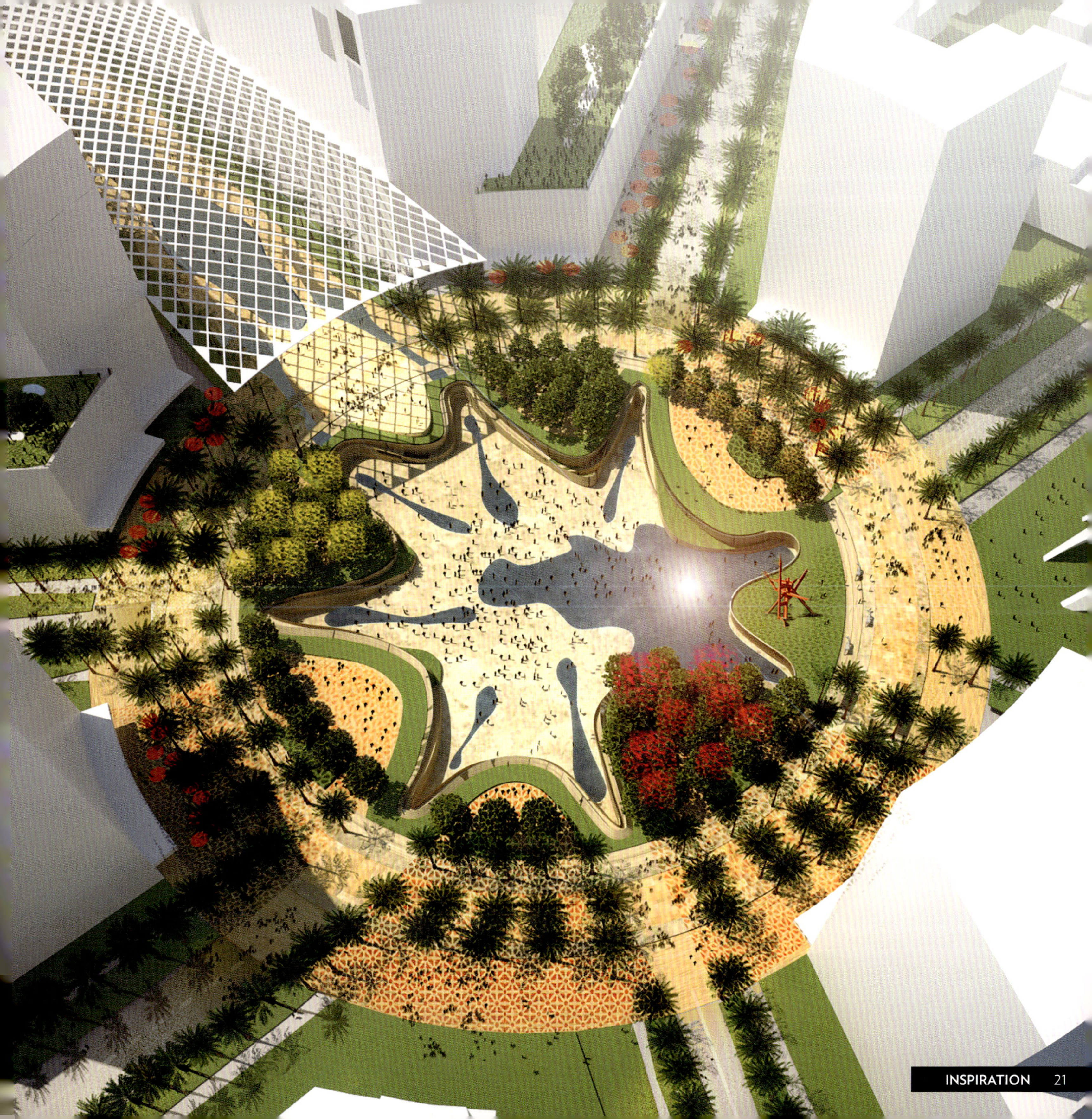

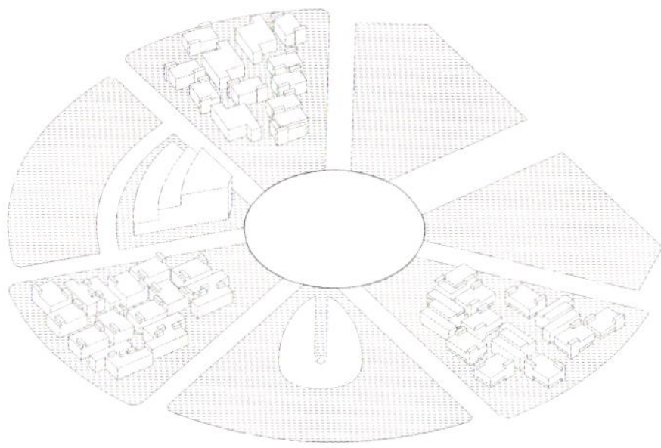

ORIGINAL MASTER PLAN

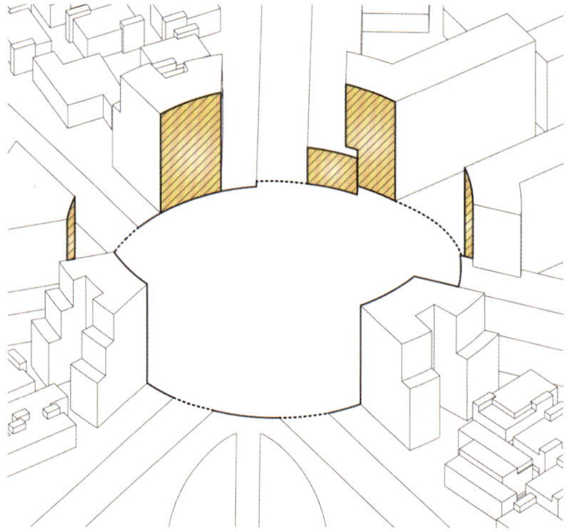

FRAME SPACE WITH ARCHITECTURE

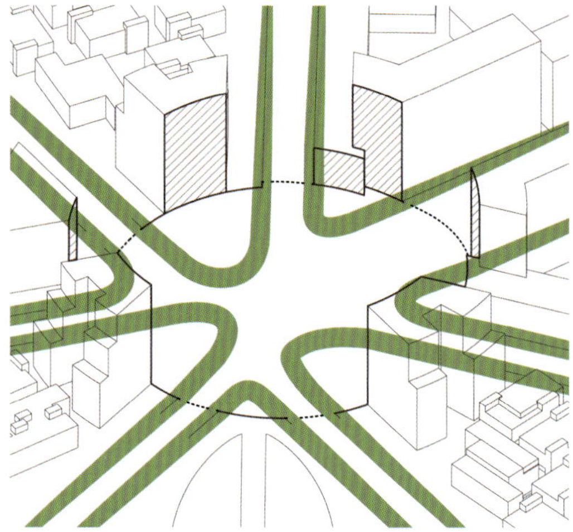

BRING DISTRICTS INTO AL WASL

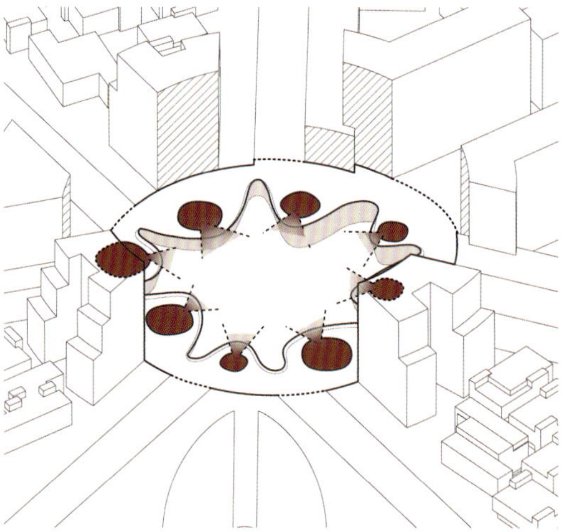

CREATE ELEVATED PLATFORMS FOR MEETING / STAGING / VIEWING

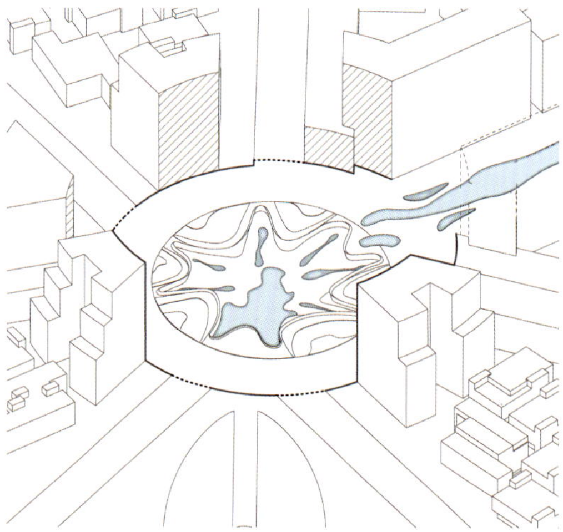

A WADI INSPIRED MEETING SPACE

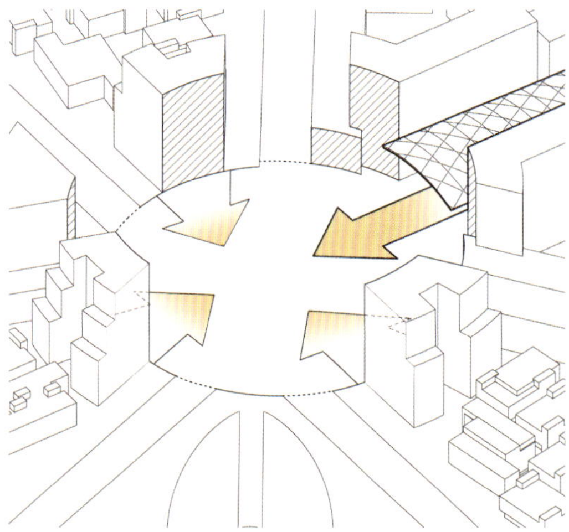

PROGRAM ARRIVAL SCENE FROM METRO AND DISTRICTS

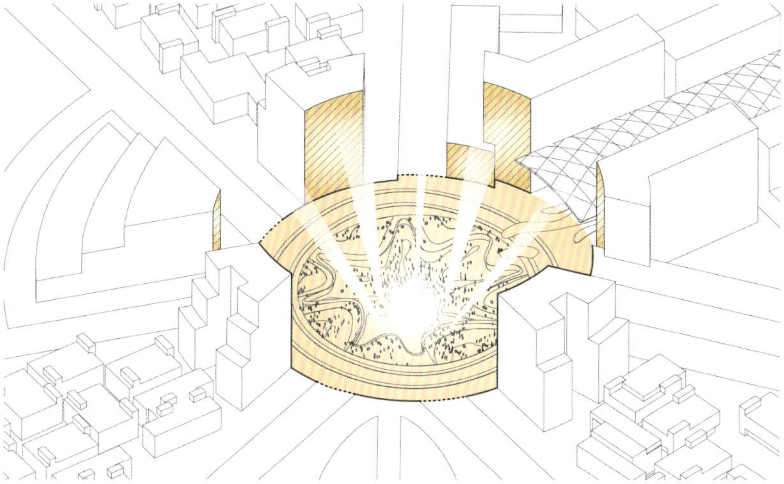

LARGE EVENT EXPERIENCE

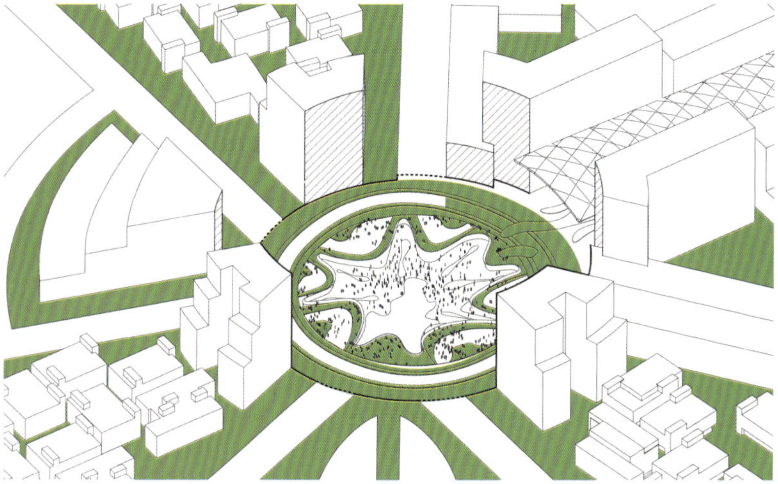

PLAZA TRANSFORMS INTO INTIMATE SETTINGS

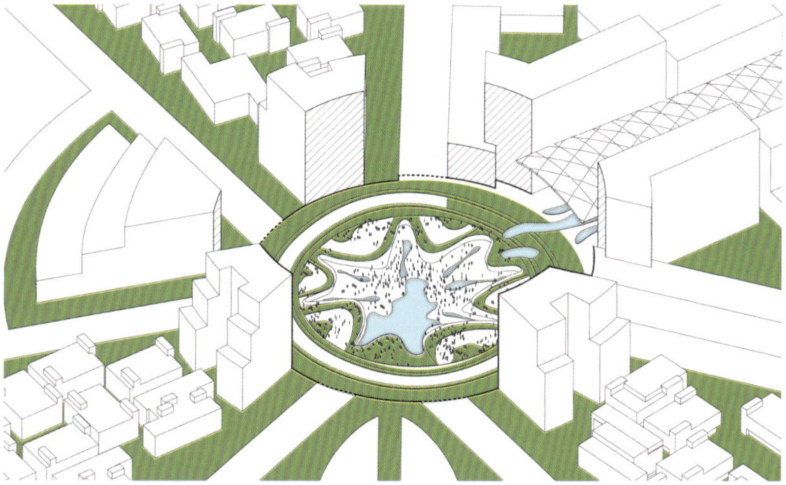

WATER AS PUBLIC AMENITY

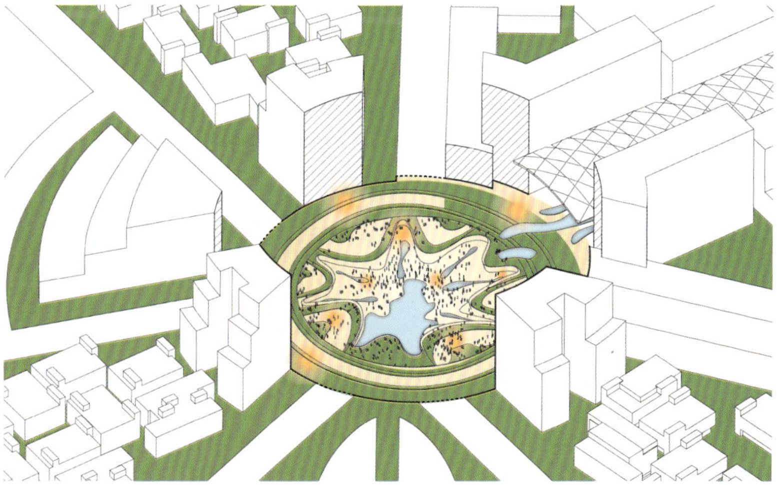

PASTORAL EXPERIENCE

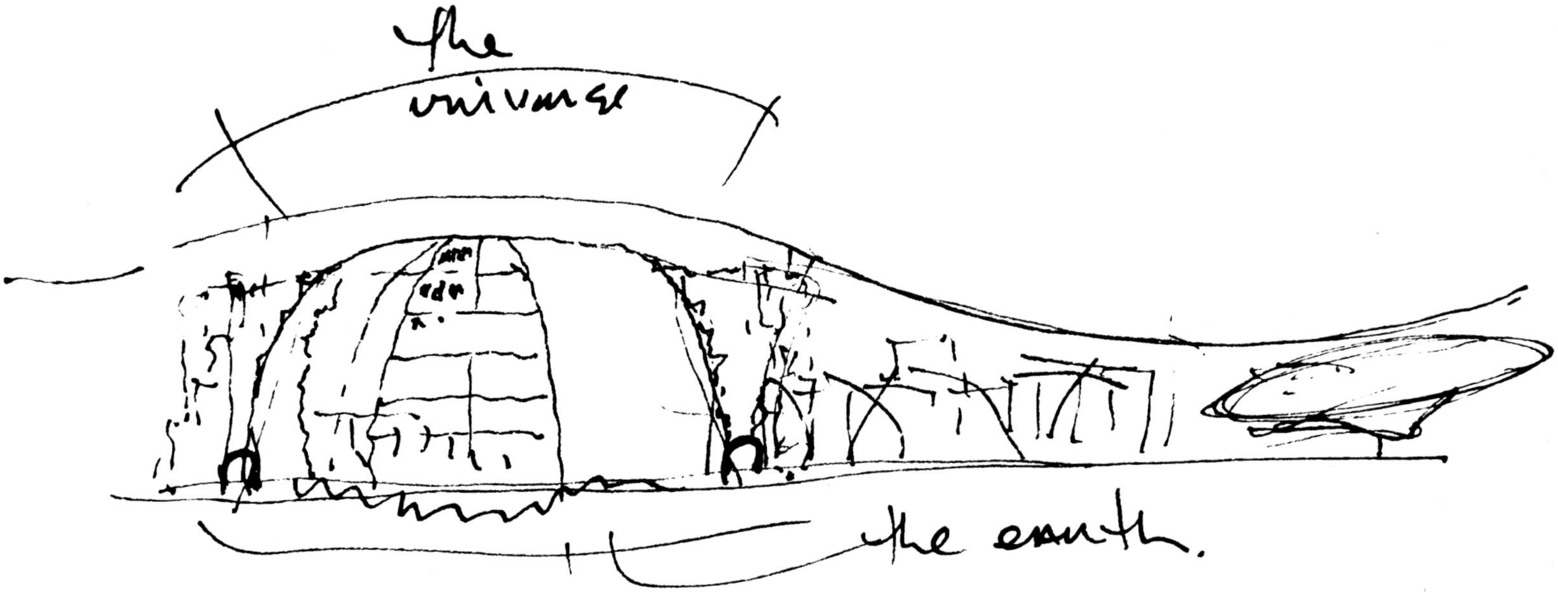

INTRODUCING THE SHADE STRUCTURE

Al Wasl Plaza was designed to create a comfortable microclimate within the hot and humid desert climate in Dubai. Shade is integral increasing the comfort of exterior spaces by reducing the intensity of solar radiation. In Dubai, the addition of shade can extend the usable life of a garden year-round, even in the hottest months of the year in combination with shade trees. The scale, form, and materiality of the shade structure was studied to define the garden and give it an identity unique to Expo 2020. To encompass the 150-meter diameter plaza, the shade system needed to be robust, requiring substantial structural support. It also needed to have an established relationship with the other elements of Al Wasl. Therefore, several shade structures were studied including forms that integrated with the adjacent buildings, offset from the buildings, and smaller scaled forms closer to the garden level. The design studies also included smaller-scale panels organized in a geometric pattern to support the veil of tensile fabric.

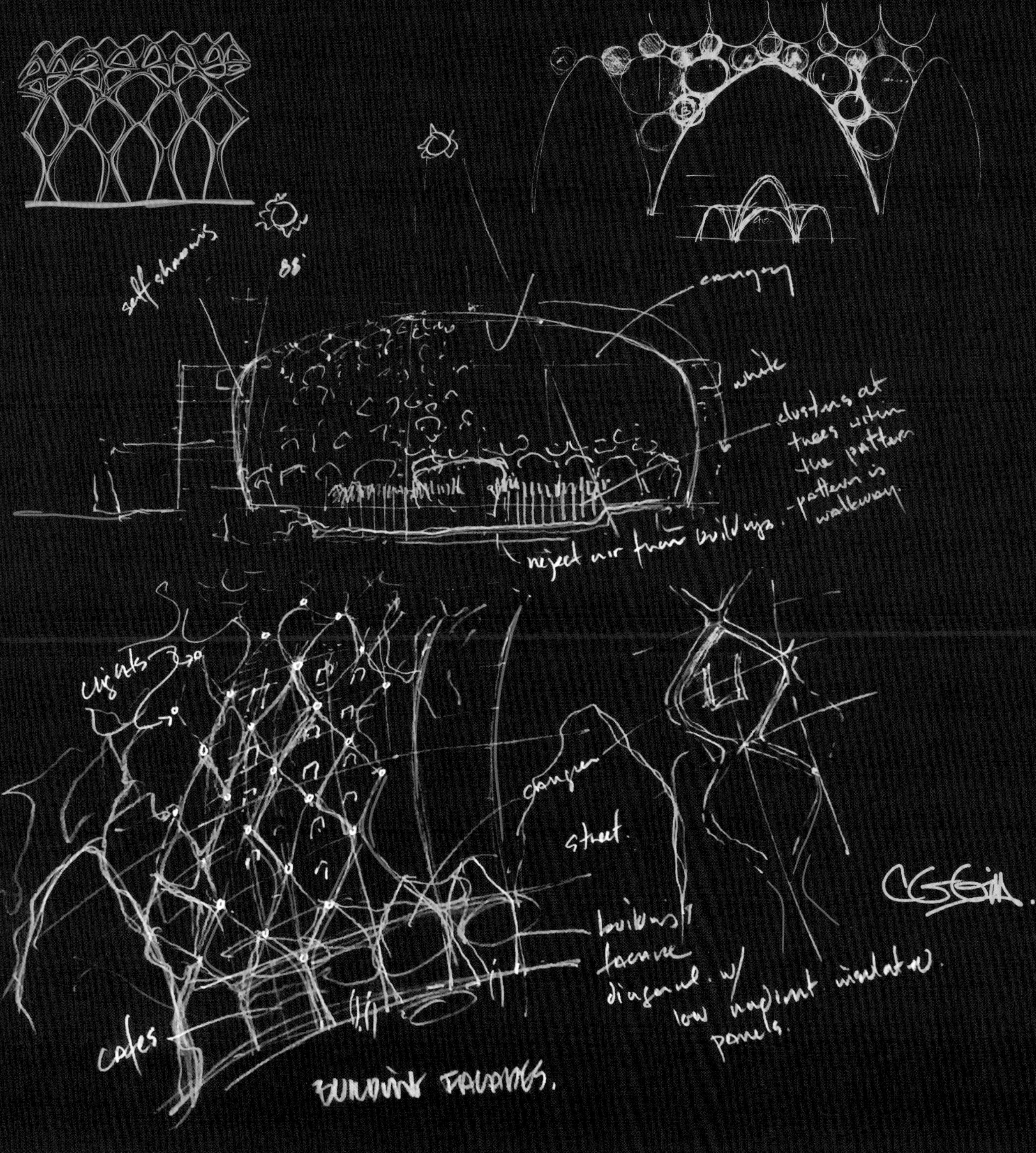
canopy
white
reject air from buildings.
lights
street.
cafes
BUILDING FACADES.

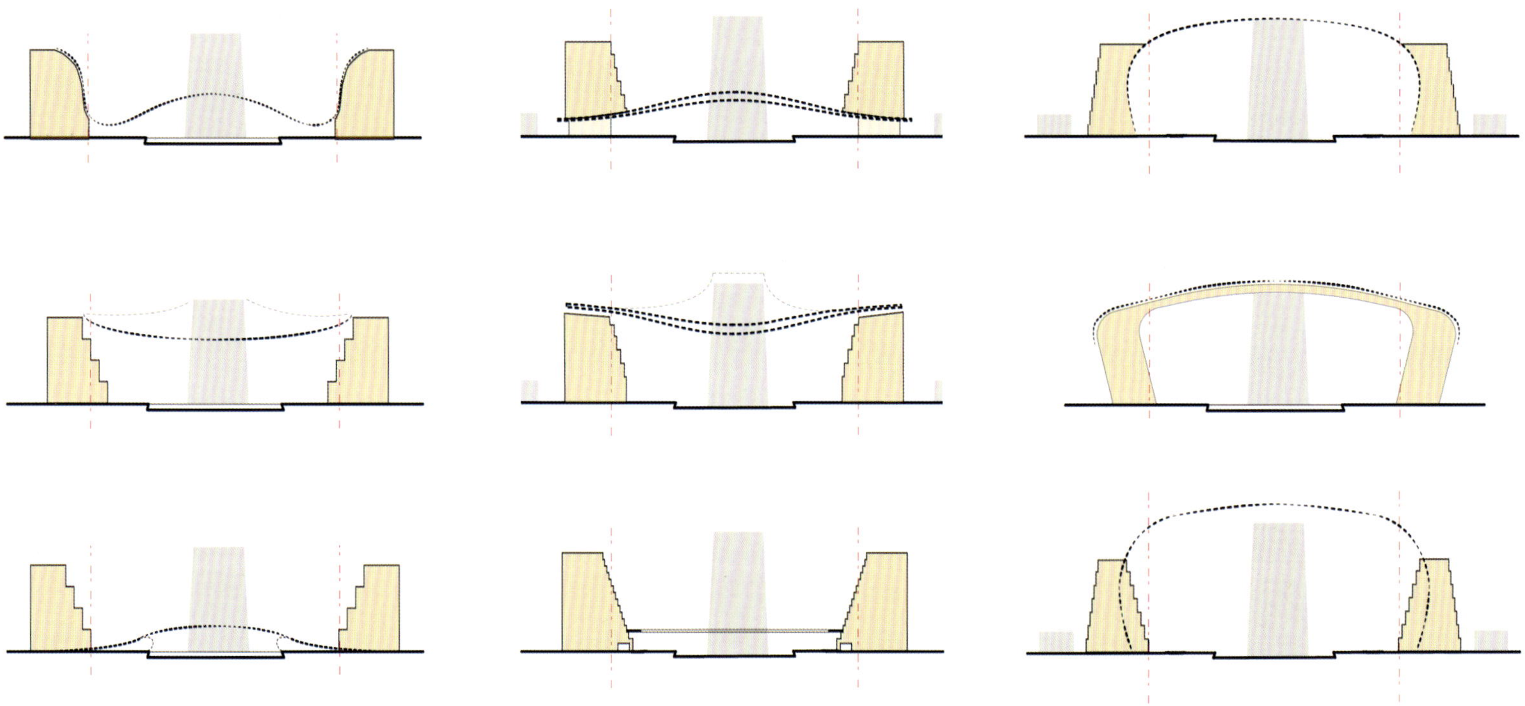

BUILDING AND SHADE STRUCTURE INTEGRATION

As the design of the garden and trellis advanced, the benefits of their symbiotic relationship became stronger. The ability of the trellis to define the urban room, the character of the space, and its presence in the district was appreciated. Shade structures were tested for engineering feasibility and environmental and architectural impact. Scale was the critical consideration; what size would achieve monumentality and shade at the intimate individual level below? The relationship to the adjacent buildings was also important. Integration with the adjacent buildings and architectural and structural independence were tested. Views from and toward the garden were relevant to the marketability of the buildings; a low-shade system would be successful at the garden level for a lower cost, however building occupants would see sun glare from the shading material which would limit views into the garden. A system fully supported from the buildings would allow maximum views to the garden but would be accompanied by structural ownership complexities and construction schedule impacts. The optimal scheme would provide structural and ownership independence, allow views of the garden from the buildings, and result in a unique expression to define the project and the expo event.

AL WASL PLAZA AS AN URBAN ROOM

A room is associated with protection and home. It has an arrival sequence and provides a sense of definition and personal space. Within a room, one feels in control while occupying the space. In Al Wasl Plaza, the idea was to translate these attributes to the larger scale of the community. A sense of arrival, protection, and community ownership were important. The plaza is connected to the district, but inside the frame of the adjacent buildings and trellis overhead, visitors are transported to a special place. Visitors have control of their visual and spatial experience within the room with a diverse series of occupiable spaces throughout the garden. The translucent nature of the trellis veil creates a subtlety to the room, allowing the experience to expand upward to the sky both day and night. The rich 360-degree spatial experience provided by the natural, architectural, and technological components offer an unparalleled experience. The ability to transform the urban room with projection allows Expo 2020 and the legacy district to reinvent the room as a platform for future events and aspirations.

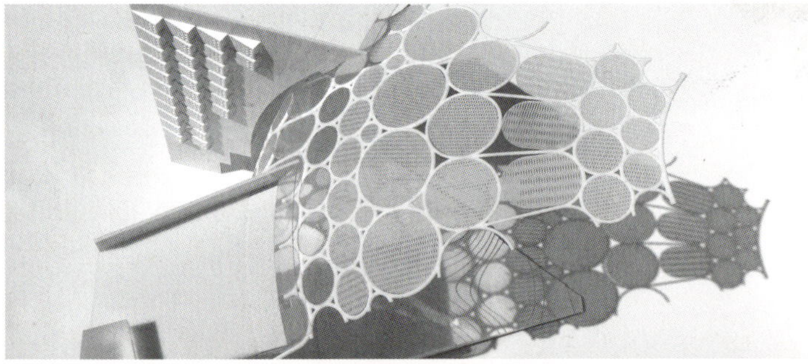

PHYSICAL MODEL TESTING

Physical models are an important part of the AS+GG design process to communicate concepts and test experiential and performance goals. The models allow the team to promptly visualize the design and adjust as needed to advance the project. The design is modeled digitally and physically in parallel using 3D printing, milling, and laser cutting to translate elements into tangible output. Scale, materiality, and natural light conditions were simulated in a small physical form. The initial Al Wasl study models conceived the urban room framed by the buildings. Several garden models communicated the power of nature as an oasis to enhance urban life in a desert environment. A series of trellis models tested the scale, quality of shade, projection potential, and articulation. A combination of materials and methods were used to construct the physical models including 3D printed plastic and rubber plastic, thermoformed plastic, CNC milled wood, acrylic and foam, and water jet cut metals.

Mobility

PHYSICAL MODEL DETAILING

A 1:500 scale model, approximately 0.3 meters in plaza diameter, was created at the end of Design Development to visualize the geometry and materiality of Al Wasl. This model allowed the team and client to appreciate the intended shading and projection on the trellis; it expressed the scale, articulation, and shading strategy of the buildings. The garden was modeled in detail, allowing a better understanding of the relative scale of components including palm trees and projection enclosures. The final physical model was considered a milestone deliverable in the design approval process. It was reviewed by the client and other stakeholders for comment and approval.

THE GARDEN

Al Wasl Plaza is the center of Expo 2020 and its legacy District 2020. It is truly a great Urban Room, marked by the monumental trellis structure and surrounding buildings. The 500,000 square-meters of mixed-use expo buildings around Al Wasl Plaza will transform into an urban innovation district that is focused on the intersections of business, technology, and lifestyle. Al Wasl Plaza will remain the center of activity as a magnet for growth serving as a dynamic and memorable public space for the district.

A lush garden for the public where visitors can engage in the simple aspects of life that are often the most meaningful: enjoying nature, walking with family and friends, participating in social events, or simply gazing up and appreciating the stars in the desert sky. At night the venue transforms, the landscape receding in focus as the trellis illuminates. This is a cultural hub for all ages and interests that educates through nature, visual arts, music and performance. In these respects, Al Wasl Plaza speaks to the inspirational and thriving nature of Dubai.

The vision for Al Wasl Plaza itself was to create a contemporary urban amenity where nature thrives in many ways. It is a place for contemplation and engagement designed to receive locals and visitors alike with lush landscape, color, sound, fragrance and fresh breeze, that transports them to a timeless experience of pure nature. The garden uses nature as a means to bring people together; it is a welcoming open space with lush plantings, varied topography and meandering paths encouraging visitors to embrace the moment. To enhance comfort in the hot desert climate, the center of the garden is sunken 3.5 meters below the perimeter roadway. The lowered landform, along with seven water features and solar shading generated by both the trellis and landscape plantings; combine to create a local microclimate, lowering the average temperature by up to 9 degrees Celsius.

"The 'Room' evokes a sense of arrival, wonder and awe. We envisioned Al Wasl as an engaging and memorable publvic space for generations to enjoy, the first of it's kind in Dubai and a strong legacy for the UAE."

- Gordon Gill, FAIA

Partner at Adrian Smith + Gordon Gill Architecture

GARDEN DESIGN

AS+GG's original 2016 design competition entry proposed a vibrant ecosystem for visitors to interact with nature and technology, focusing on the longevity of the plaza beyond Expo 2020. Seven landforms extended inward from the surrounding parcels. Access to the center of the plaza sloped between these landforms to create a sunken micro-climate with paths leading to a large, amoeba-shaped waterbody four meters below the upper plaza. The valleys descended into a cooler air environment and the refreshing water provided peaceful sounds, reflection, and tranquility. Cafes opened onto the plaza in the space below the landforms. Each of the seven irregularly shaped topologies had a distinct character and landscape design. The garden was designed as a series of small-scale gardens that supported intimate encounters under the grand dome. Lush, native plantings provided a refreshing contrast to the harsh desert environment. The soft landscape purposefully contrasted the sharp lines of the urban context. Most importantly, the contoured landform is designed to bring the joy of discovery to the pedestrian experience.

As a result of the desert context, the proposed oasis resembled a wadi, a term referring to a natural valley that floods to create an oasis in the desert. Many elements of the wadi are relevant to Al Wasl Plaza: lowered elevation, water, lush landscape, shade, and diverse landforms. When configured in an optimized manner; these elements can improve comfort, just as they do in nature. This blend of architecture and nature does not exist locally. Crafting such a space within the urban context of Dubai that is rooted in regional landscape creates an amenity for the city that was not previously present.

With the continued evolution of the initial concept and input from expo leadership, Al Wasl Plaza evolved into a venue able to support Expo 2020 ceremonies and expo and legacy visual and audio immersive events. Advancement of the trellis and event design transformed the garden to a more sinuous landform to accommodate an audience capacity of up to 10,000 people. Accessibility was prioritized to create a walkable garden without obstructions to views. The original large-scale undulating topography was softened into a rolling meadow. Two winding pathways lead from the upper pedestrian ring down to the central plaza. The wide paths descend 3.5 meters below the street level to the central fountain plaza reflecting the circular trellis oculus above. Visitors may stroll freely within the garden along these paths, which gradually twist through the topography and are integrated with rolling landforms, stepped seat walls, and grand stairs. The paths modulate the topography and allow the entire plaza to function as an open-air theater with both central and peripheral focal points.

-4.0
CENTER STAGE/ FOUNTAIN/MIST POOL
POOL

CAFE
CAFE TERRACE
CENTER STAGE/FOUNTAIN

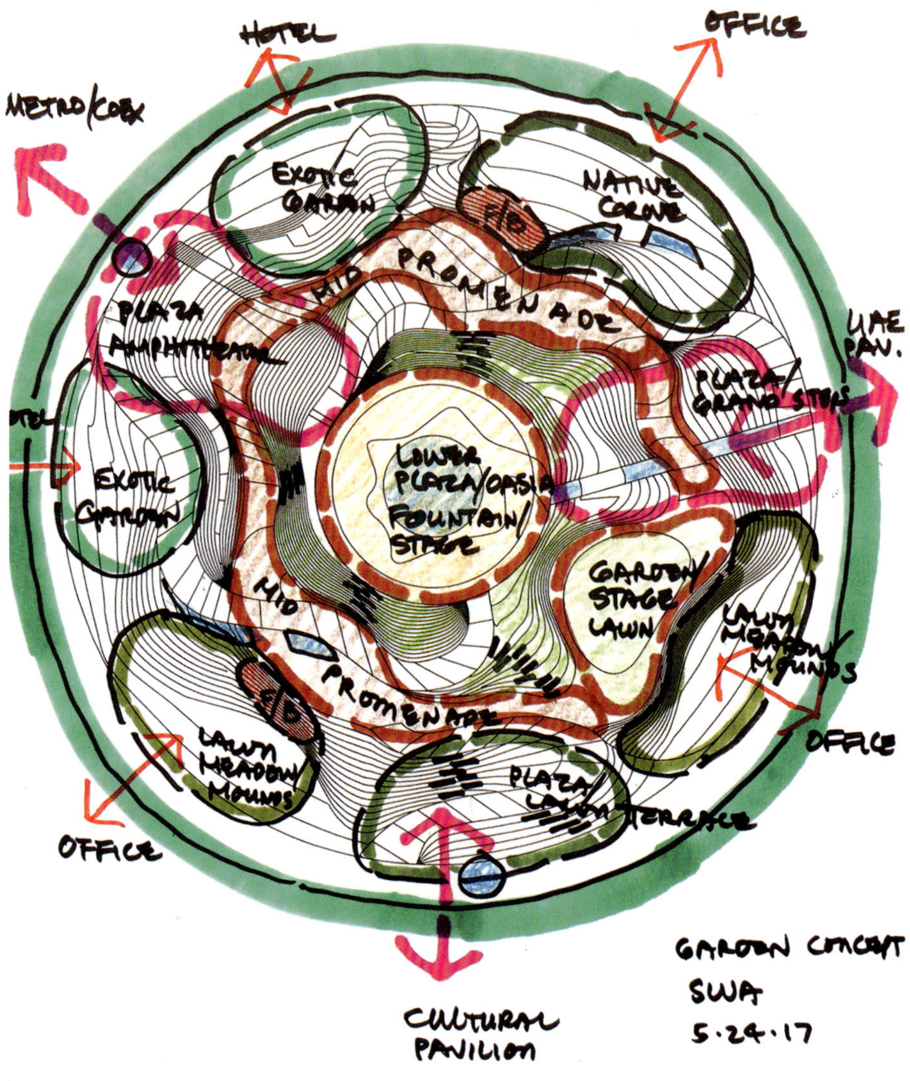
HOTEL
OFFICE
METRO/COEX
EXOTIC GARDEN
NATIVE GROVE
MID PROMENADE
PLAZA AMPHITHEATER
UAE PAV.
PLAZA/ GRAND STEPS
HOTEL
EXOTIC GARDEN
LOWER PLAZA/OASIS
FOUNTAIN/ STAGE
GARDEN/ STAGE LAWN
LAWN MEADOW/ MOUNDS
MID PROMENADE
OFFICE
LAWN MEADOW MOUNDS
PLAZA/ LAWN TERRACE
OFFICE
CULTURAL PAVILION
GARDEN CONCEPT
SWA
5.24.17

± 10M
CAFE / ENTRY
COLUMN LINE
±4.5M
2M
2M
BIKE
7M
ROAD
3M
HORSE TRAIL
2M
PLAZA
CAFE ZONE
TRELLIS
GRAVEL HORSE PATH
AMPHITHEATER SEATING
LAWN AREA
KIOSK ARCHITECTUR
IN LANDFORM

PLAZA
2M
3M
7M
2M
2M
4.5M
HORSE TRAIL/ LANDSCAPE
ROAD
LANDSCAPE
BIKE
MAIN PLAZA/ARRIVAL
A - A
1:125 SWA
0 1 2 5M
CASCADING WATER FEATURE
UPPER PEDESTRIAN PATH
CENTRAL WATER FEATURE
LAWN AREA

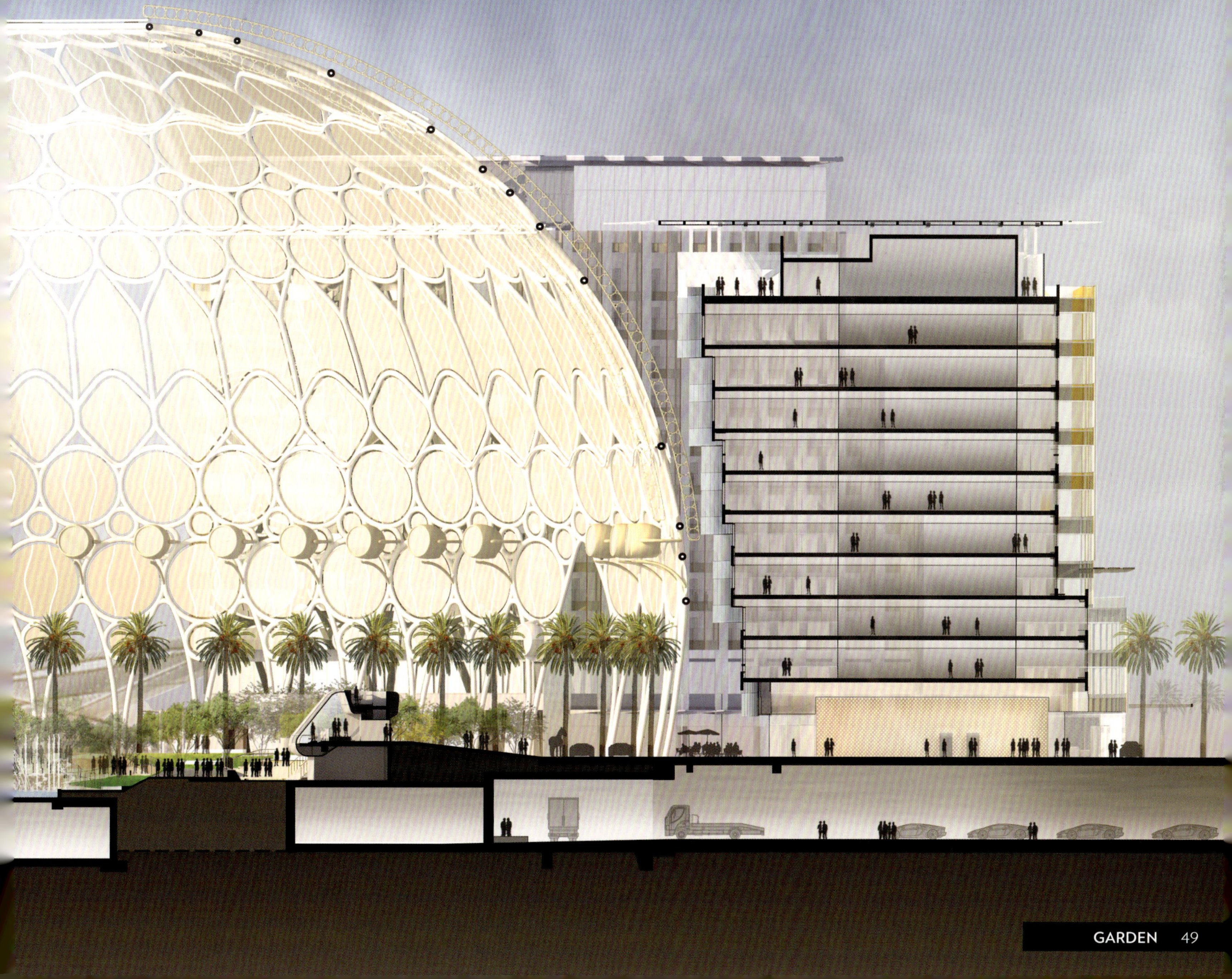

GARDEN LANDSCAPE DESIGN

AS+GG worked in collaboration with SWA Group, on the landscape design of Al Wasl Plaza and the adjacent public realm spaces. They have an extensive portfolio of built work, including the Burj Khalifa and other well-known spaces around the world. SWA brought a natural sensitivity to the project incorporating native species, bold paving patterns, and intricate water features to define intimate spaces within the overall plaza.

Three areas along the upper pedestrian ring provide the main access into the garden, with each relating to important adjacencies. Along the axis of the Arrivals Plaza is the Sunrise Plaza; on axis with the UAE Pavilion is the Sunset Plaza; and on the southeast axis with Jubilee Park is the Moonlight Plaza. Fountains at the center of each entrance are programmed to respond to sunlight throughout the day and provide focal points along the perimeter. The fountains are level with the paving and can be turned off to accommodate high pedestrian traffic when large crowds are anticipated. A series of grand stairs and seat walls cascade down from the plazas to provide amphitheater seating.

The garden functions both as a singular event venue to entertain thousands and as a series of intimate gardens that can be occupied individually for rest, relaxation, or small-scale entertainment. The ring of gardens provides a variety of landscape amenities. Starting at the Sunset Plaza clockwise they include: the Exotic Garden featuring unusual species from around the world; the Interactive Garden with playful spaces for children; the Vista Garden with views of the garden below; the Stage Lawn features an open meadow for small performances surrounded by lush planting; the Secret Garden is a small area of seating hidden in vegetation; the Art Garden is a space for exhibitions and installations; the Summer Garden is a lush space shaded during the hottest months of the year; the Landform Garden has low growing species that hug the ground to reveal the topography; the Star Garden has sparkling LEDs for a dreamy quality after dusk; and the Tropical Garden has rich colorful planting.

The Central Plaza, which is directly below the trellis oculus, is the heart of the garden. Its intricate radial paving pattern emphasizes the centrality and hosts an interactive water feature that is programmed based on the sun patterns to control the microclimate at the lowest portion of the plaza. At the center of the water feature is a stage lift, which can be lowered to the basement and raised to 1.5 meters above the level of the paving during live performances.

The planting design responds to the specific program of each of these unique spaces with a diverse selection of species while maintaining a unifying palette through the plaza. Solar analysis was performed to identify the sun and shade patterns from the trellis and buildings on the garden. As a result of the solar analysis, palm trees stretch across the plaza below the sun path of the oculus.

The beauty of the trellis is in the shade it provides, creating a cooler microclimate for visitors in the garden. However, shade is anomalous to local desert species requiring the planting design to react accordingly. Except for the Exotic Gardens, where unusual exotic species are displayed, 50% of the species are considered native and 100% of the plants are grown locally in Dubai nurseries. The species within the garden facilitate habitat creation for birds, butterflies, and bees.

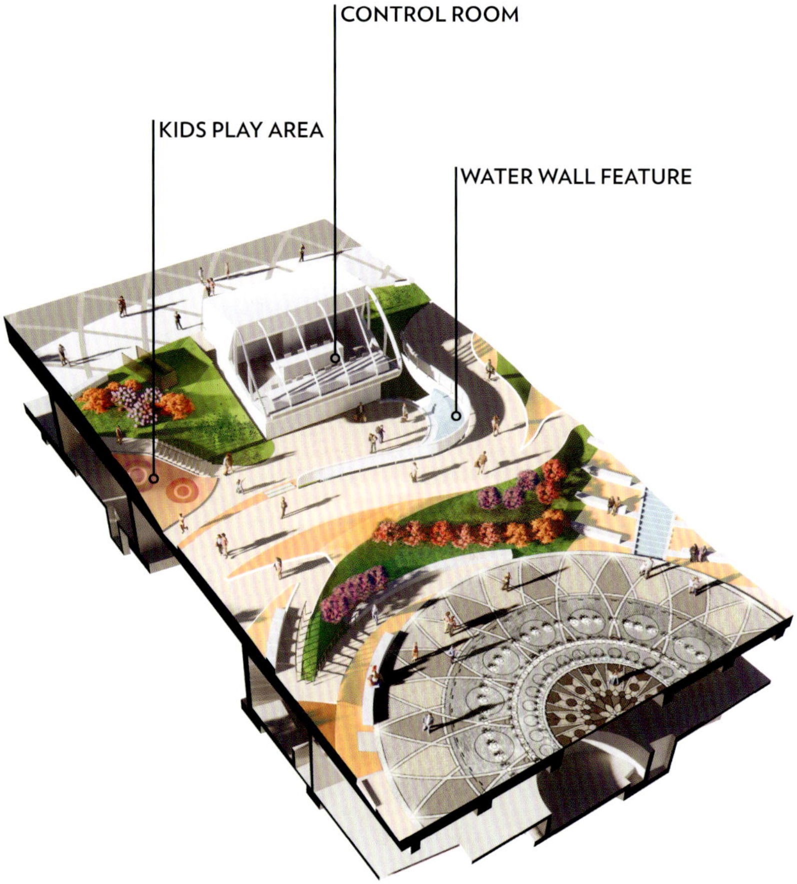

CONTROL ROOM - EXPO GARDEN

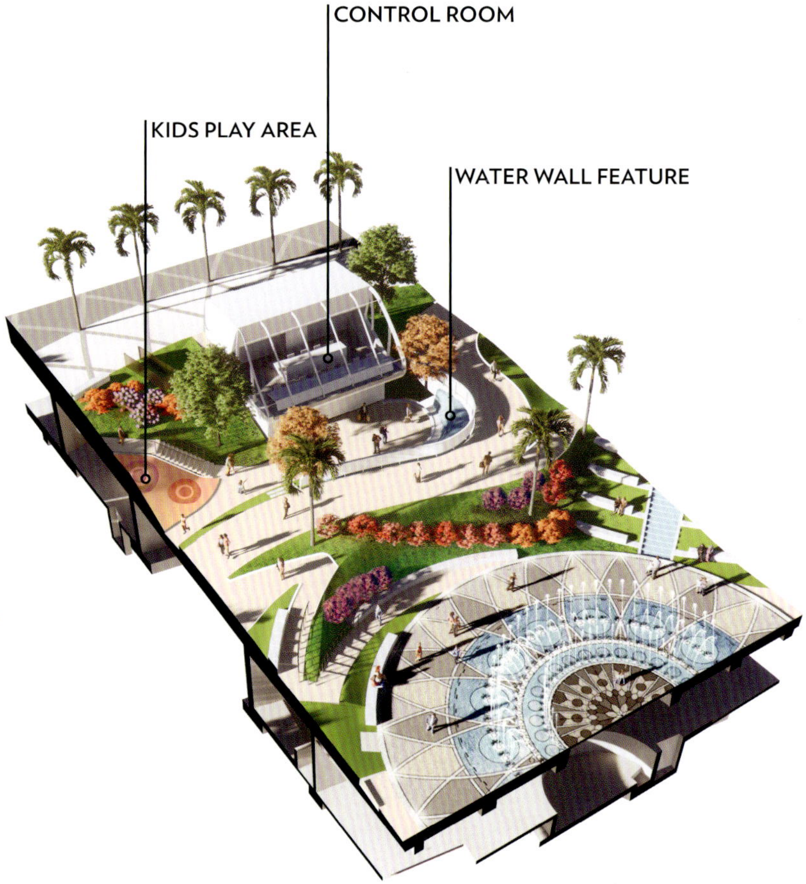

CONTROL ROOM - LEGACY GARDEN

GARDEN EXPO TO LEGACY TRANSITION

As introduced in the Inspiration chapter, Al Wasl Plaza was conceived as a legacy asset to Dubai and the greater UAE to thrive for generations. Support for the long-term vision came from UAE leadership and was reinforced by AS+GG's legacy master plan vision. Thus, Al Wasl Plaza was designed as a legacy project; a grand centerpiece of the district for locals and visitors to relax and enjoy an endless array of events, large and small, in the garden, the office spaces, and when visiting the hotels. The first six months in the life of the plaza anticipates 25 million visitors for Expo 2020. As a result, the design for the event was twofold: a subtractive approach for permanent elements such as planting and trees and an additive approach layering technology to support large expo ceremonies. Some trees, plantings, and water features were withheld from installation until the close of the event to facilitate crowd flow and allow for the opening and closing ceremonies to encompass a larger area within the plaza. Areas where plantings are withheld are replaced with a colorful walkable recycled rubber surface. A district designed for a temporary use is of no value without a transition strategy to propel the investment forward. The legacy transition plan for Al Wasl Plaza was designed to require minimal construction at the close of the event to facilitate quickly reopening for public use; a distinction that will propel economic activity in District 2020.

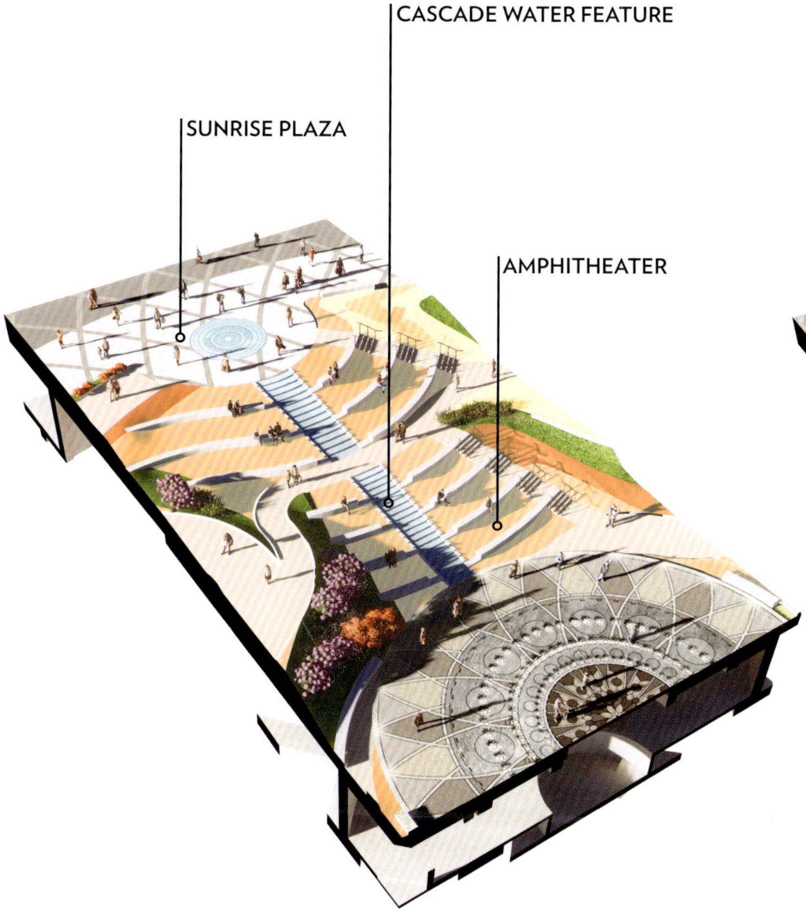

AMPHITHEATER - EXPO GARDEN

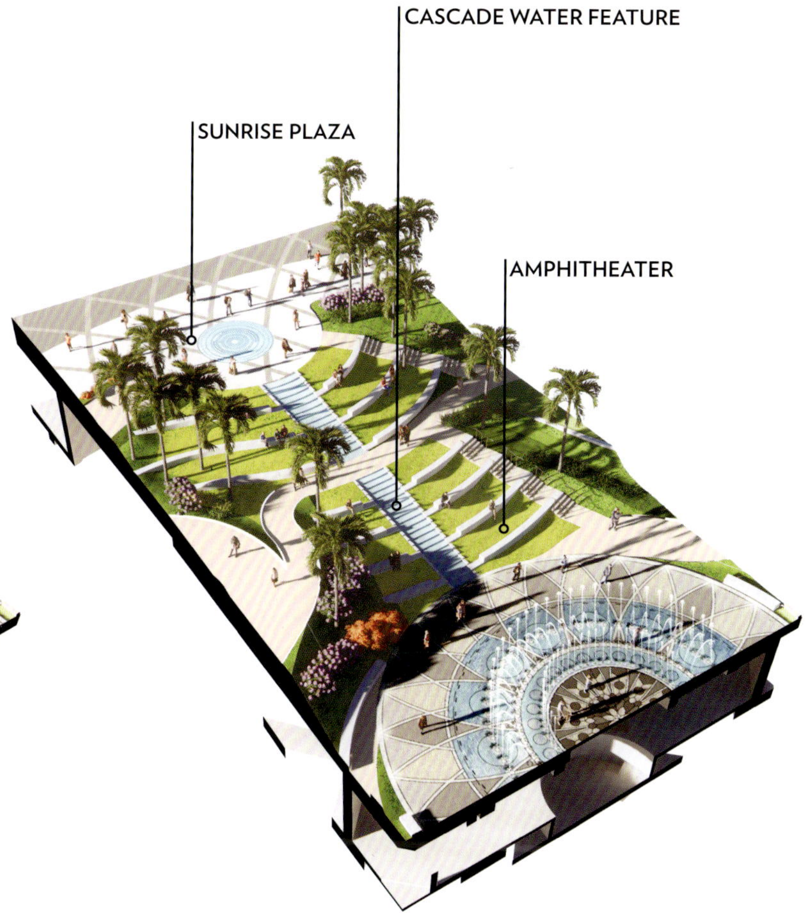

AMPHITHEATER - LEGACY GARDEN

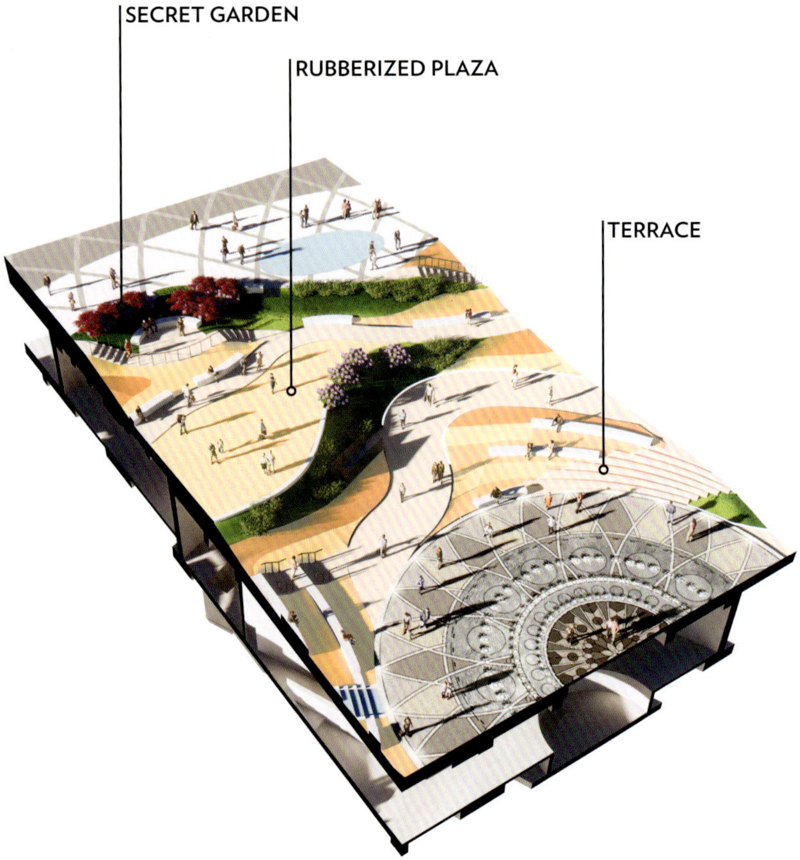

THE LAWN - EXPO GARDEN

THE LAWN - LEGACY GARDEN

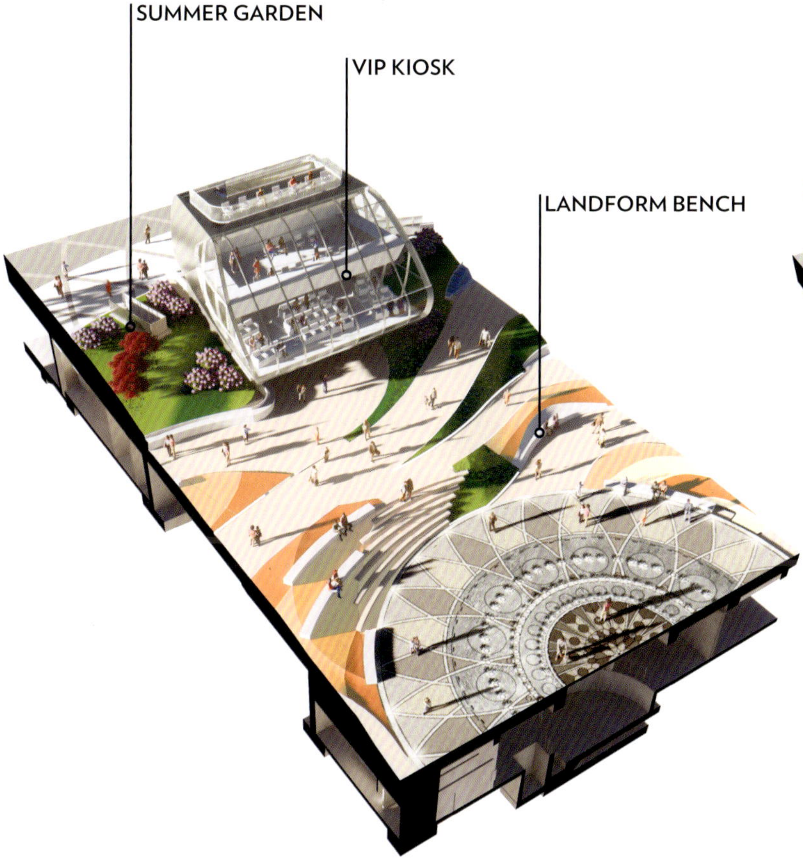

VIP KIOSK - EXPO GARDEN

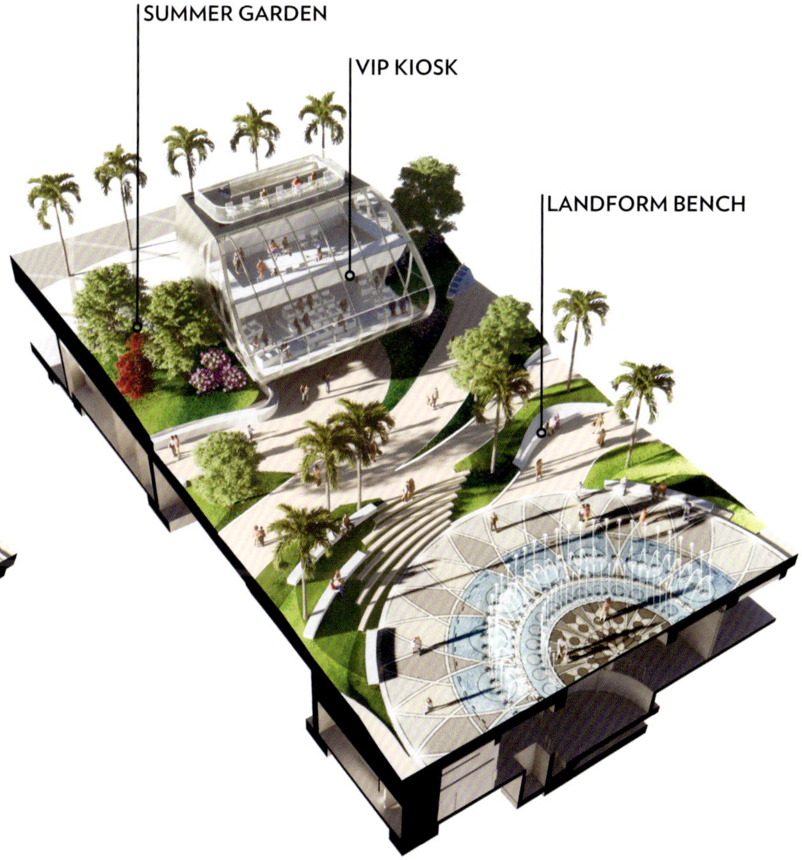

VIP KIOSK - LEGACY GARDEN

LEGACY PLAN

EXPO RUBBERIZED PAVING

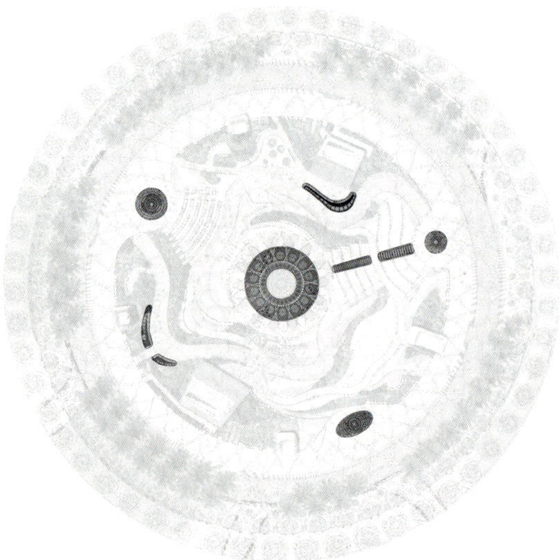

WATER FEATURES ACTIVE/INACTIVE
DURING EXPO

EXPO OUTER PALM TREES

EXPO PLAN

LEGACY PLANTING
REPLACES EXPO
RUBBERIZED SURFACE

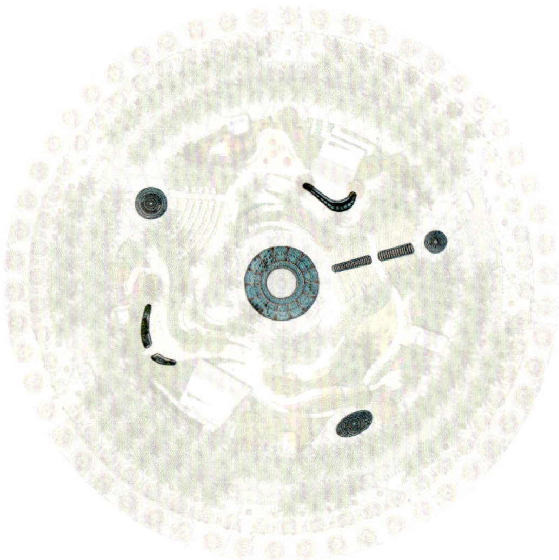

WATER FEATURES
ACTIVATED

INNER TREES PLANTED

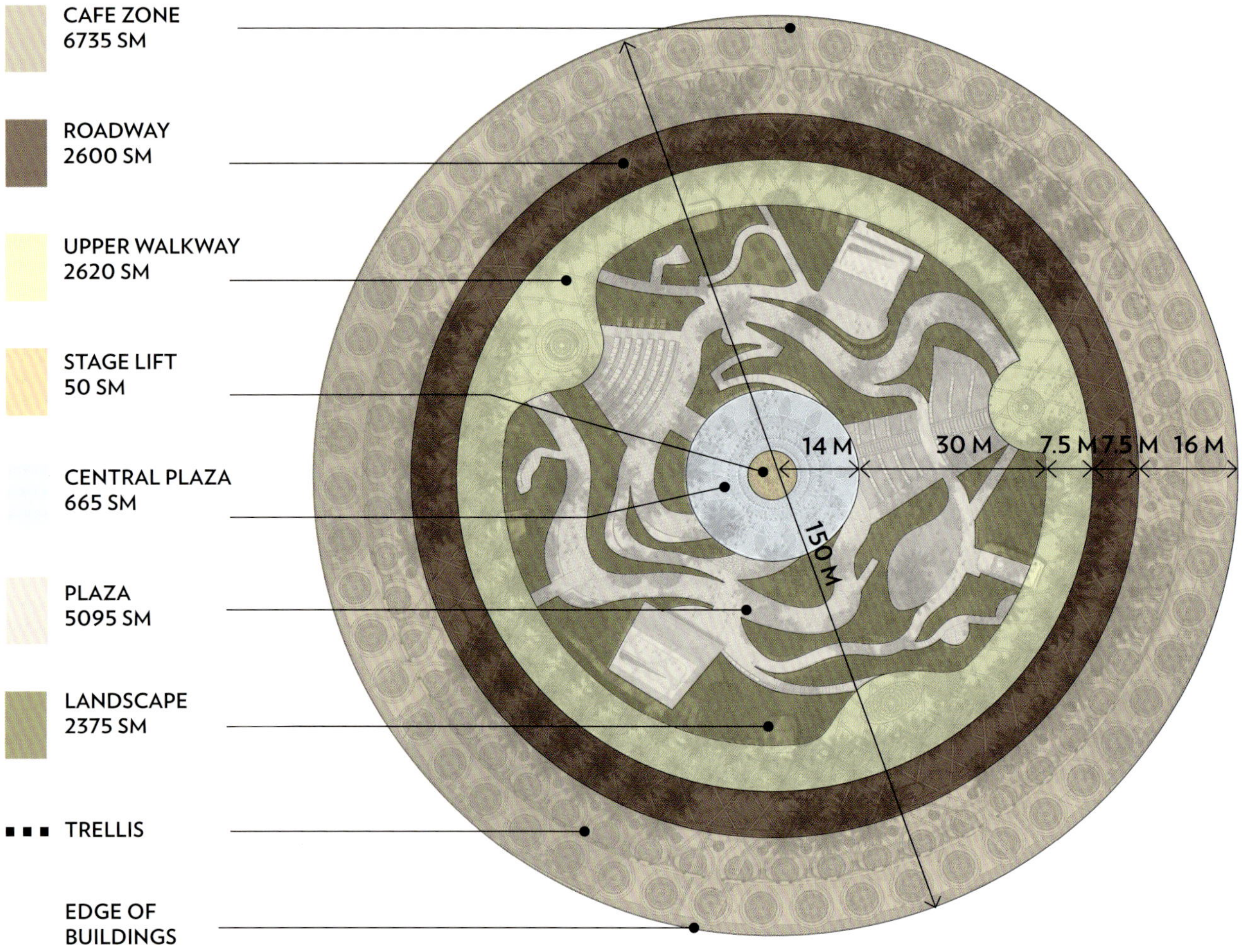

1 SUNSET PLAZA
2 SUNRISE PLAZA
3 MOONLIGHT PLAZA
4 ART GARDEN
5 SUMMER GARDEN
6 EXOTIC GARDEN
7 DISCOVER WALK
8 LAWN TERRACE
9 KID'S PLAY AREA
10 INTERACTIVE GARDEN
11 VISTA GARDEN
12 LAWN AMPHITHEATER
13 SECRET GARDEN
14 STAGE LAWN
15 TROPICAL GARDEN
16 LANDFORM GARDEN
17 STAR GARDEN
18 CENTRAL PLAZA + STAGE LIFT
19 KIOSK
20 UTILITY BUILDING
21 WATER FEATURE
22 CAFE ZONE
23 HORSE PROMENADE
24 ROADWAY

GROUND LEVEL PLAN

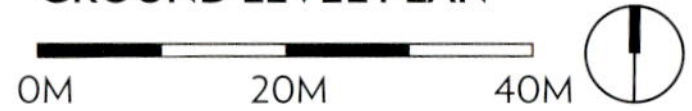

22
20
9
11
6
10
19
1
7
23
21
21
17
8
2
24
23
12
21
21
21
18
6
16
20
14
20
7
21
15
13
5
19
4
21
20
3
22

OFFICE
HOTEL
District 2020

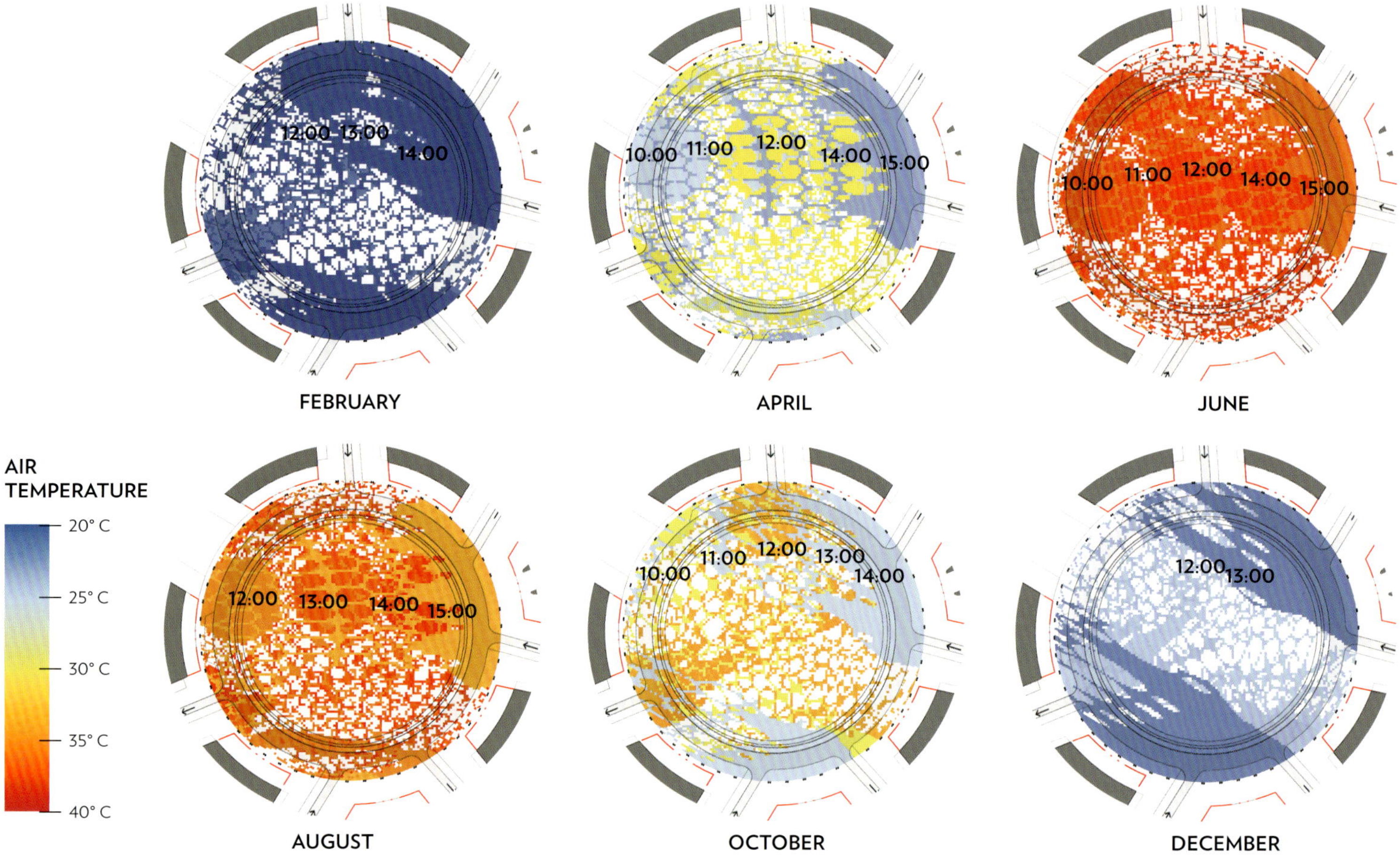

GARDEN DAYLIGHT ANALYSIS

The garden's arrangement of planting and programming was designed based on solar radiation within Al Wasl Plaza. As the sun passes across the sky, the trellis and oculus create a dynamic pattern of light and shade. These natural patterns were simulated to program the space and locate various tree and plant species in response to their sun exposure needs. The sun path of the large 35-meter diameter oculus spans across the plaza each day. In the hottest summer months, it spans the central portion of the garden, and the sun moves toward the northern portion of the site when the sun is lower in the sky in spring and fall. Although shade is ideal for human comfort in warm weather, it is not ideal for native landscape that thrives in direct desert sunlight. The garden plantings were designed accordingly, with palm trees spanning from the Arrivals Plaza to the UAE Pavilion in the direct sunlight. Small gathering areas are positioned along the northern and southern edge of the plaza where visitors are shaded throughout most of the year.

GARDEN ARCHITECTURE

The beauty of Al Wasl Plaza is in its blend of nature and technology. Nature is in focus while technological support is seamlessly integrated to support a diverse platform for events. The garden conceals a concentric district truck tunnel and technical basement below grade. It is the heart of the district and the center of logistics. To maximize views within the trellis, most of the infrastructure in the plaza is hidden from view, allowing visitors to fully occupy the garden without obstruction at grade. As the design developed, certain spatial requirements emerged that would enhance either the visitor experience or provide necessary technical support for events that needed to be enclosed at the plaza level.

If buildings were to be inserted within the garden, the forms would need to integrate into the design of the plaza, landforms, and planting. A small pavilion was envisioned to either hide inside the landforms or integrate organically on top of the plaza to create unparalleled viewing experiences. In early iterations, two kiosks were designed into the landform as small café stands for visitor refreshments while visiting the garden. These small spaces were not intended to service the high anticipated visitor count during Expo 2020, as food vendors were designated elsewhere. Their function was dual: as venues during the expo and as technical support for the opening and closing ceremonies during the event.

In late 2018, AS+GG began coordination with the Expo 2020 Ceremonies design team of audiovisual, lighting, rigging, and theatrical specialists. The Expo client's request for additional audiovisual capacity prompted the design team to add equipment enclosures and support spaces. The enhanced ceremony design required approximately 200 sm of space dedicated as control rooms for event operators. Interior temperature-controlled workstations and equipment rooms, as well as exterior event viewing platforms, called for prominent views of the trellis and garden. This required AS+GG to test a series of architectural solutions inside the trellis, both temporary and permanent.

To maximize views for the control personnel and event attendees throughout the plaza, AS+GG initially proposed a series of prefabricated modular pavilions on stilts to be located adjacent to the trellis legs. The perimeter location was temporary and allowed for easy installation and removal after events. During the development of this concept, the team presented the potential of occupying the pavilions after the event as special immersive experience viewing rooms. The client agreed with this vision to add value to the legacy of the project. This shift prompted relocation of the control space from being placed at the edge of the plaza to placement more central to the experience. The architects shifted the focus to redesigning the two kiosks at the prime locations of the intersecting paths of the garden for this use. This was a mutually beneficial solution for both the event operators as well as the client.

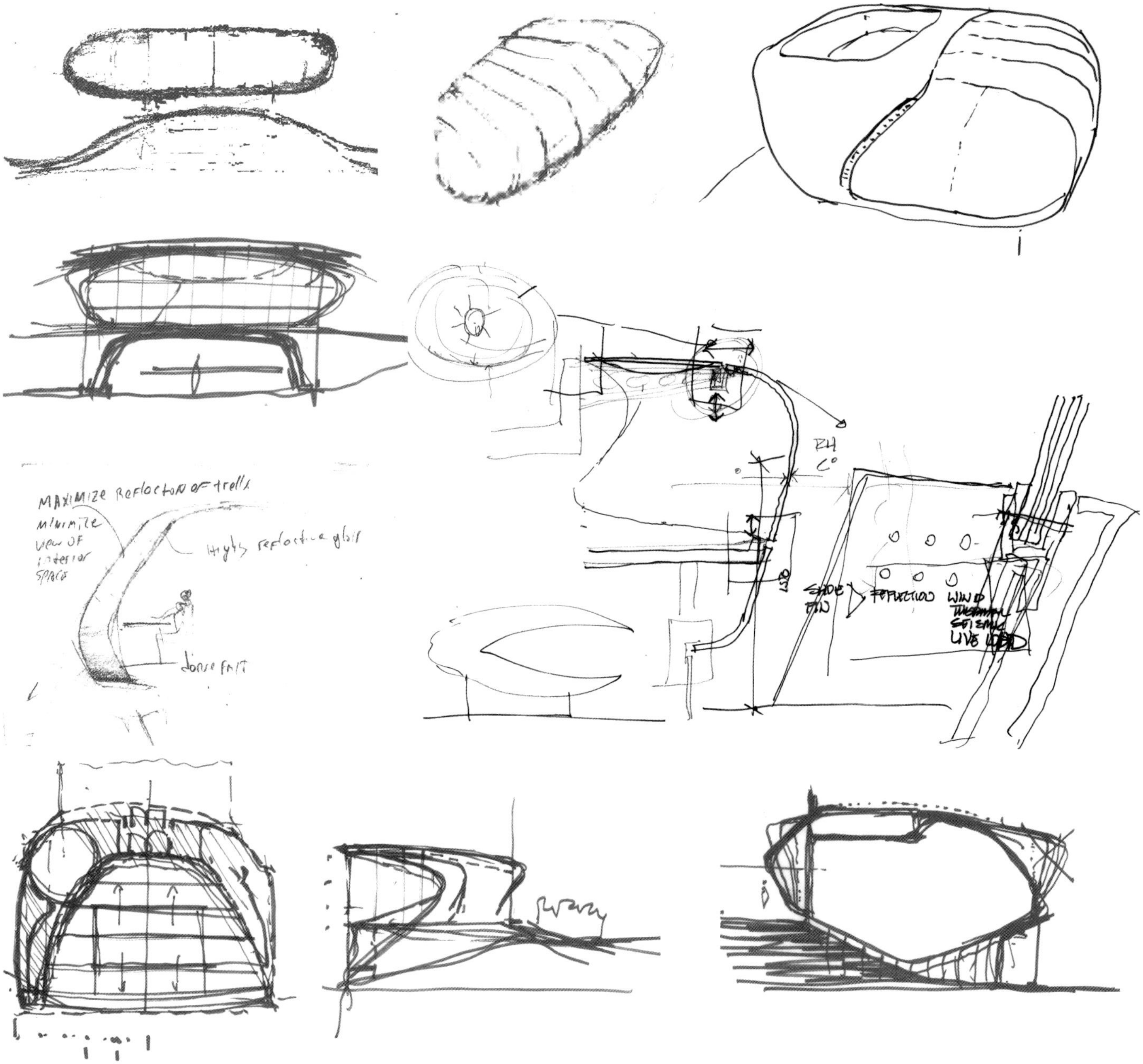
MAXIMIZE Reflection OF trellis
minimize view of interior space
Highly reflective glass
REFLECTION
WIND
LIVE LOAD

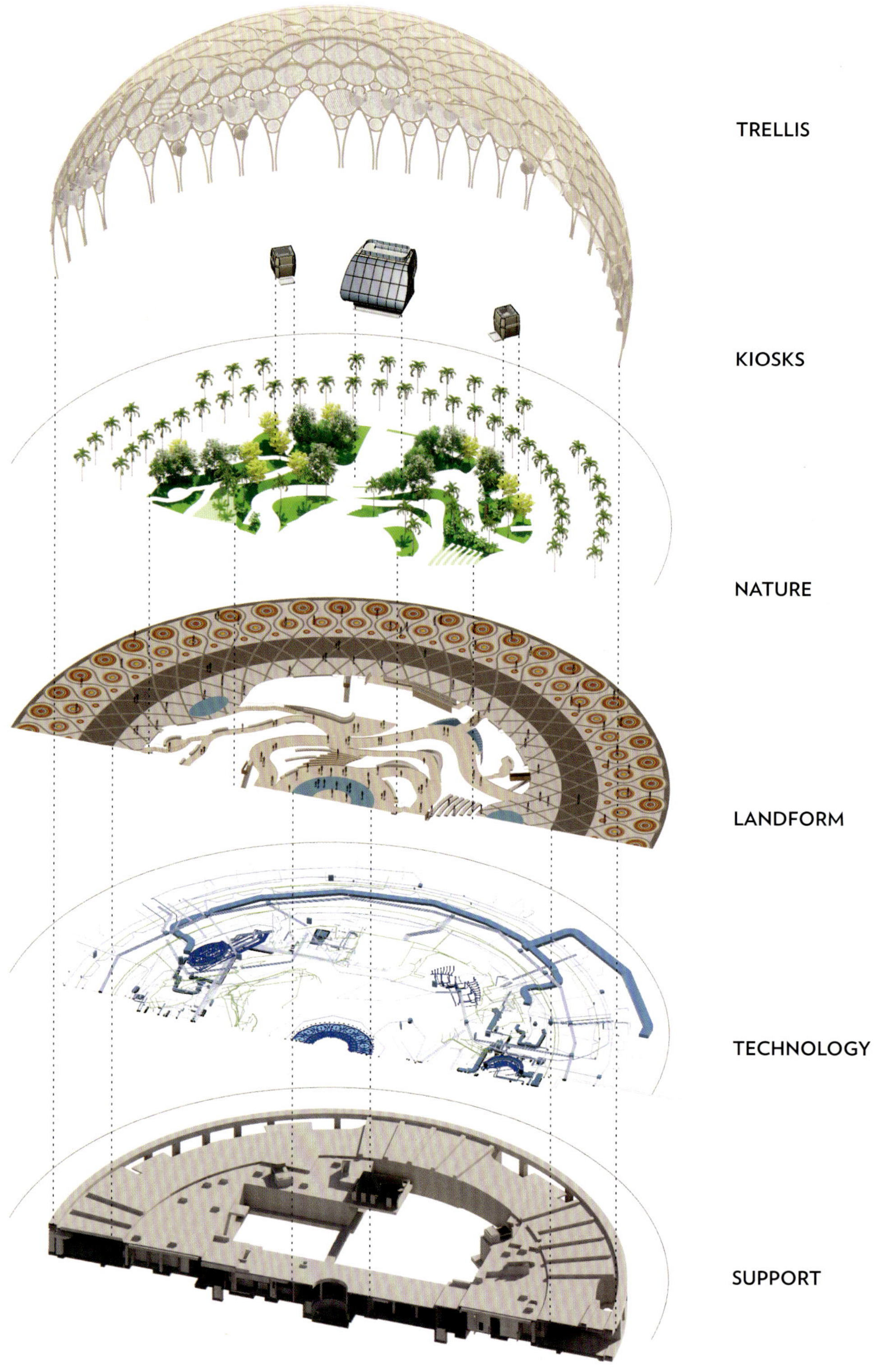
TRELLIS
KIOSKS
NATURE
LANDFORM
TECHNOLOGY
SUPPORT

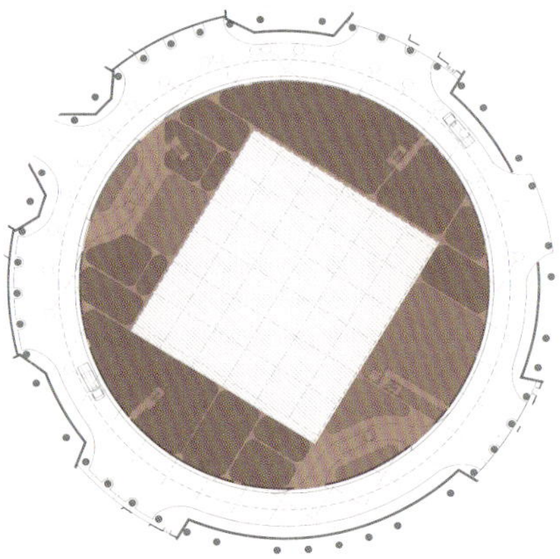

APRIL 2017

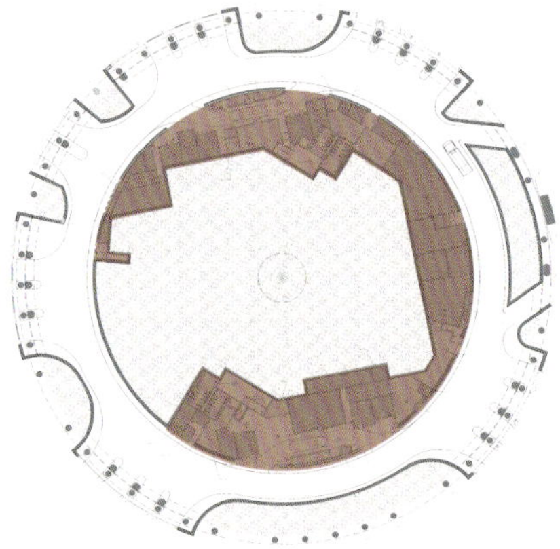

MAY 2017

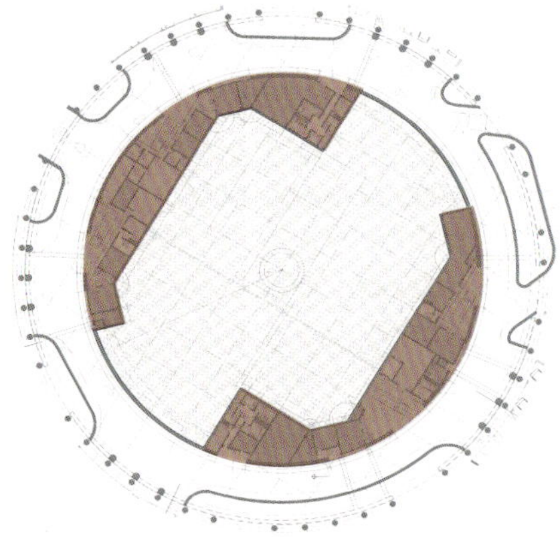

JUNE 2017

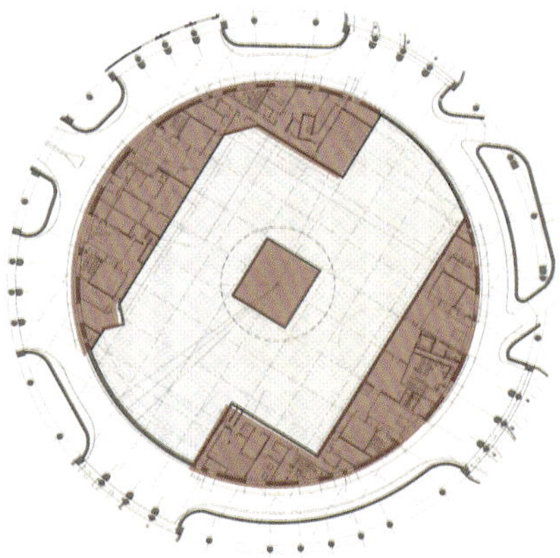

AUGUST 2017

SEPTEMBER 2017

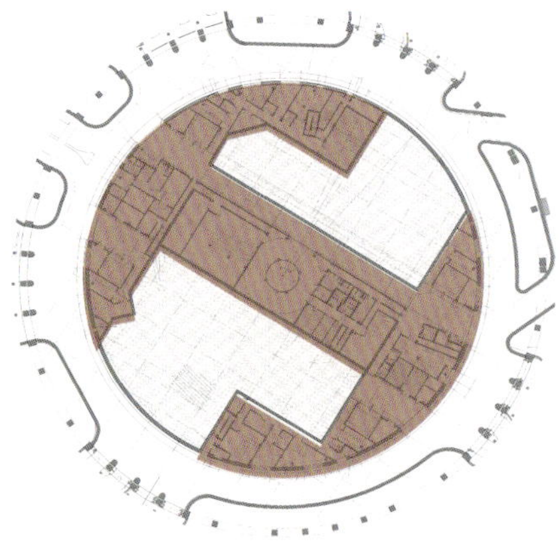

DECEMBER 2017

AL WASL BASEMENT

As the program for the garden and trellis became more ambitious during the design process, it became clear that a significant amount of support space would be required. The infrastructure supporting Al Wasl Plaza is contained below grade in a 4260 sm basement, located below the garden, within the ring of the district truck tunnel, corresponding with and at approximately eight meters below the grade level of Al Wasl roadway. These below grade spaces contain services for electrical, telecommunication, information technology, water features, mechanical, storm water, immersive experience, audio visual, estate management, security, and event support. The basement also contains a tunnel roadway linking the district truck tunnel to the central stage lift and the event support area. As the garden slopes 3.5 meters down to the central plaza, the basement structure steps down in the center to allow at least 1.7 meters of soil to accommodate the lush plant and landscaping materials, including the large number of trees planned for the legacy concept. Due to the fast-track nature of the project and continual enhancements for the immersive experience and expo ceremonies program; the basement design adjusted many times while the project was under construction. This central hub was perfect for logistical access to all parcels and parking, as well as back of house stage operations for major events.

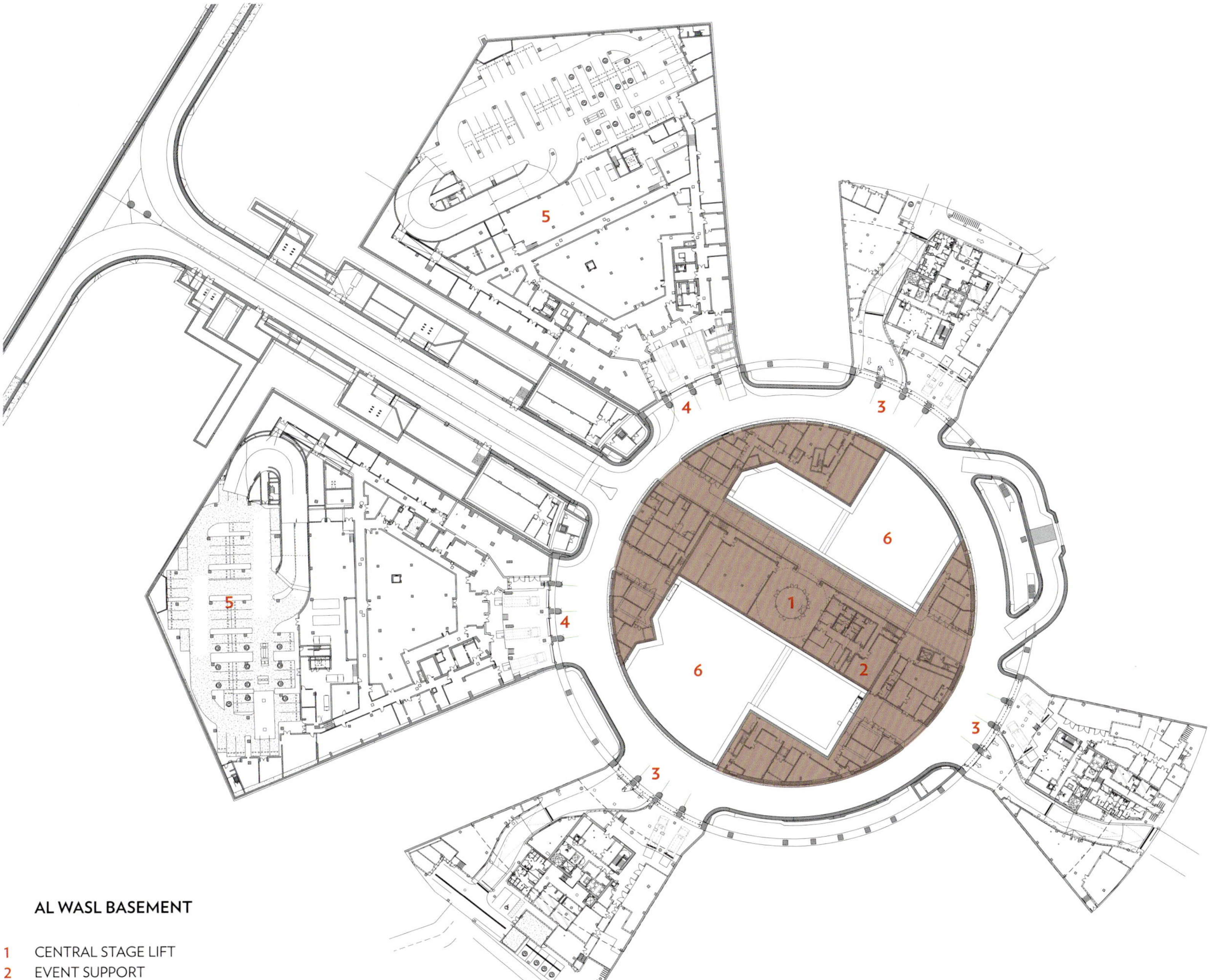

AL WASL BASEMENT

1 CENTRAL STAGE LIFT
2 EVENT SUPPORT
3 OFFICE LOADING
4 HOTEL LOADING
5 PARKING
6 UNEXCAVATED

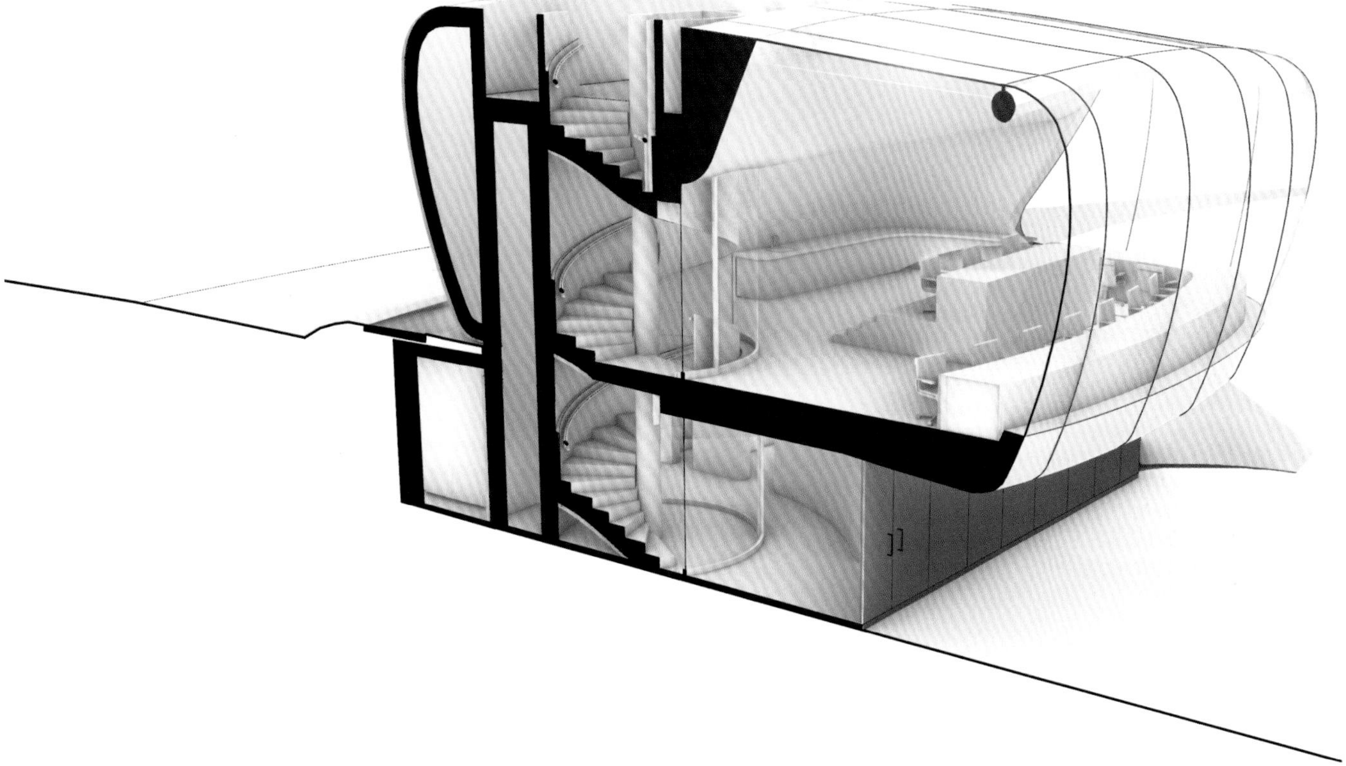

AL WASL EXPERIENCE CONTROL ROOM EARLY CONCEPT

To integrate organically into the soft language of the garden, AS+GG studied iterations of control room structures using glass forms nestled into the landforms and surrounded by nature. Glass on the front, sides, and a portion of the roof were essential to provide unobstructed views of the plaza and trellis. The curved glass surfaces merge with their context and eliminate sharp contrasting lines. The original café at the lower plaza level became a technical equipment room on which the glass room was placed. The form was optimized using parametric software and generative design. It allowed the scale to be minimized based on parameters for the interior program area, structural size, and the limits of curvature for the glass. An occupiable rooftop was required for event sound control monitoring and is accessed by spiral stair. The design of the control rooms integrated with the ongoing construction of the structure below, the intricate garden design at grade, and a series of technological constraints while also following an unyielding cost and construction schedule.

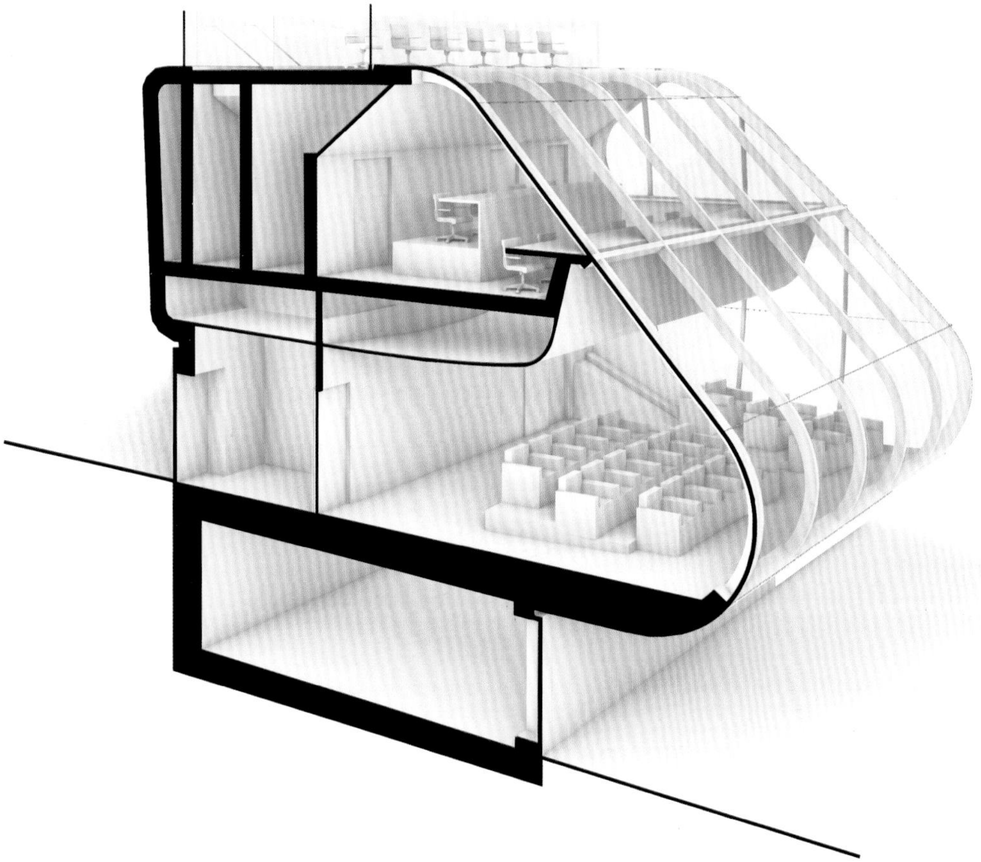

AL WASL EXPERIENCE CONTROL ROOM FINAL DESIGN

The glass pavilion design was so well received for its architectural integration with the garden, and its potential to provide an optimum viewing experience, that the client requested additional space within the buildings. The viewing space originally envisioned for legacy use, was requested for Expo 2020. In October 2019, it was decided to add a second level above the plaza to the south building to serve the technical control function. The northern pavilion remains a single level above the plaza with a total area of 167 sm. To the south, 326 sm of area is compacted into three levels and a rooftop. The buildings remain small in comparison to the overall scale of the trellis enclosure. The final building design is a concrete structure clad in glass and aluminum panels. The glass front of the viewing room curves back to disappear, allowing the trellis to take the foreground. Due to a constrained timeline, construction of the concrete structure commenced immediately while the geometry of the building was being optimized. Detailed coordination with glass fabricators was essential to meet cost expectations, streamline timely procurement, and meet the construction schedule. These pavilions are the ultimate viewing experience in Al Wasl Plaza: to see and be seen while fully immersed in the experience.

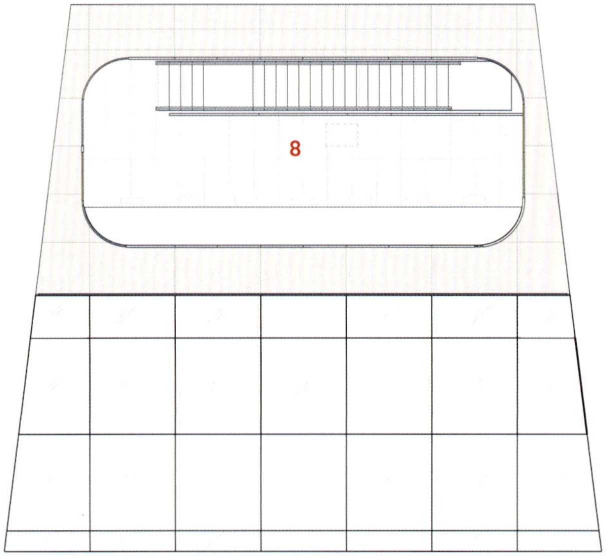

ROOFTOP

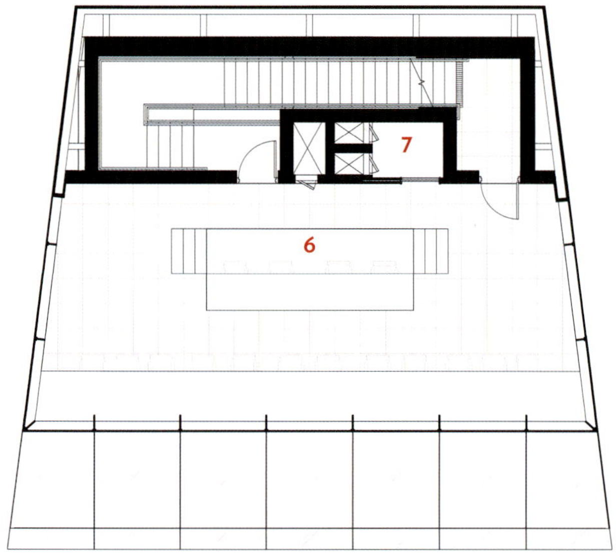

UPPER LEVEL

AL WASL EXPERIENCE ROOM

1 EXPO VIEWING
2 LOUNGE
3 ENTRANCE VESTIBULE
4 WASHROOM
5 PANTRY
6 CONTROL ROOM
7 MEP
8 AUDIO CONTROL PLATFORM
9 TRANSLATION BOOTH
10 RACK ROOM

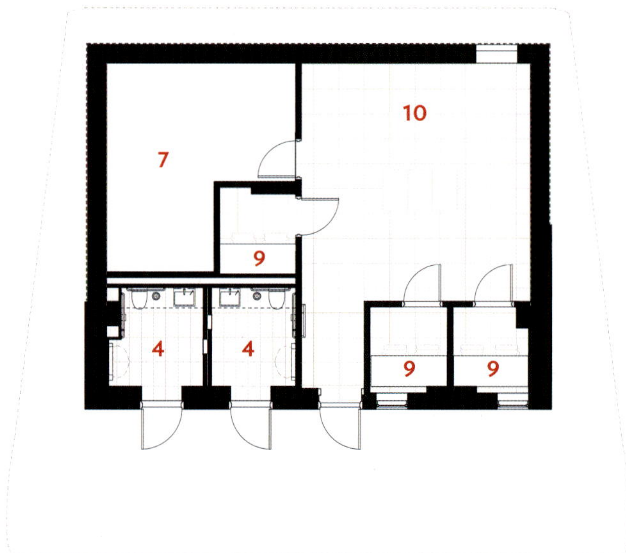

LOWER LEVEL

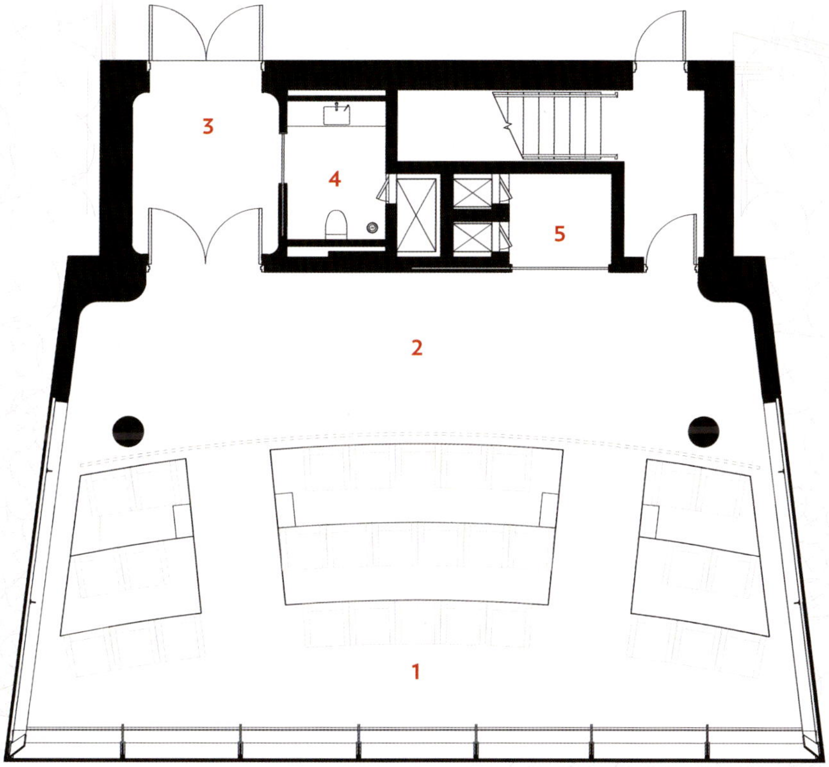

MAIN PLAZA LEVEL

AL WASL UTILITY BUILDINGS

There are four utility buildings distributed approximately equidistant along the upper perimeter walkway in Al Wasl Plaza. These buildings are multi-functional, supporting the systems of the plaza architecture in numerous ways. The enclosed portion of the buildings each contain an RMU (Ring Main Unit) or switchgear unit for electrical power distribution to Al Wasl from the district. Three of the buildings are a typical size, the fourth is larger, incorporating elevator access to the basement from the garden and an integrated staircase for event support and maintenance. The utility buildings are surrounded by plantings that conceal fresh air intake grilles and act to keep pedestrians at a safe distance. This air supply connects to the basement fan rooms for mechanical ventilation. Plumbing vent stacks are also integrated, supporting the infrastructure below the plaza.

These buildings also act as spotter locations for events and are designed with occupiable rooftops for one or two camera operators or projection supervisors. The side facade hinges open for the operator to access an integrated ladder to the roof; equipped with power and data outlets necessary for operations during events. Standing at 3.5 m above the ground level, the operators have unobstructed views of the complete garden and dome above. Their operations can be linked to the event control room in the basement as necessary.

The exterior cladding is a double skin system that has several benefits. The base GFRC (glass fiber reinforced concrete) panels create the curved form and provide a shell for mounting components. The secondary system is an aluminum frame supporting panels of open weave PTFE fabric matching the trellis. The cladding design concept was developed to integrate security cameras, 5G antennae and Wi-Fi antennae on the exterior. Security cameras and Wi-Fi antennae are in the reveal of the cladding because they cannot be shielded behind fabric. On the upper facade, 5G antennae are concealed behind the fabric. The technology of 5G was in constant development in parallel to the design and construction of these utility buildings. The design had to respond with flexibility and the antennae were tested in a mock-up to confirm that the proposed PTFE fabric was a suitable cladding that would not obstruct the 5G signal.

Integration of technology into a garden comes with many requirements. For example, digital signal and security provisions have prescribed mounting heights, power stations must be accessed from a roadway at grade and air intake and exhaust need to be separated from public space for safety. The circular, amphitheater form of Al Wasl, does not have a back facade or a place to store service and utilities. The entire plaza is open and accessible to the public, requiring careful design consideration and exposure of the various infrastructure and technology powering the immersive space. Overall, the design required flexibility to accommodate the changing service requirements as the event design progressed. These utility buildings absorbed many of the technical project requirements and connect the plaza to the service zone below grade to make the plaza function seamlessly. These buildings are the connective technological tissue of Al Wasl.

TYPICAL UTILITY BUILDING

1 METAL GRILLE
2 PTFE FIBERGLASS MESH PANEL
3 GALV STEEL FRAME SUPPORT
4 GFEP COPING
5 CONCRETE WALL
6 LOUVER DOOR
7 FIBERGLASS MESH PANEL ON OUTER DOOR
8 TRENCH PLACEMENT
9 VENT STACK
10 ROOF ACCESS LADDER

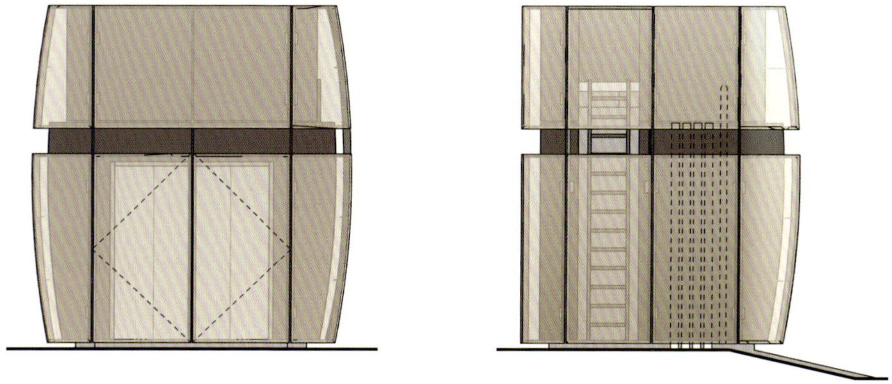

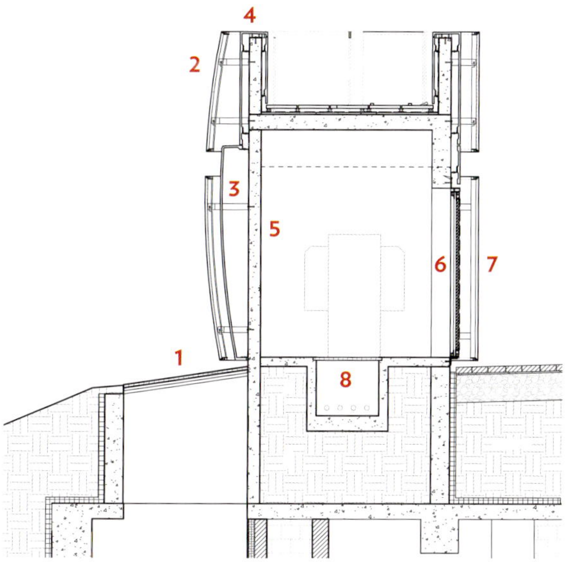

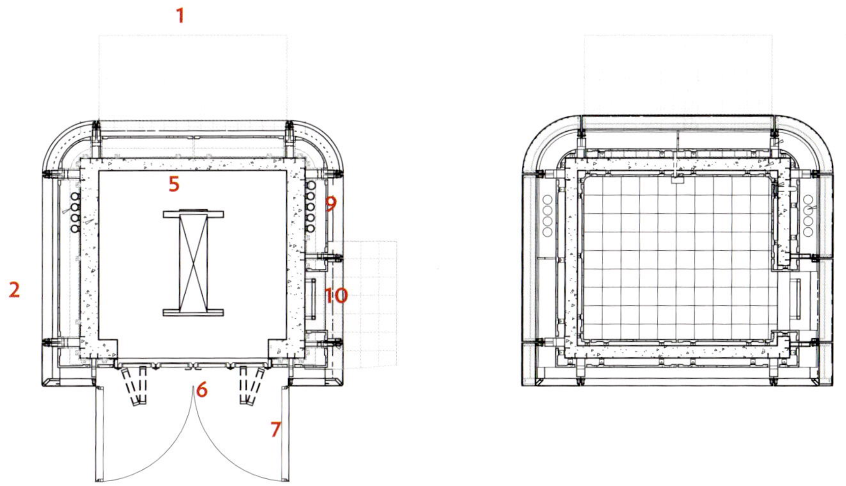

TREE UPLIGHTING

LIT BOLLARDS

BENCH LIGHTING

FOUNTAIN LIGHTING

PATH ILLUMINATION

AL WASL PLAZA LIGHTING

The lighting in Al Wasl Plaza was designed to celebrate and simulate the night sky. Stargazing is often challenging in urban developments, and it is also difficult to experience the amazement brought on by the expanse of the night sky. Over 2,600 LED lights are positioned at the nodes of the trellis structural shapes. The programming of these lights can highlight patterns of the trellis in sync with projected content or in moments of silence, they can be controlled in isolation to create a twinkle of stars. Each light is capable of 281 trillion shades of color with a range of intensity. This allows the lights to be integrated with the video projection system to enhance the immersive experience. The garden lighting compliments the overall immersive experience with low levels of light designed for pedestrian safety. Lighting in the water features, benches, and paving illuminates the ground plane. Bollards and lights mounted on trees provide an additional controllable layer of illumination as necessary for the public realm. All the lighting is controllable with the latest technology to provide a seamless experience for any event imaginable. Al Wasl Plaza is a theater; a platform for an endless array of performances.

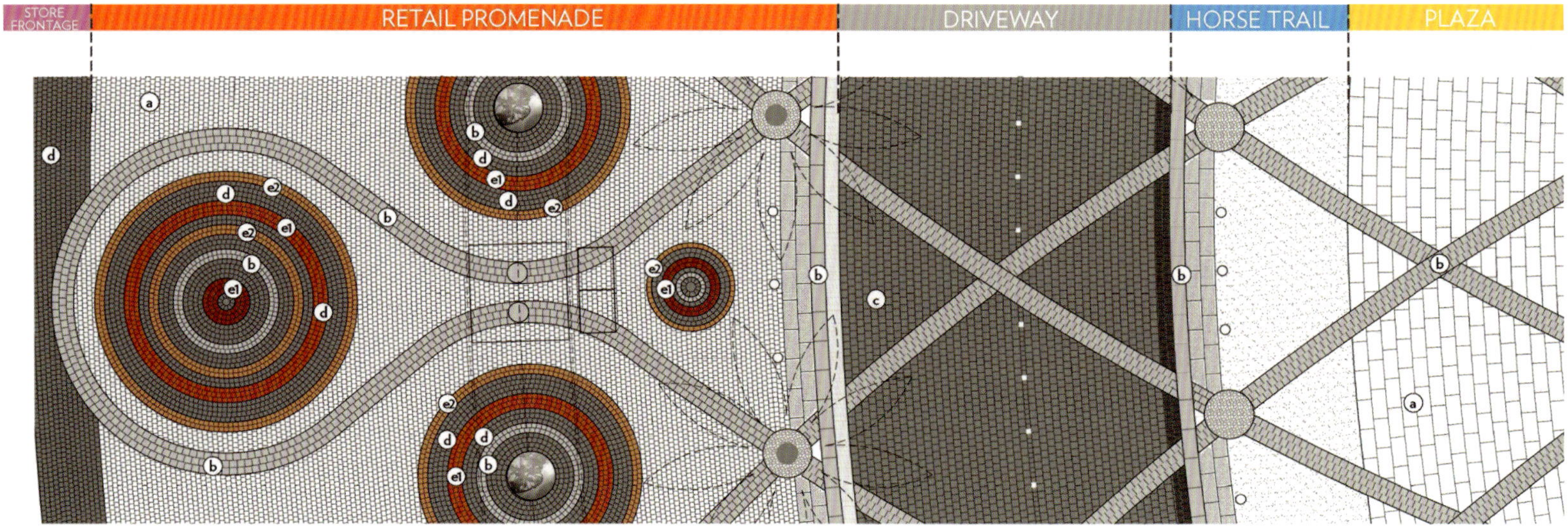

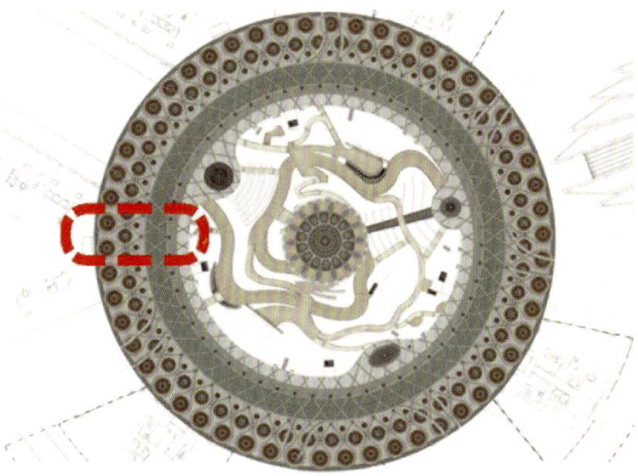

SHARED STREET DESIGN

The Al Wasl ring road is designed as a shared street where vehicles are participants in a vibrant public space that prioritizes safety and pedestrian right-of-way. Shared street design removes the formal distinctions and traditional barriers between zones dedicated to pedestrians, cyclists, and motorized vehicles. The street is shared by everyone, with each user becoming increasingly aware and respectful of the others. Formal shared street environments are considered in places where pedestrian activity is high and vehicle volumes are low or discouraged. Shared streets use traffic calming and unique streetscape features to create a safe environment for pedestrians and can be easily converted to 100% pedestrian use on weekends or for special events. Prior to Al Wasl Plaza, there were no public spaces of this design, scale, character, or function in the UAE. Therefore, as a progressive city, Dubai will experience Al Wasl as a precedent for future similar streetscape projects. It will be the new promenade for Dubai.

TRELLIS

The centrality of Al Wasl presented an opportunity to create an inspirational plaza for gathering. In the hot Dubai climate, the need for shade led the design to a grand trellis tying a lush garden at the ground to the diffused sunlight above during the day. At night, Al Wasl is a stage that heightens the experience and appreciation of the beautiful night sky. The sky is framed, and the stars are experienced from the culturally inspired and technologically enhanced modern garden. The space is the first of its kind, a new typology of civic space and the largest 360-degree audio and visual immersive experience in the world. The pattern of the trellis structure symbolizes the truly Emirati nature of the Expo 2020 logo. Inspired by a 4,000-year-old gold ring found in a desert archaeological site by Sheikh Mohammed, the logo is authentic to the UAE. It beams at the center with gold light as a beacon of life and prosperity, just as the sun shines through the oculus of Al Wasl trellis to the garden below.

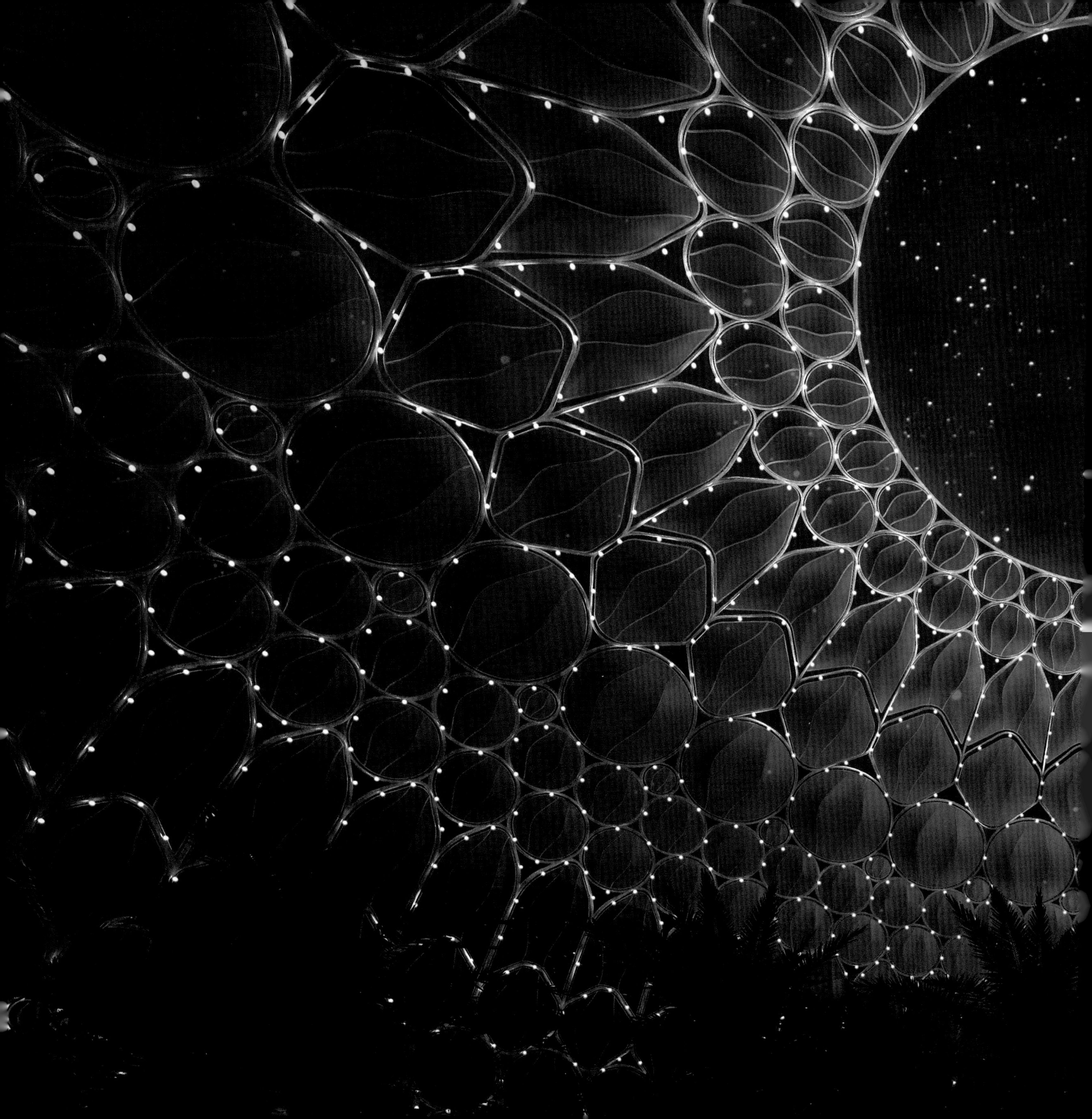

TRELLIS DESIGN

World Expos have a long history of prominent and innovative structures from London to Paris to Milan that form the centerpiece of the event and attract visitors from all over the world. In late 2016 and into early 2017, AS+GG teamed with world-renowned structural engineering firm Thornton Tomasetti (TT) in the design competition for the Al Wasl parcels.

During the early stages of the competition, the design team explored a wide variety of rectilinear and diagonalized gridshells. These early iterations concentrated on sizing of the module, and the openings at the base and the oculus. The openings at the base are aligned with the six major pedestrian and vehicular arteries converging into and out of Al Wasl Plaza, with the alignment of the structure and context studied through many iterations. The largest portal opens to the UAE pavilion, defining the prominent relationship between the two important cultural icons.

Midway through the competition, Expo 2020 leadership asked the design team if the official event logo, which is an abstraction of the 4,000-year-old ring, could be incorporated in some fashion, into the design of the trellis. The logo has important meaning in the context of Expo 2020's central theme of connection—Connecting Minds, Creating the Future—and Dubai's status as a hub that connects the world both culturally and geographically. This idea elevated the project to a new level, solidifying its prominence in the heart of the Expo.

Concentric in form, the logo is a radial array of circular and fileted poly shapes that increase in scale toward the perimeter. The conceptual framework translated well into the curved forms, allowing the design iterations to focus on the scale of the openings. The first three iterations were not dense enough in structural form, requiring the architectural team to continue to add additional layers of geometry.

The height of the arch openings at the base was optimized during these studies in parallel with the design of the adjacent buildings. A slender parabolic arch was selected to satisfy the structural and aesthetic requirements of the project while maintaining the resemblance to the Expo 2020 logo. Arches are historically significant and prevalent in Middle Eastern architecture. In Al Wasl, the base creates an arcade defining an intimate relationship between the buildings, the outer pedestrian zone, and the inner plaza.

The final design for the Al Wasl Plaza trellis is an optimized curvilinear geometry of steel pipe members in keeping with the iconic Expo 2020 logo. The geometric voids between the steel elements are infilled with lightweight, stressed fabric panels with a transparency of about 30% that provides shade during the day, and functions as a projection surface during the evening hours. The simplicity of the overall form, combined with the intricacy of the fabric panels, achieves the desired intent to provide shade to the plaza below with a rich array of dappled light, while maintaining a level of transparency that allows the sun to animate the garden as it travels across the sky.

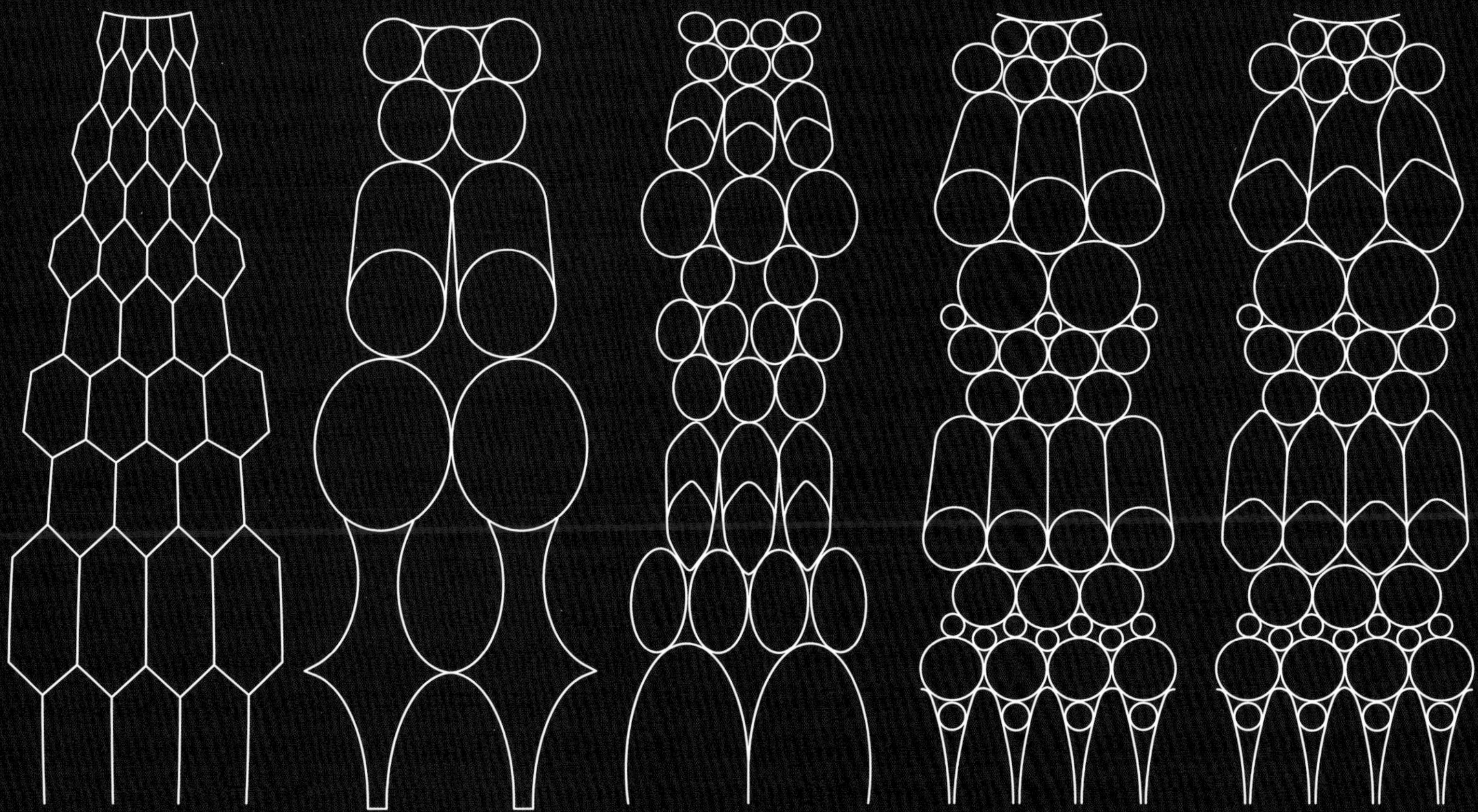

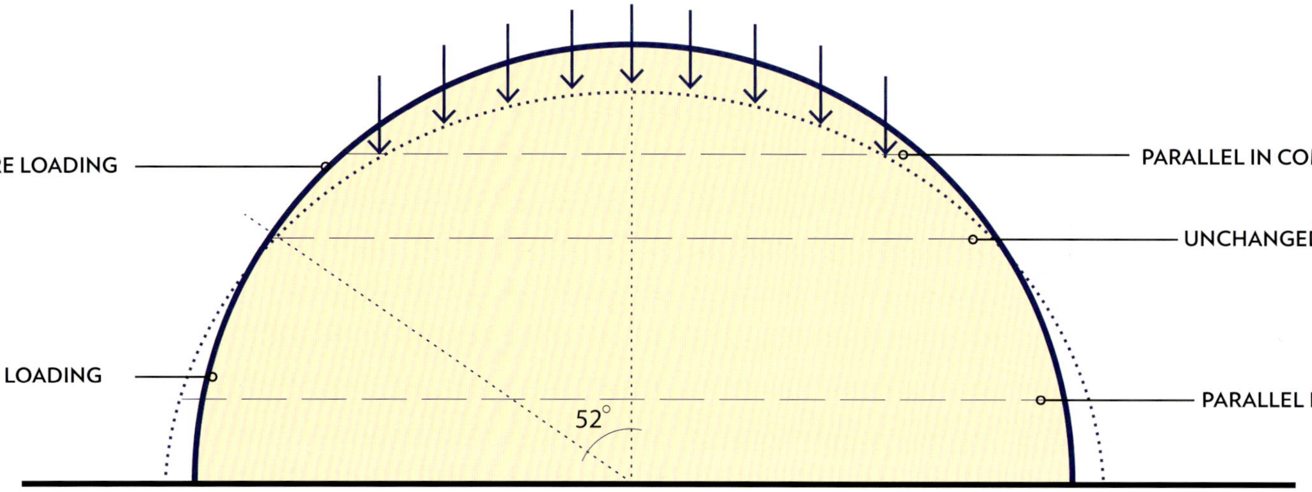

TRELLIS STRUCTURAL DESIGN CRITERIA

The trellis dome geometry is constructed as a revolved surface. Two pure 55-meter radius spheres are offset at a distance of 13 meters from a central axis and revolved 360 degrees. The oculus opening at the top is 35 meters in diameter. Meridional forces act in the longitudinal direction, increasing in magnitude from the crown to the base. Hoop forces act in the latitudinal direction and contribute significantly to the stability of the dome. The oculus adds complexity as this open edge is susceptible to additional stresses. Most of the steel pipe members are in compression as they align vertically in the meridional force direction. Horizontally aligned members in the lower two thirds of the dome are in tension as hoop forces that restrict the surface from bowing out due to the vertically applied loading. As a cultural landmark, the structural design accommodates a multitude of superimposed loads and conditions including the following: wind, gantry access cleaning unit, suspended lighting, fabric and fabric support brackets, maintenance access live load, ambient thermal gradients, seismic, event rigging loads, suspended projector and speaker enclosures, connection material at joints, MEP infrastructure, and accumulated drifting sand.

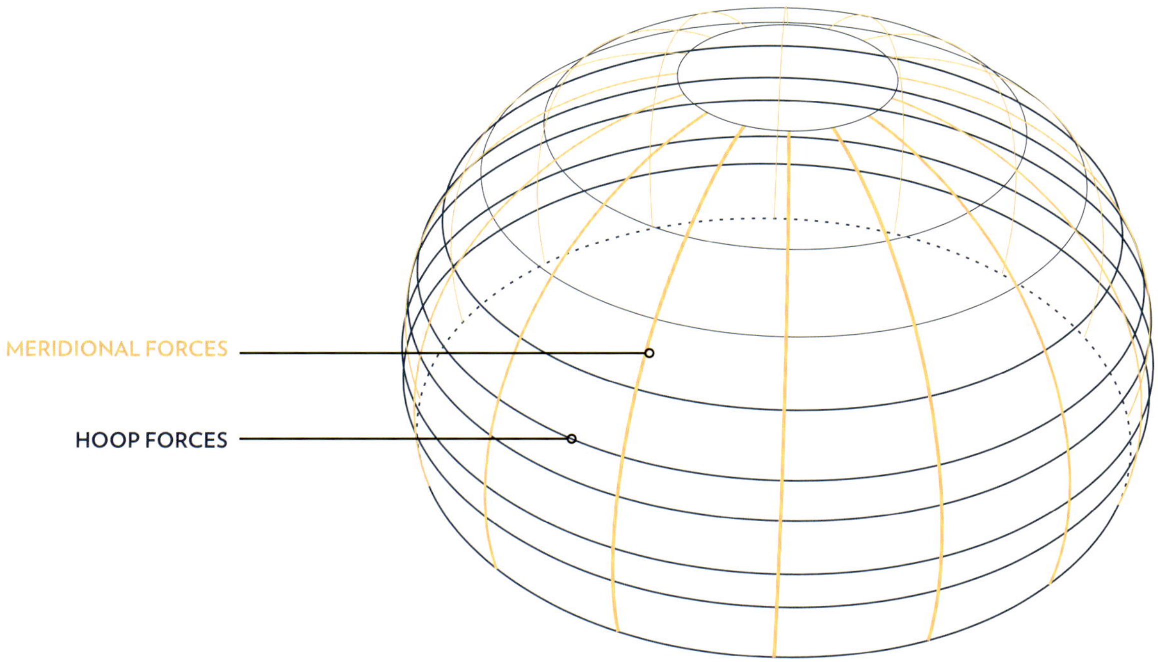
MERIDIONAL FORCES
HOOP FORCES

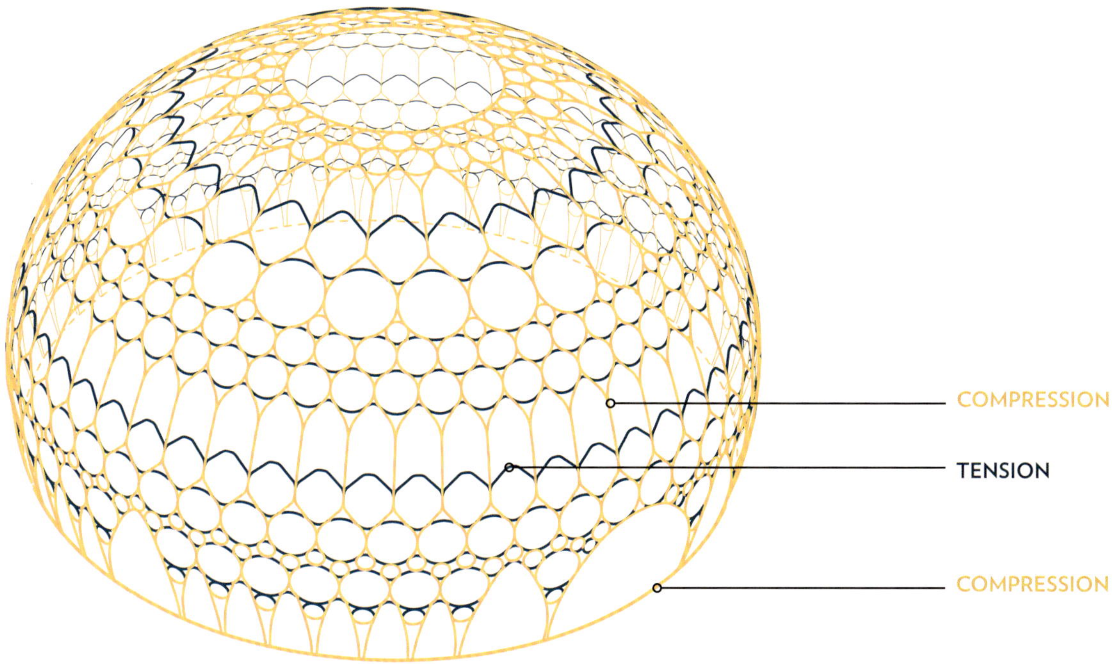
COMPRESSION
TENSION
COMPRESSION

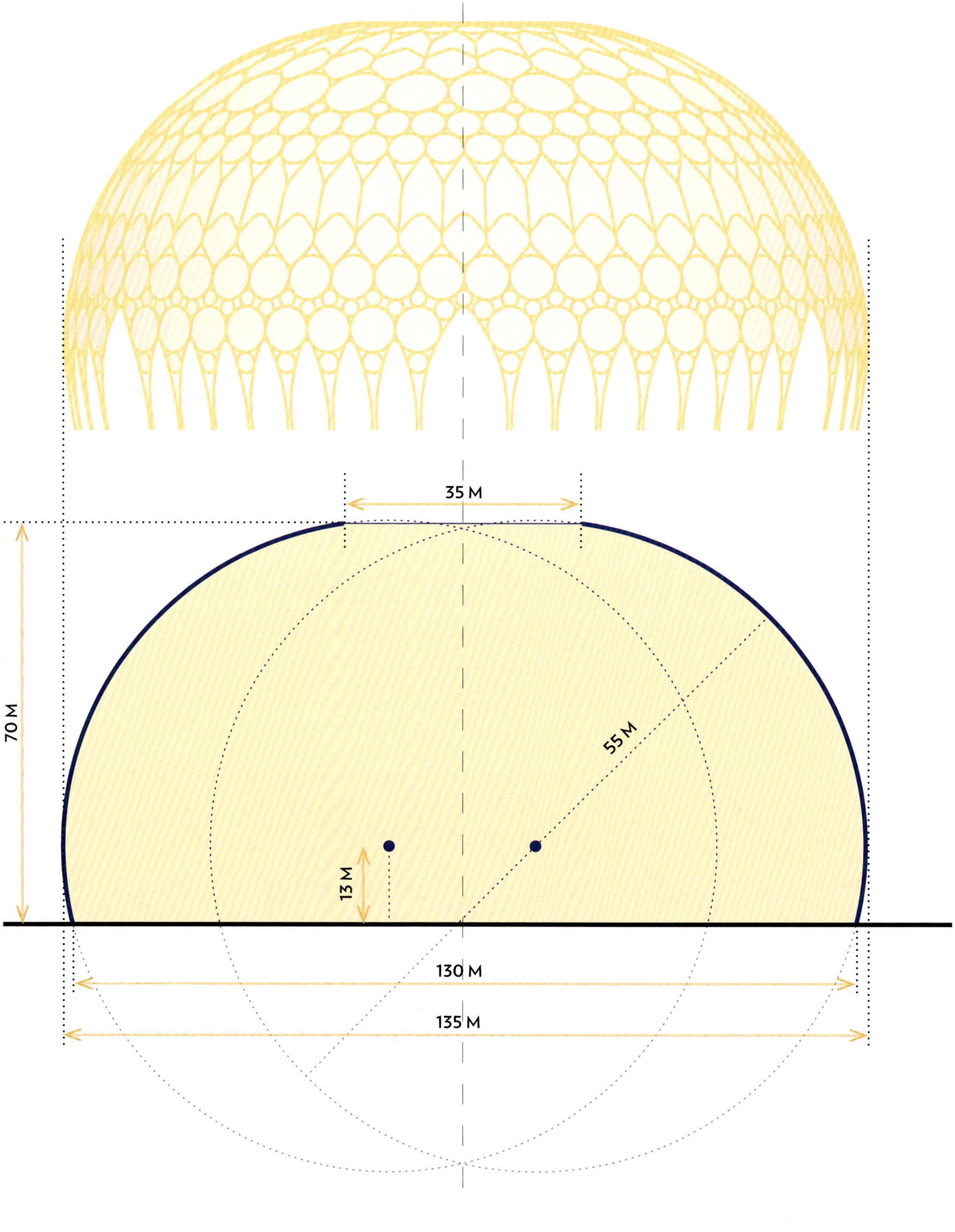
35 M
70 M
55 M
13 M
130 M
135 M

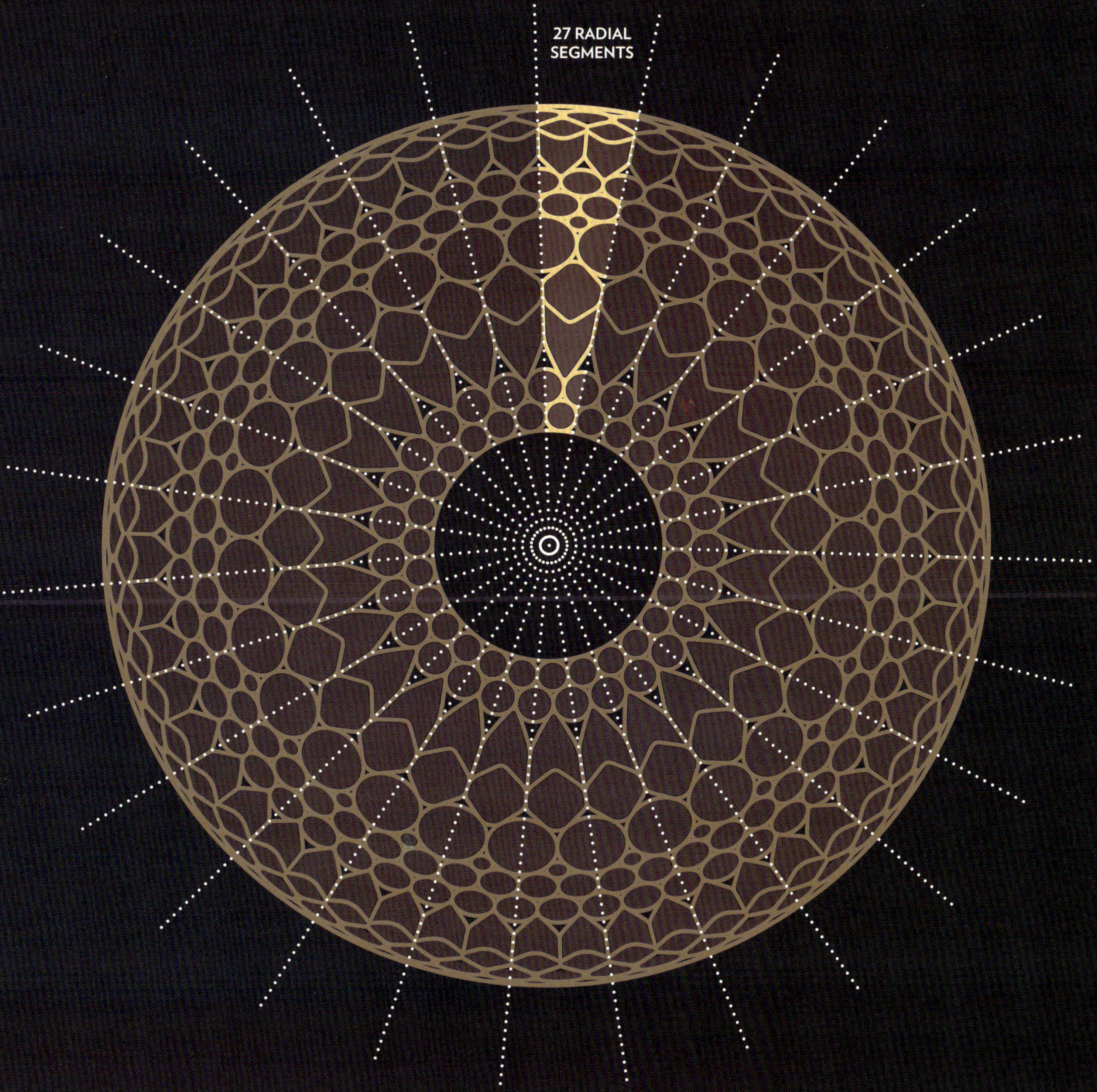
27 RADIAL
SEGMENTS

ARC DE TRIOMPHE, PARIS

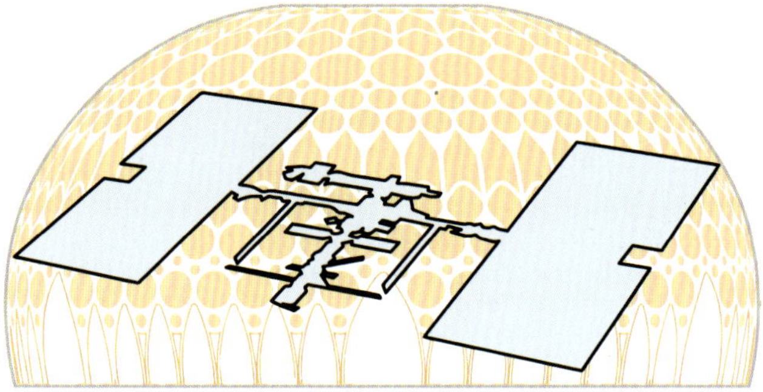

INTERNATIONAL SPACE STATION

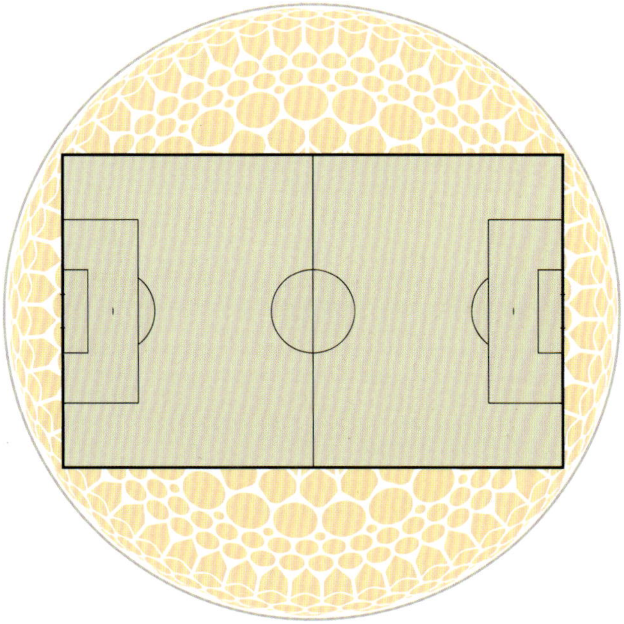

FIFA FOOTBALL FIELD

BOEING 777 PLANES

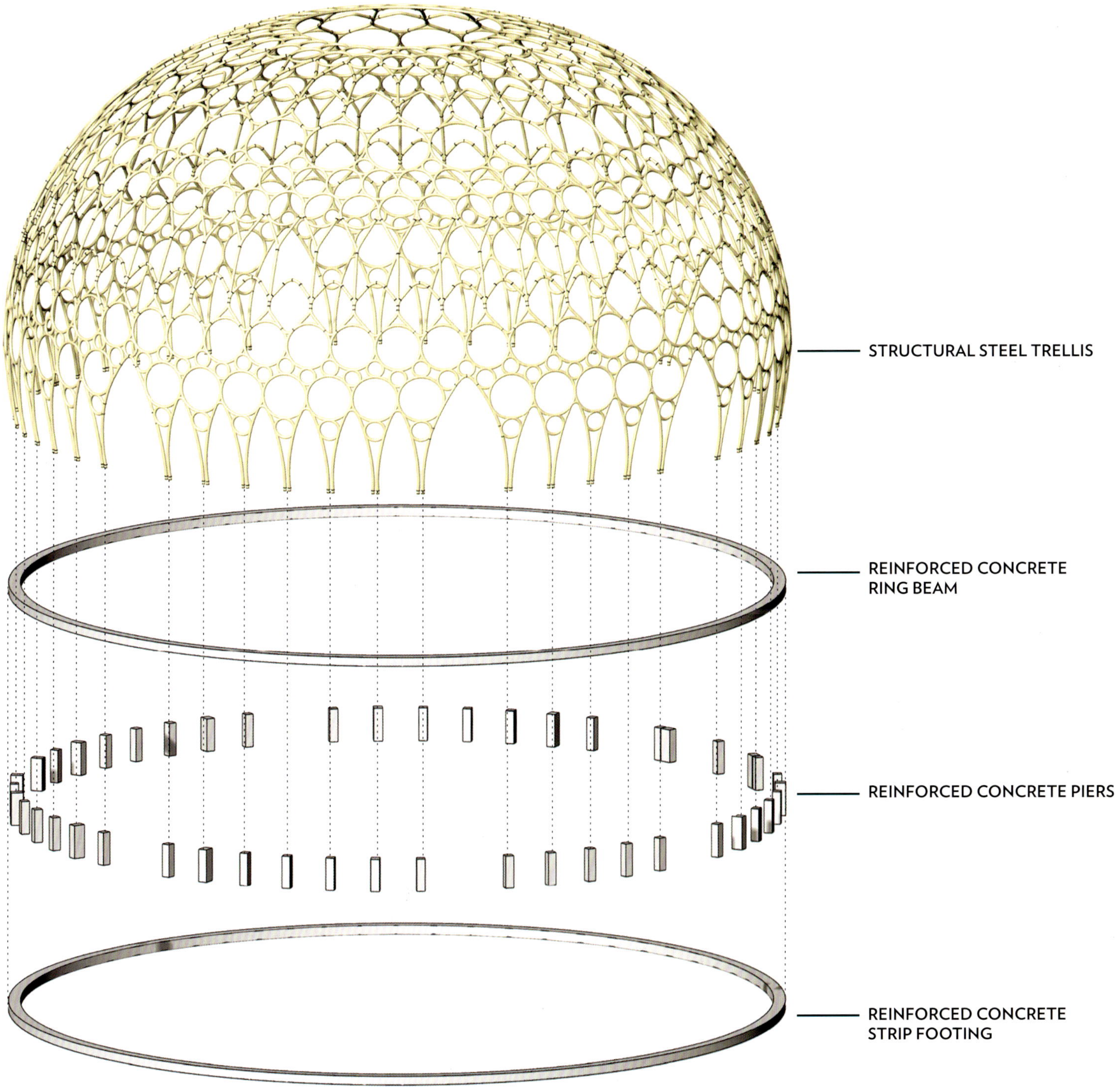
STRUCTURAL STEEL TRELLIS
REINFORCED CONCRETE RING BEAM
REINFORCED CONCRETE PIERS
REINFORCED CONCRETE STRIP FOOTING

TRELLIS GEOMETRY + STRUCTURE OPTIMIZATION

The rationalization of the wireframe, or the centerline geometry of the trellis, was an iterative process between the architectural and structural engineering design teams, which continued between the design team and the steel fabricator and erector Cimolai Rimond Middle East (CRME) following the contract award and mobilization. There were three primary goals of the optimization process for the geometric definition of the trellis steel framework. The first was to facilitate the steel fabrication through a rationalized series of tangent, circular arcs with the least number of pipe-to-pipe splices. Second, to promote repetition of the steelwork thereby improving cost-effectiveness, and finally, to maintain the aesthetic of the competition design.

Steel pipe, which is more properly called circular hollow sections (CHS), was determined very early in the process to be the most suitable steel shape for the trellis primarily due to aesthetics and efficiency. Given the three-dimensional nature of the trellis shape, these structural members need to be bent and connected to adjacent members that are never in the same plane. Using pipe of the same diameter allows for the creation of a seamless appearance, avoiding the warping and discontinuity inherent in rectangular hollow sections or open shapes such as I-sections. The internal void of the CHS elements also provide the desired advantage of being the main arteries within the trellis to route the lights, speakers, cameras, and projector pods discretely out of public view.

The nature of the connections at the confluence of the steel pipes was a source of substantial aesthetic and structural considerations. A variety of schemes were studied both aesthetically and analytically from the two pipe centerlines meeting in perfect tangency to the two pipes passing without interruption. Ultimately the tangent scheme prevailed because it best addressed the design vision. Although this approach created challenges that required creative engineering solutions in the fabrication of the nodes, the resulting look was agreed on by the architects and engineers and endorsed by the Expo client. The physical fabrication of these connections was also a subject of much development by both the design team and fabricator/erector and some geometric modifications were introduced to facilitate construction without compromising the overall design aesthetic.

Apart from the varying arched openings at the base of the trellis, there are 27 identical sectors, or modules of 13.33-degree sweep defining the centerline geometry. The uppermost oculus compression ring is 35 meters in diameter, and 70 meters above the floor of the central plaza offering unobstructed views to the sky above. Combining the use of high strength S460, EN 10210-1, hot-finished seamless steel material sourced in Europe and China, and a consistent 500mm nominal pipe diameter throughout the dome (with varying wall thicknesses between 10mm and 50mm) proved to be the most cost-effective solution. This constant pipe size allowed the completed structure, its pipes and intersecting steel connections, to have a slim, refined, and continuous appearance.

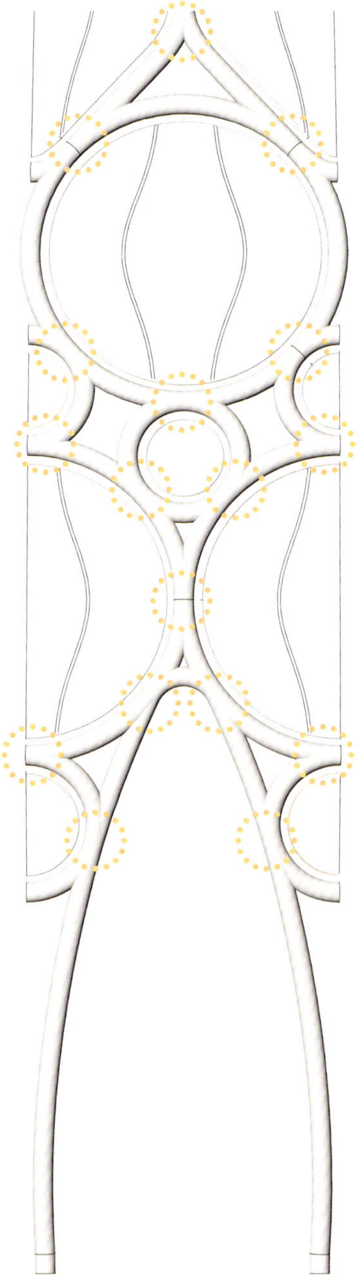

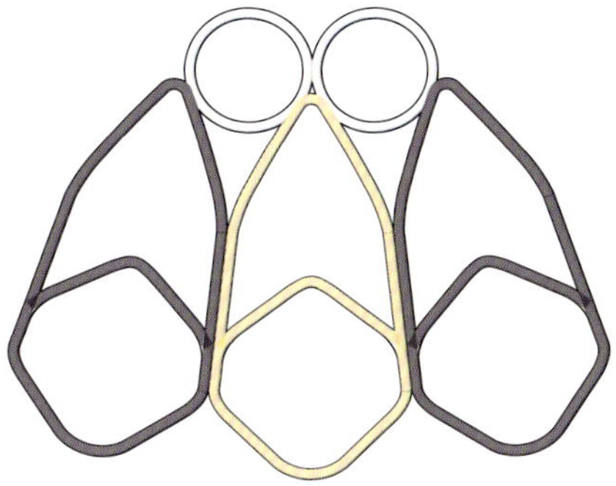

DOUBLE TUBULAR SYSTEM

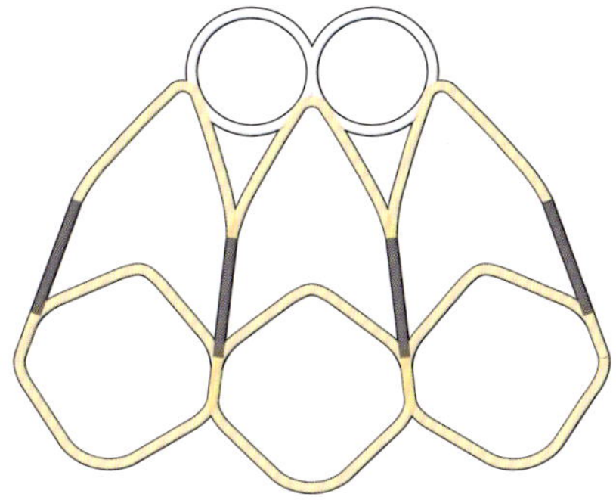

SINGLE TUBULAR SYSTEM

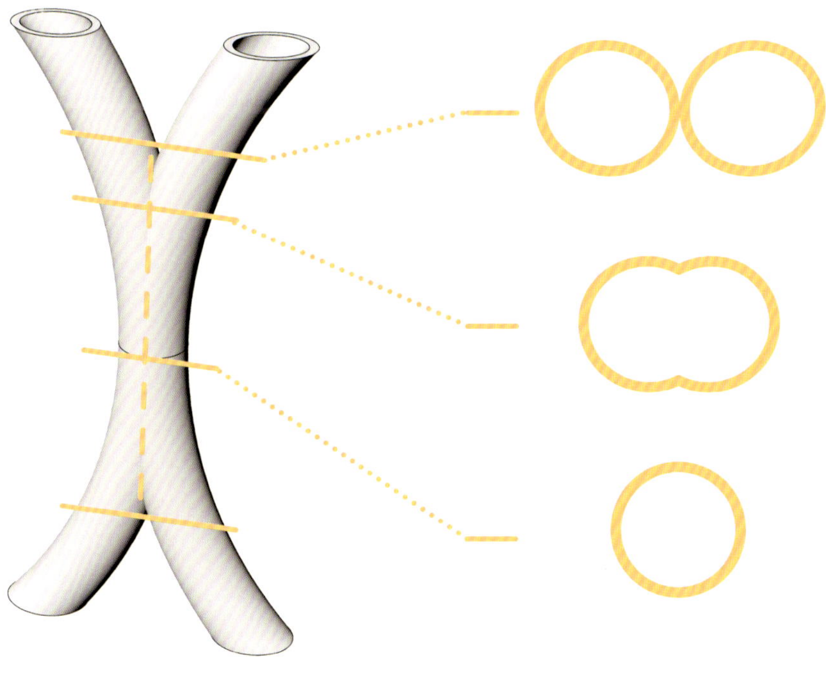

MERGED

INDICATES NODES OF CONNECTION

ENGINEERING OF TRELLIS JOINTS

The issue of the localized stresses within the nodal regions where the pipe sections merge required additional simulation beyond the overall global modeling of the trellis. As the unique merged joint geometry has no basis in any published literature from which to develop design checks, it was necessary to address the localized stresses with a detailed local finite element analysis investigating possible stress concentrations. To do this, the global model was used with only local intersections fully meshed with shell elements constrained to the surrounding frame elements. Thus, there was no need to determine the forces at the ends of the isolated connection pieces as they are determined directly by the global FEA frame element model. Local imperfections related to ovality of the pipes based on assumed tolerances were also considered, but the tolerances were tight enough as to not have significant impacts on the localized stresses.

For this analysis of the stresses within the overlapping joints, localized yielding was permitted provided it was demonstrated through non-linear analysis that the overstress was highly localized and resulting strains did not exceed the material fracture criteria. Auxiliary shell models included the effects of penetrations for services through the walls of the pipe sections, particularly for LED installation and maintenance. Other detailed connection studies included the effect of the rigging brackets and projector pod supports on the primary steel framework. A substantial amount of analysis effort was required as there are many different types of overlapping connections with differing wall thicknesses of pipe joined.

Upon award of the steelwork contract, CRME requested to adjust the longitudinal welds within the overlapping joints from the full penetration welds specified by TT to partial penetration square groove welds to simplify the fabrication of the joints. TT worked with CRME's on-staff engineers for the revised connections to re-analyze and re-verify all the overlapping joint configurations on the trellis. Pipe-to-pipe butt welds for splices away from the nodal regions remained full penetration groove welds, with most performed in the shop and the remaining achieved on site.

Connection node designs were also analyzed for impacts related to the erection of the structural system with a series of static load multipliers applied to the element demands based on the construction sequence analysis as performed by CRME's engineer, Maffeis. TT collaborated closely with Maffeis to ensure the locked-in stresses due to the contractor selected erection sequence were minimal.

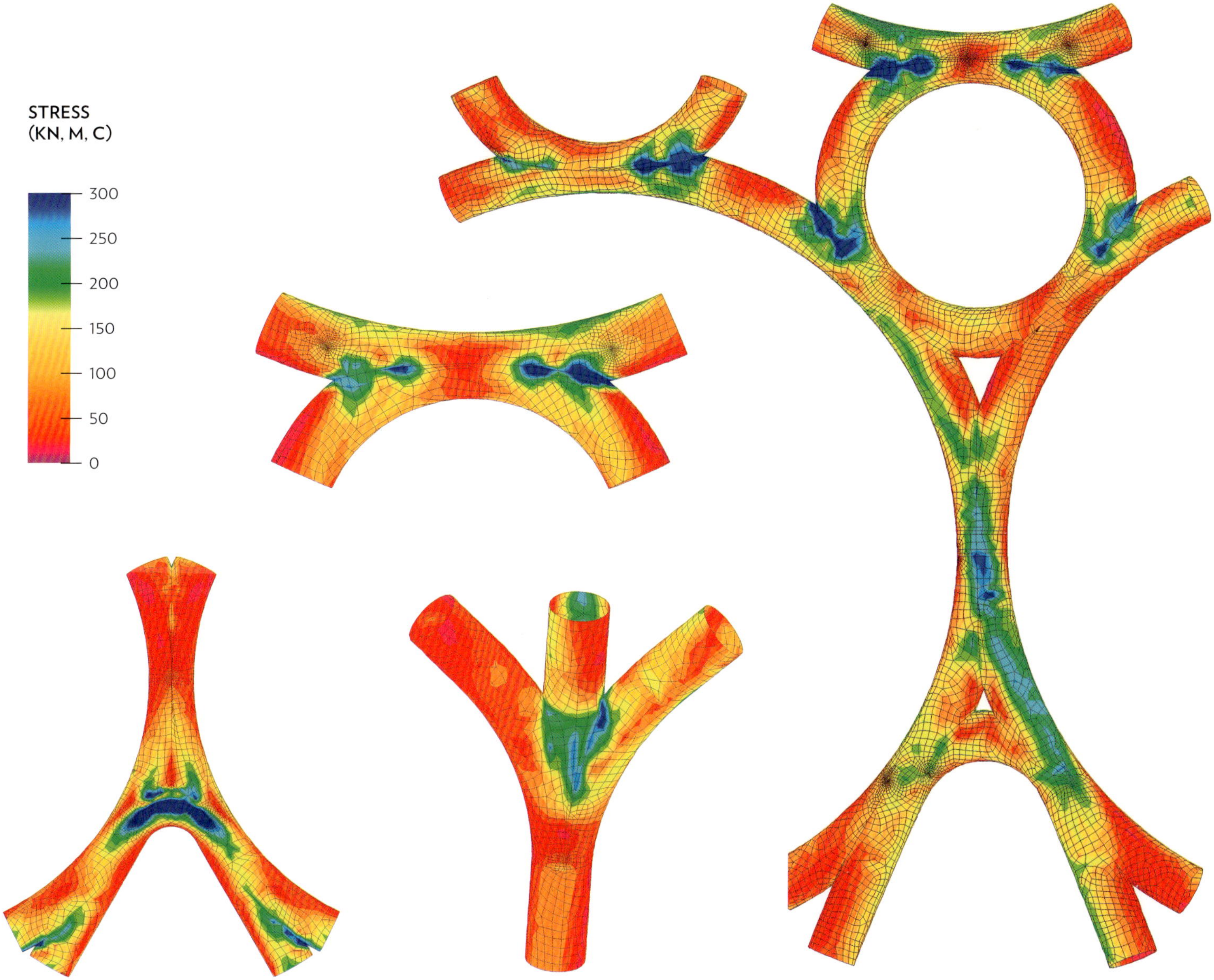
STRESS
(KN, M, C)
300
250
200
150
100
50
0

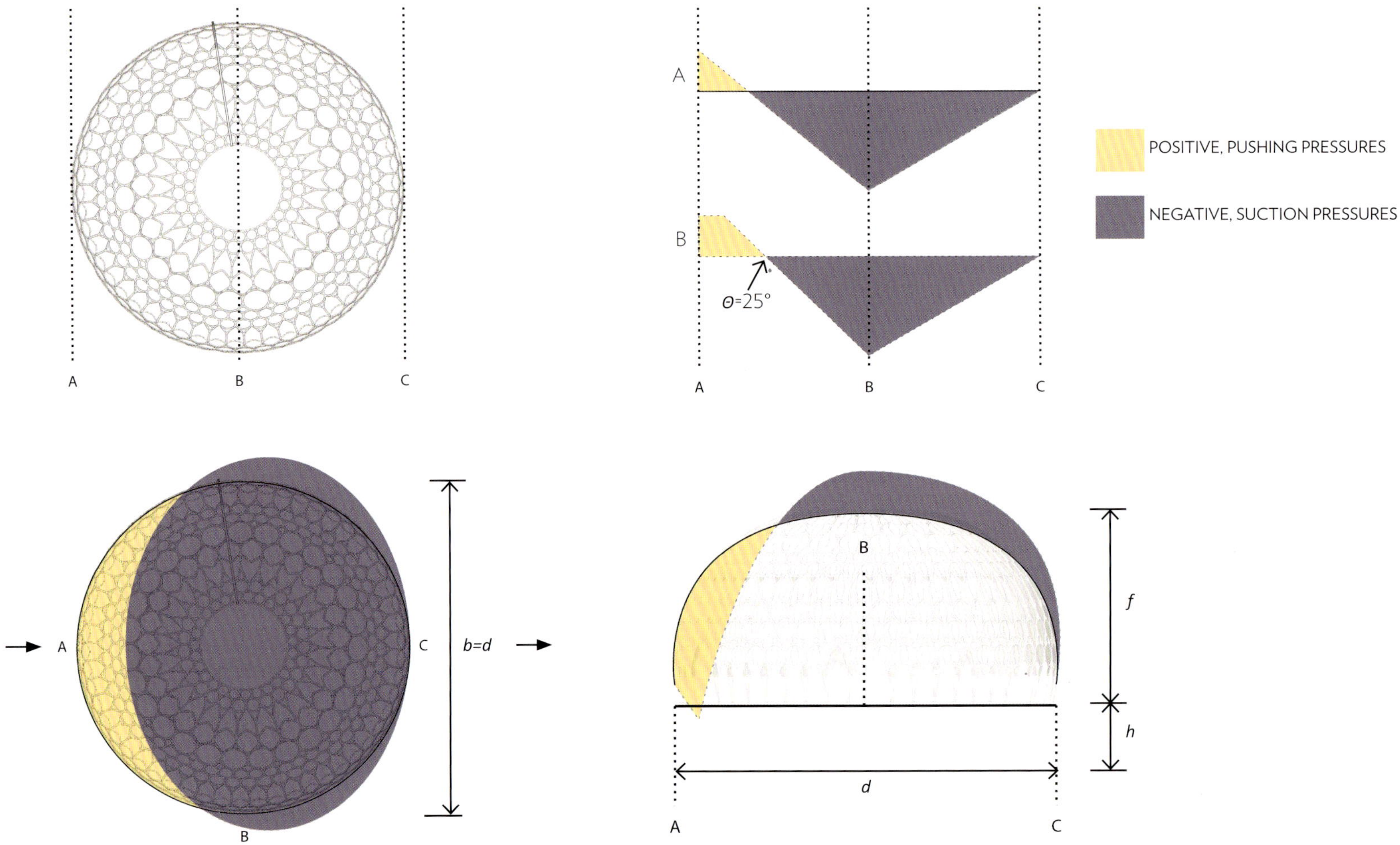

TRELLIS WIND FORCE ANALYSIS

As the trellis is nearly fully enclosed from a wind sail standpoint, wind loads were determined through use of a High Frequency Pressure Integration (HFPI) wind tunnel test performed by Rowan Williams Davies + Irwin Inc. (RWDI) at their laboratories in Ontario, Canada. The trellis was tested for two configurations: the full Expo build-out and a configuration without the adjacent five buildings and utilized the locally mandated wind speed of 45 m/sec as the basis of testing. The five adjacent buildings tend to shield the trellis, although some deleterious funneling of wind between the buildings onto the trellis was detected from the testing. However, overall test results indicated a significant reduction in the peak negative design pressures observed at the apex of the dome when compared to codified references for wind pressure gradients on closed spherical surfaces. This reduction is attributed to the vented regions of the center oculus and openings at the base of the structure and the design of the trellis was able to take advantage of these reductions to achieve a slenderer and more elegant structural framework.

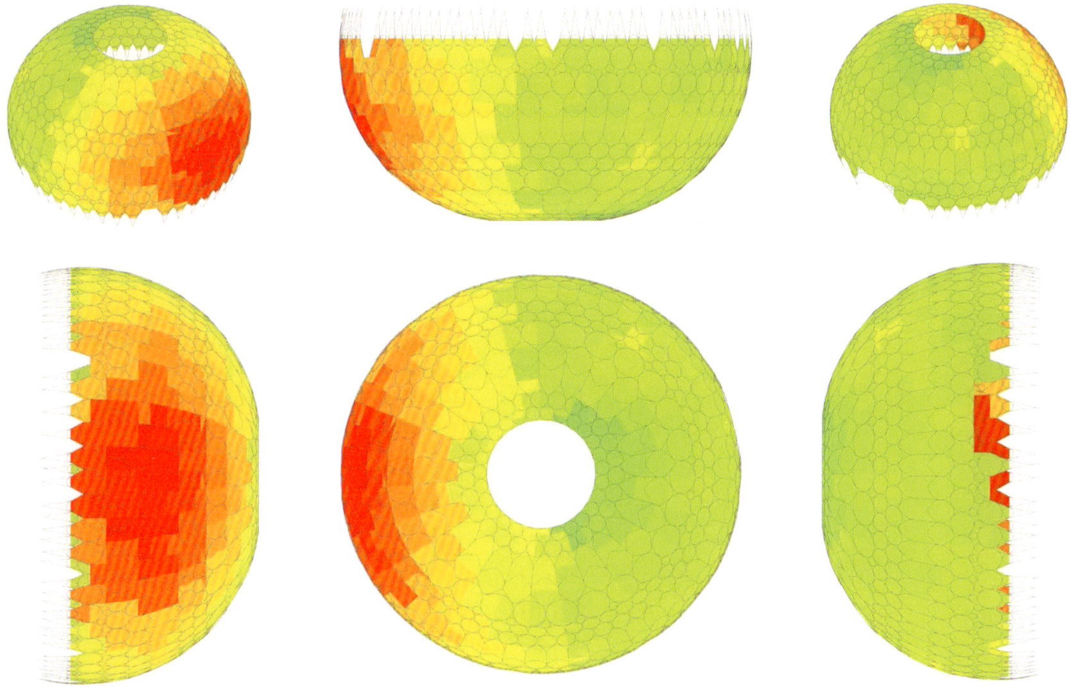

WIND TUNNEL RESULTS

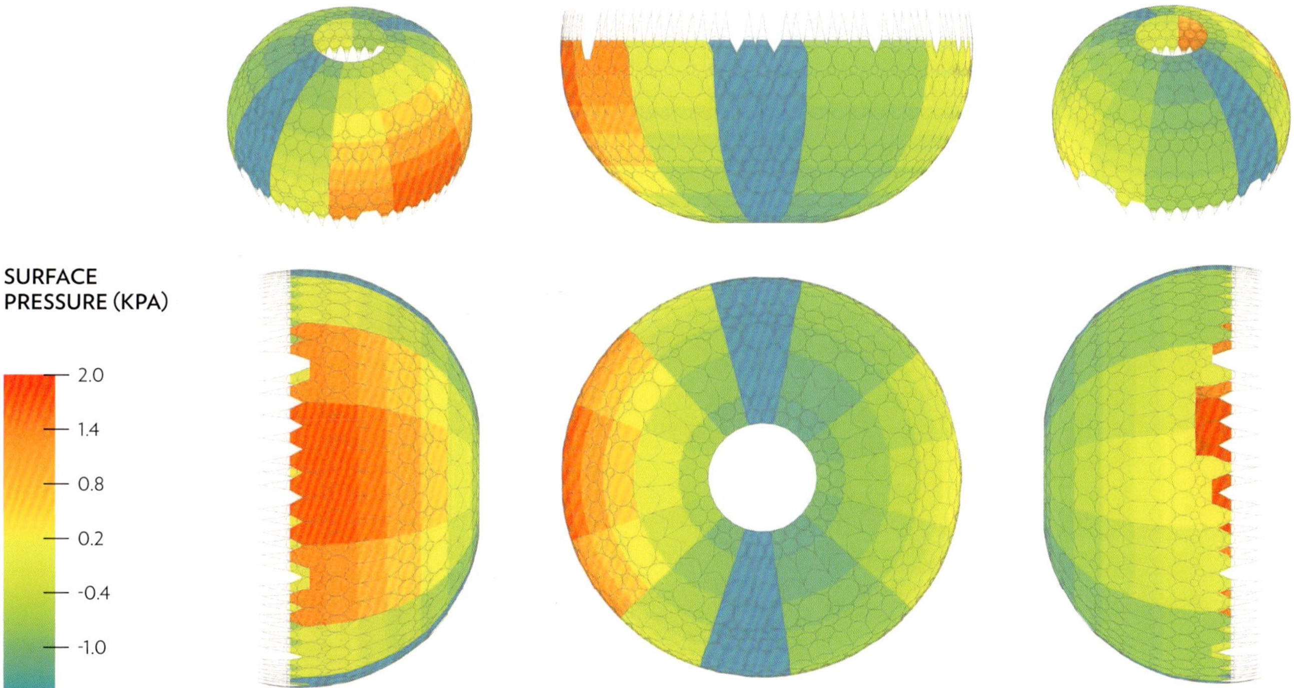

DESIGN CODE APPROXIMATION

TRELLIS FABRIC MATERIALITY

Central to the function of shading the plaza, the trellis materiality must effectively respond to the local climate. The design team faced the challenge of sourcing, or creating, a material that met the varied requirements of this unique application. To allow sunlight to the plants below, the fabric must be translucent. Additionally, it must allow air movement to avoid stagnancy. As hot air rises and escapes out the trellis, fresh air circulates within. In this desert climate, dust accumulation must be minimized as it could collect and turn into a maintenance problem with infrequent but strong seasonal rainfall. If the material were not porous, this infrequent rainfall would collect on the surface requiring a significant channeling drainage system. Therefore, it was determined that a porous material allowing light, air, and water to pass, while still providing shade, was to be procured.

Although the original intent of the trellis was to shade the plaza, it quickly assumed a secondary purpose as its design evolved into an armature for and container of a very ambitious audio and visual immersive experience. The desired materiality for the infill panel took on a dual quality; in addition to the environmental requirements, it must also receive projected light. Solid fabrics would provide a stable projection surface but would not meet the environmental requirements, nor would it achieve the architectural desire to view the projected light from both sides. Metal meshes were considered, but the desire to see projection from the outside narrowed the material search to fabrics.

The architecture of the office and hotel buildings was developing as an offset from the trellis, simultaneous to the trellis design. This raised new considerations prioritizing fire and life safety regulations. The fabric was required to comply with Dubai Municipality fire and life safety requirements to protect large groups of users below in the garden as well as the occupants inside the adjacent buildings.

Once the material properties were determined, the architects visited fabric manufacturers in Europe to understand the potential to custom fabricate the desired material. The companies are leaders in their markets and showed an interest in altering their existing product lines to meet the project requirements. The manufacturing facilities required a loom to produce the fabric at large scales up to 10 meters in width. In collaboration with the manufacturers, several materials were selected for testing that seemed to provide all the required characteristics.

Initially the design team selected a PTFE fiberglass mesh fabric with two densities. Fabric with 50% nominal translucency was positioned in front of the buildings to allow occupants to participate and more clearly see events in the garden and fabric with 30% nominal translucency was located everywhere else. Upon further consideration and testing, it was determined that the 30% translucent fabric with 20% open area should be used everywhere to improve the clarity of the projected image. A beacon of light at the center of the master plan, the trellis was designed for visibility from afar, not only from the Expo district, but from a plane landing at the nearby Dubai Al Maktoum International Airport.

PTFE coated fiberglass mesh with 20% nominal open area allows views from the garden to the outside and from the adjacent buildings into the garden.

Hot air escapes through the porous fabric and voids between the structure.

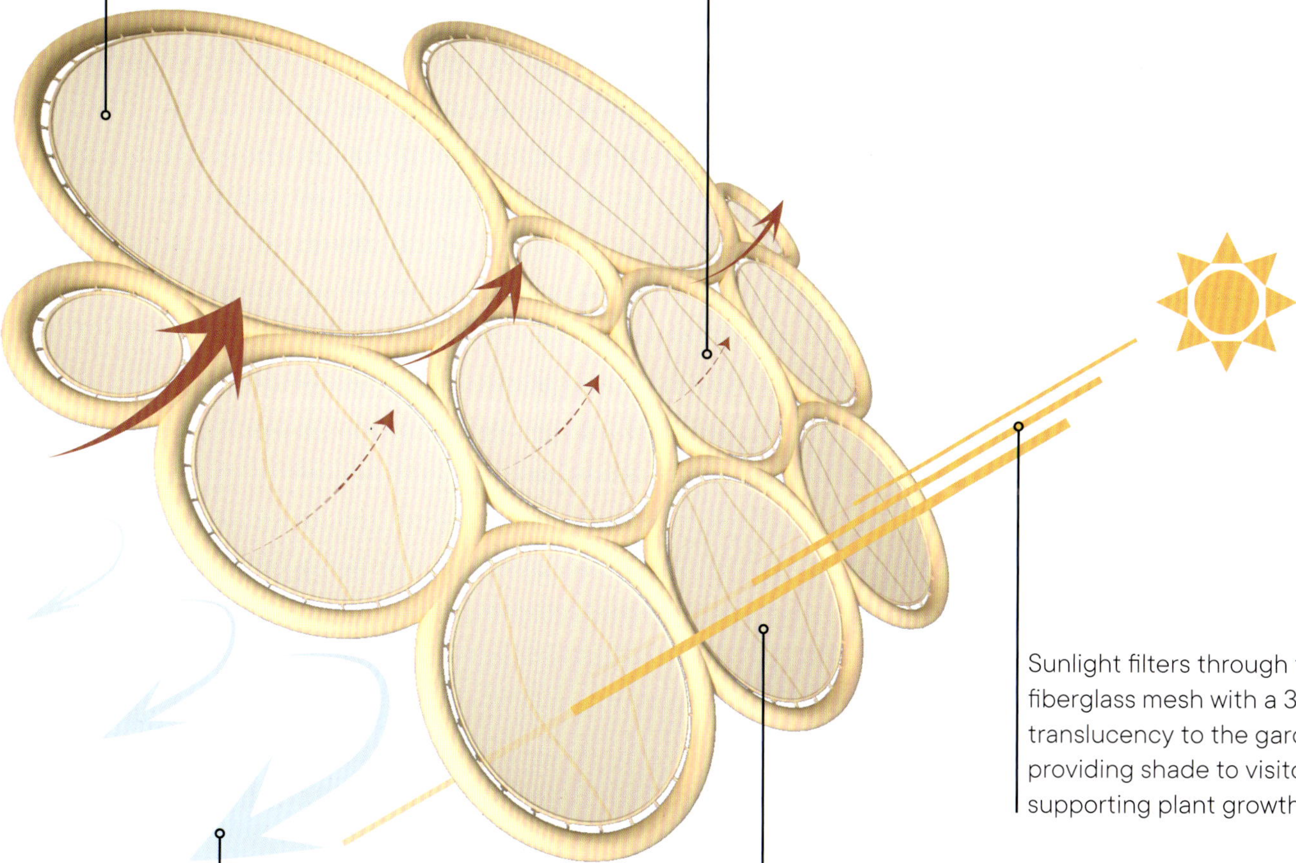

Sunlight filters through the fiberglass mesh with a 30% nominal translucency to the garden below providing shade to visitors, while also supporting plant growth.

Cooler air circulates under the canopy in the shaded garden below the trellis.

Seams are designed into the panels over 3.8 meters wide, the maximum fabric width, allowing them to be prefabricated and efficiently installed on site.

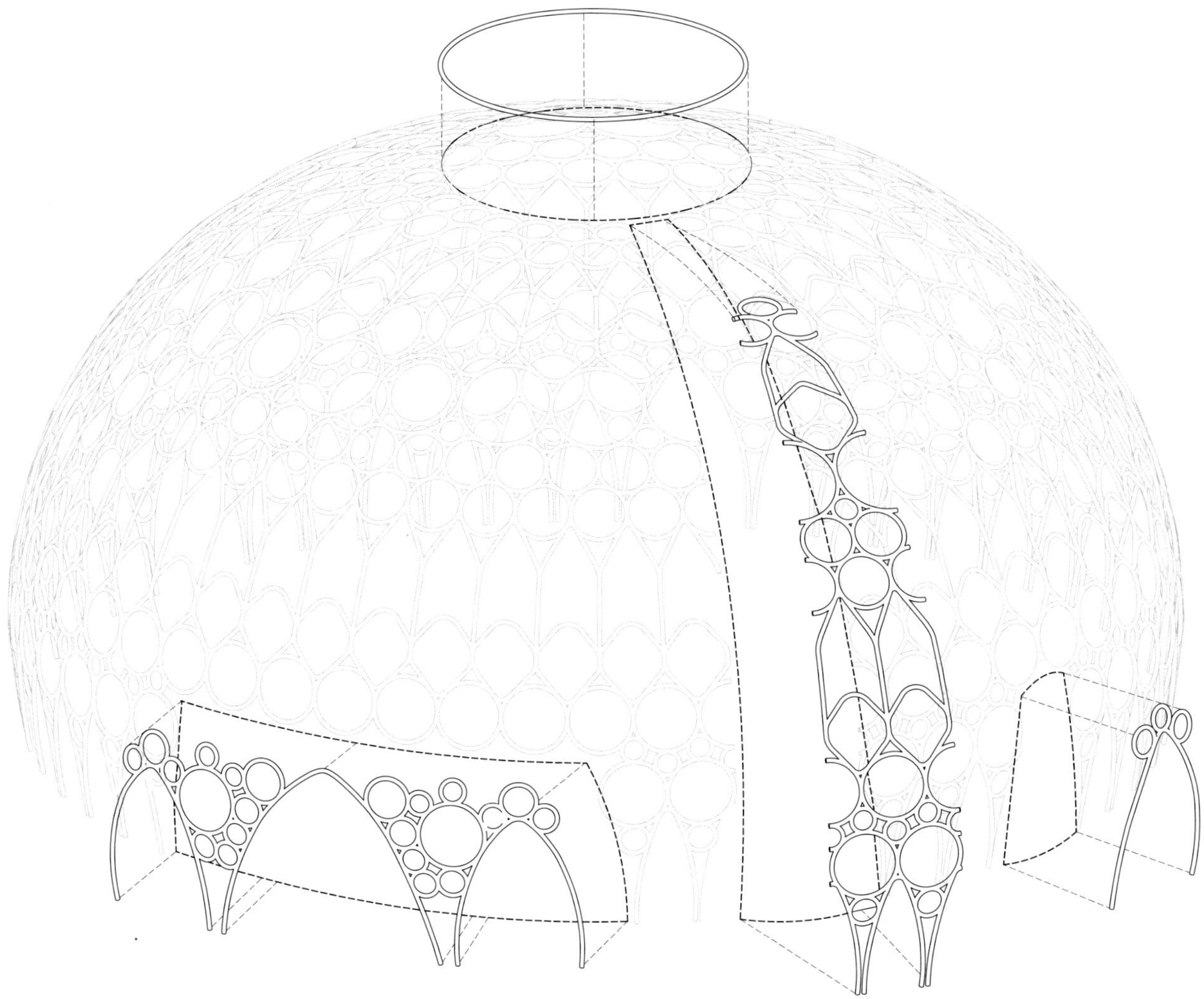

TRELLIS INFILL SYSTEM

In parallel with the design and optimization of the trellis structure, the attachment system for the infill material was designed. The relationship between the infill panels and the structure has a critical role in the overall expression of the trellis. Several options were studied including a near-continuous surface with no gaps between the structure and fabric and systems attached above or below the structural members. Most of the options failed to highlight the elaborate geometry of the structure. The selected scheme is offset in from the structural members to celebrate the Expo 2020 logo geometry. A framed fabric system was developed to tension the fabric. The void between the frames and main structural members was not only useful for installation purposes, but it was desired to allow dappled direct light into the garden below. Another reason for creating the tensioned panels was to meet the tight construction schedule. The prefabricated panels were installed on site in phases.

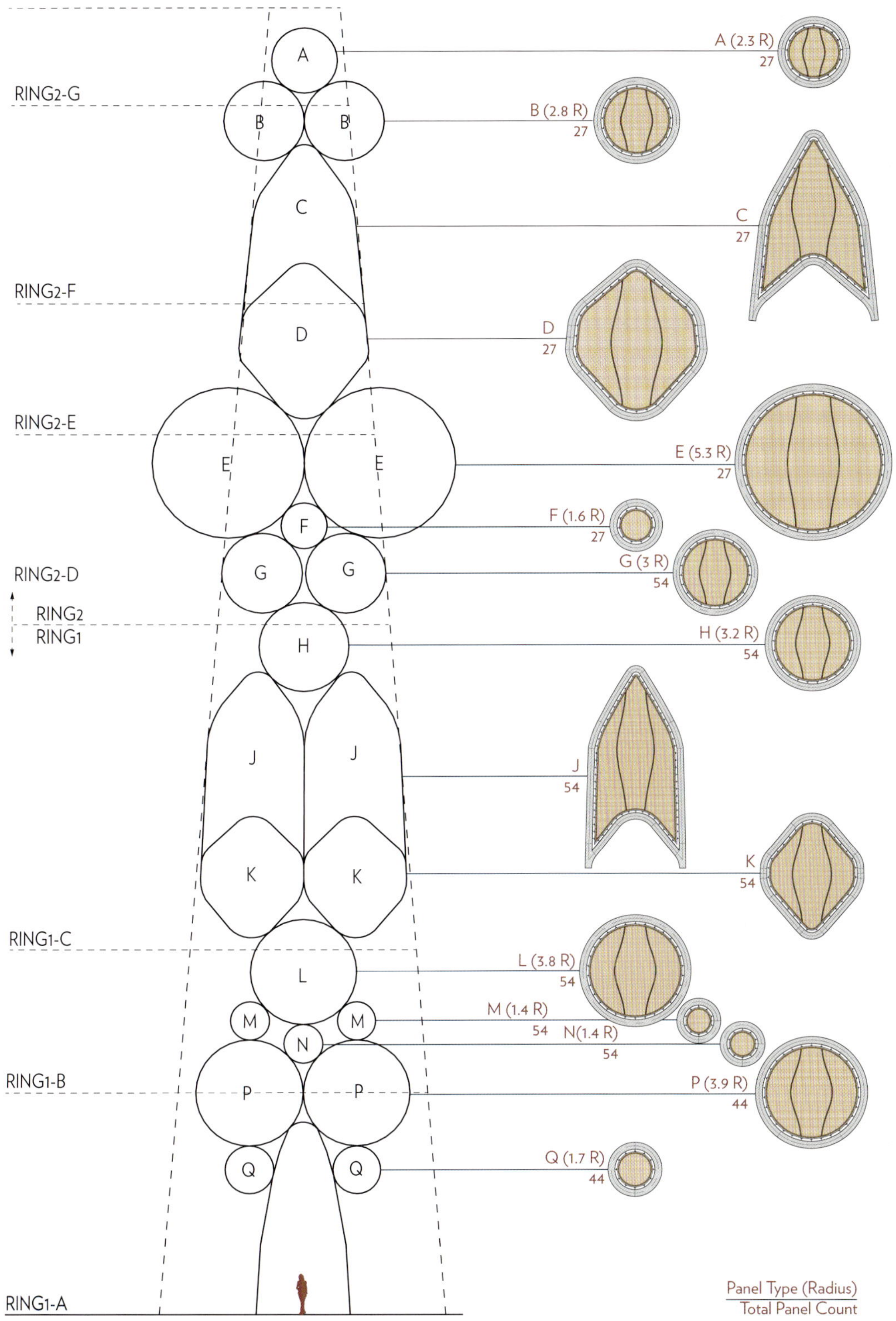
RING2-G
RING2-F
RING2-E
RING2-D
RING2
RING1
RING1-C
RING1-B
RING1-A
A
B
B
C
D
E
E
F
G
G
H
J
J
K
K
L
M
M
N
P
P
Q
Q
A (2.3 R)
27
B (2.8 R)
27
C
27
D
27
E (5.3 R)
27
F (1.6 R)
27
G (3 R)
54
H (3.2 R)
54
J
54
K
54
L (3.8 R)
54
M (1.4 R)
54
N(1.4 R)
54
P (3.9 R)
44
Q (1.7 R)
44
Panel Type (Radius)
Total Panel Count

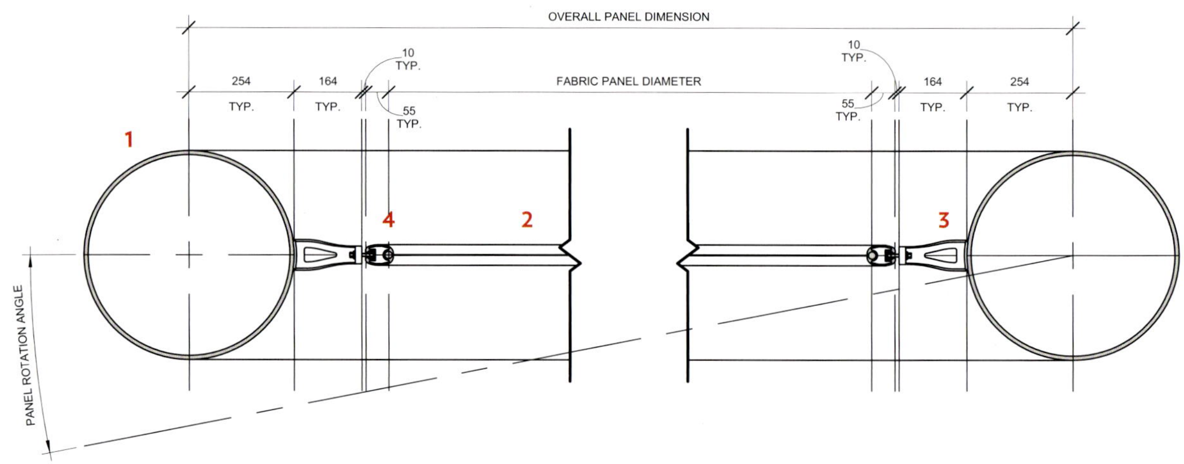

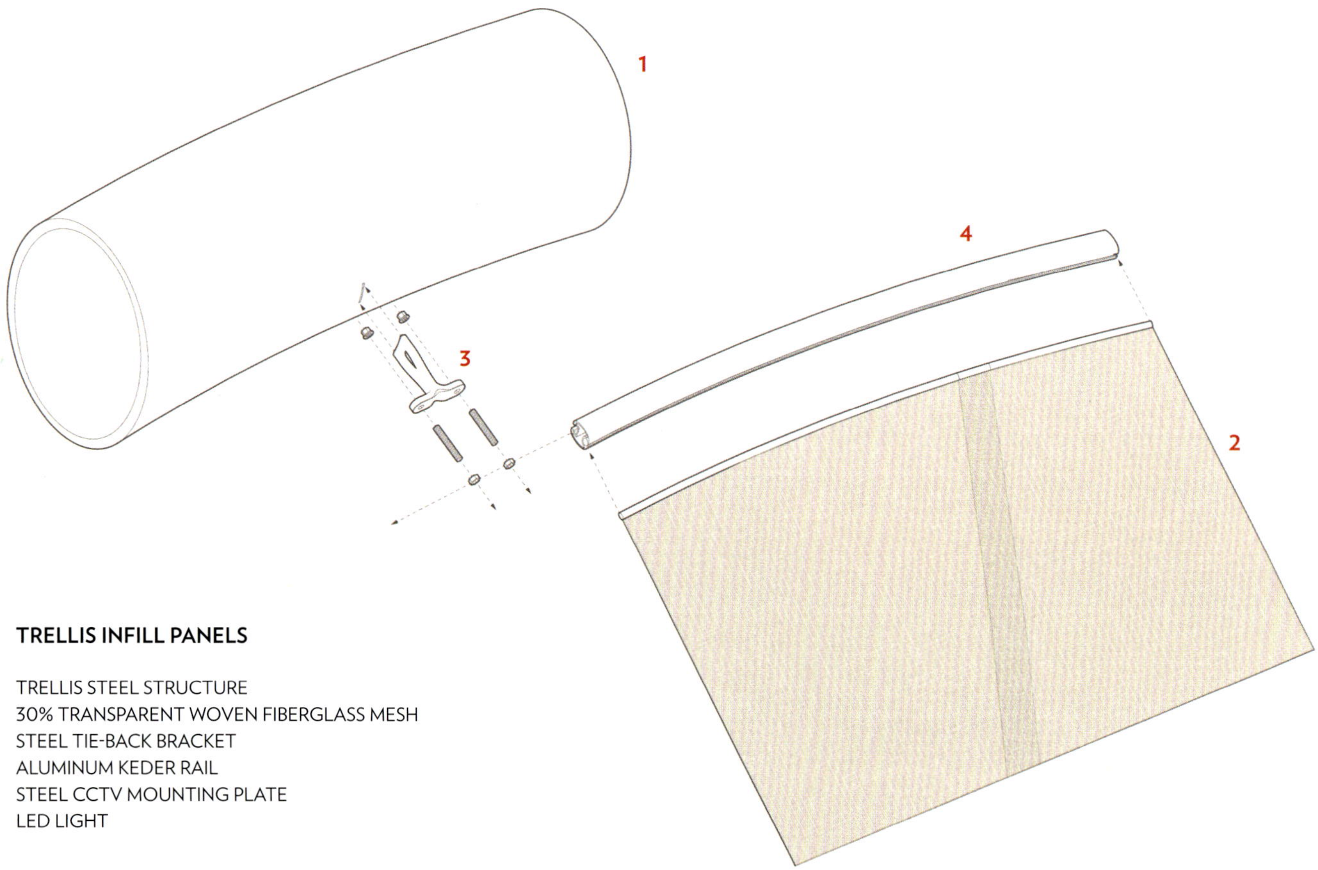

TRELLIS INFILL PANELS

1 TRELLIS STEEL STRUCTURE
2 30% TRANSPARENT WOVEN FIBERGLASS MESH
3 STEEL TIE-BACK BRACKET
4 ALUMINUM KEDER RAIL
5 STEEL CCTV MOUNTING PLATE
6 LED LIGHT

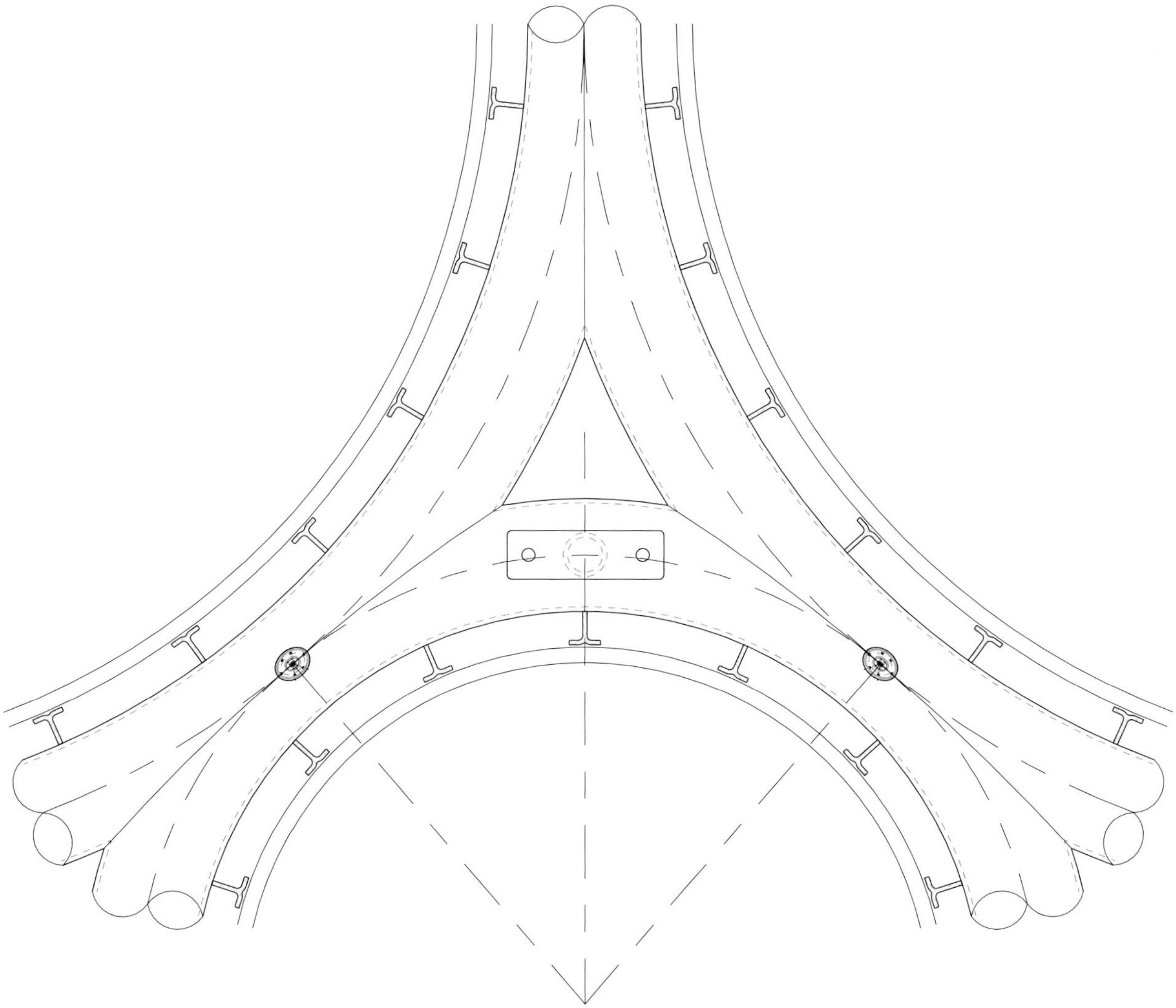

TRELLIS FABRIC BRACKET OPTIMIZATION

To maintain a planar surface, the fabric is stretched within an aluminum clamping frame. These clamping members are called Keder rails. The framed fabric panels are in turn attached to the trellis structure by cast steel brackets. There are 27 different fabric panel types and a total of 629 panels installed on the trellis. Over 17,000 custom cast steel tie-back brackets anchor the fabric panels to the trellis structure. The bracket was developed based on several design principles, primarily material efficiency, whilst preserving structural integrity and design intent. To accurately determine where material could be removed, a process known as topology optimization was carried out. This metaheuristic process also validated the structural integrity of the new bracket against the original, including all stresses and deflections. The resultant optimized bracket only employs material along the structural load path and has several benefits in the form of a 45% reduction in material which translates to reduced overall carbon footprint that aligns with the sustainability goals of the project.

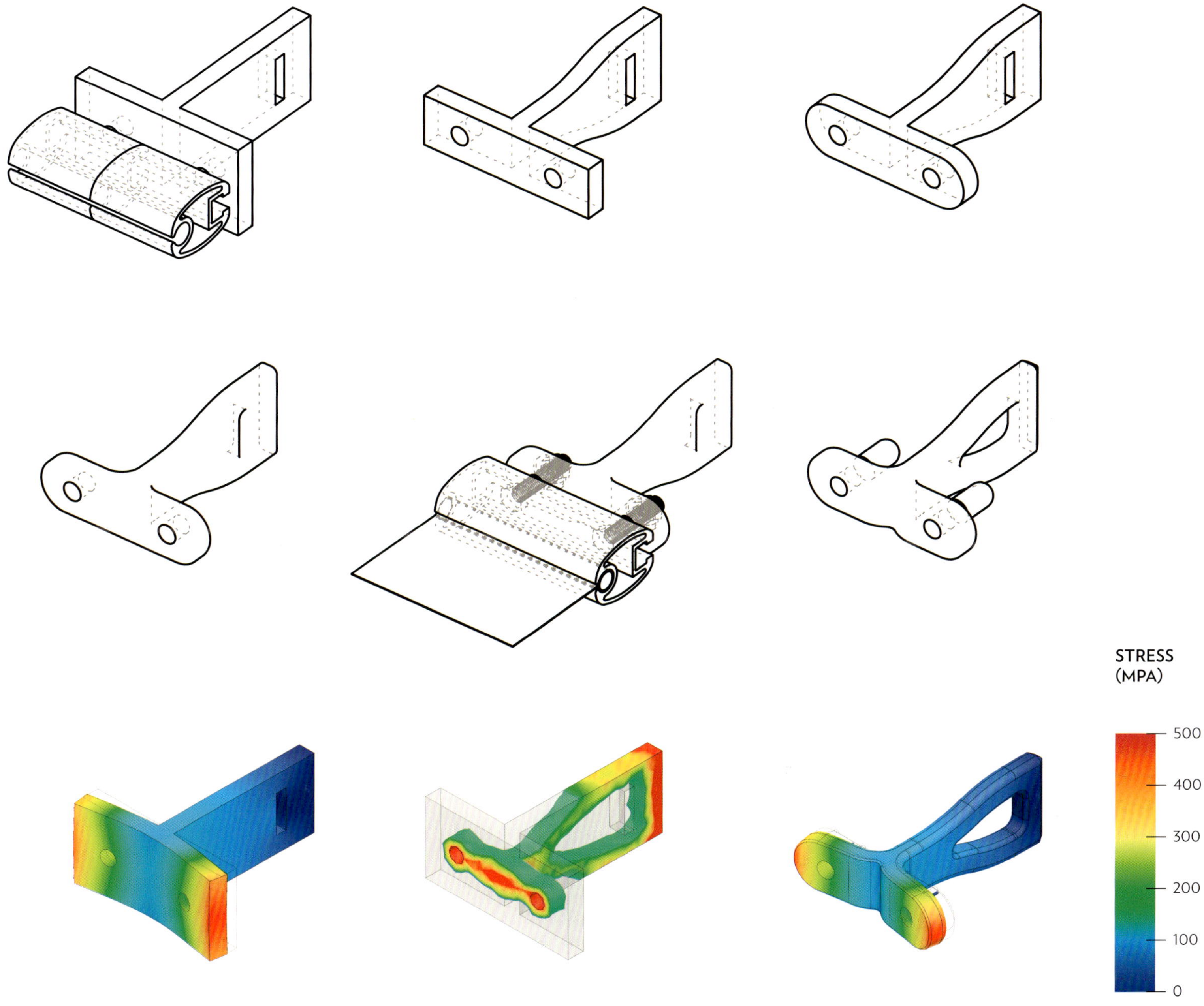
STRESS
(MPA)
500
400
300
200
100
0

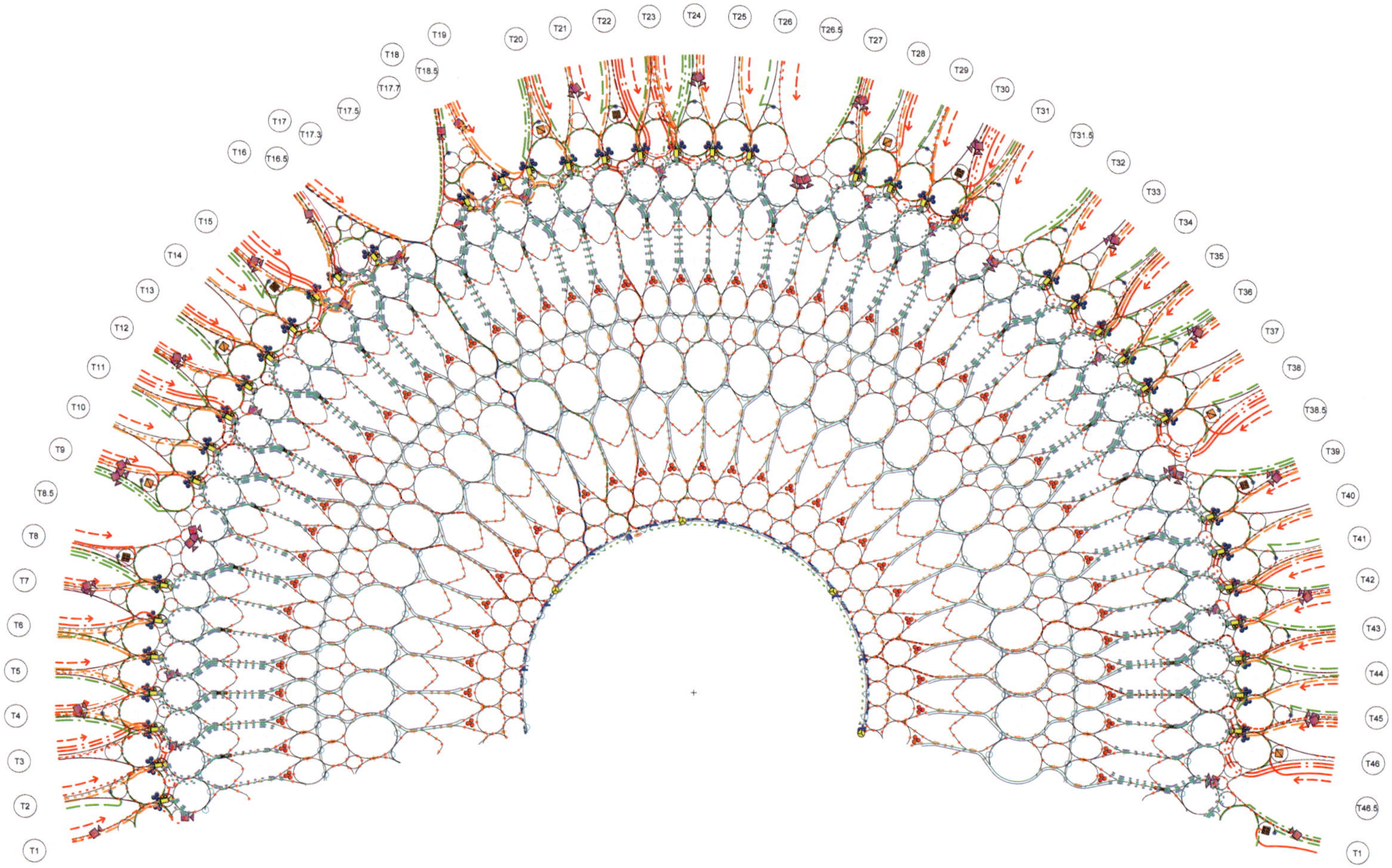

TRELLIS INFRASTRUCTURE

To maintain a planar surface, the fabric is stretched within an aluminum clamping frame. These clamping members are called Keder rails. The framed fabric panels are in turn attached to the trellis structure by cast steel brackets. There are 27 different fabric panel types and a total of 629 panels installed on the trellis. Over 17,000 custom cast steel tie-back brackets anchor the fabric panels to the trellis structure. The bracket was developed based on several design principles, primarily material efficiency, whilst preserving structural integrity and design intent. To accurately determine where material could be removed, a process known as topology optimization was carried out. This metaheuristic process also validated the structural integrity of the new bracket against the original, including all stresses and deflections. The resultant optimized bracket only employs material along the structural load path and has several benefits in the form of a 45% reduction in material which translates to reduced overall carbon footprint that aligns with the sustainability goals of the project.

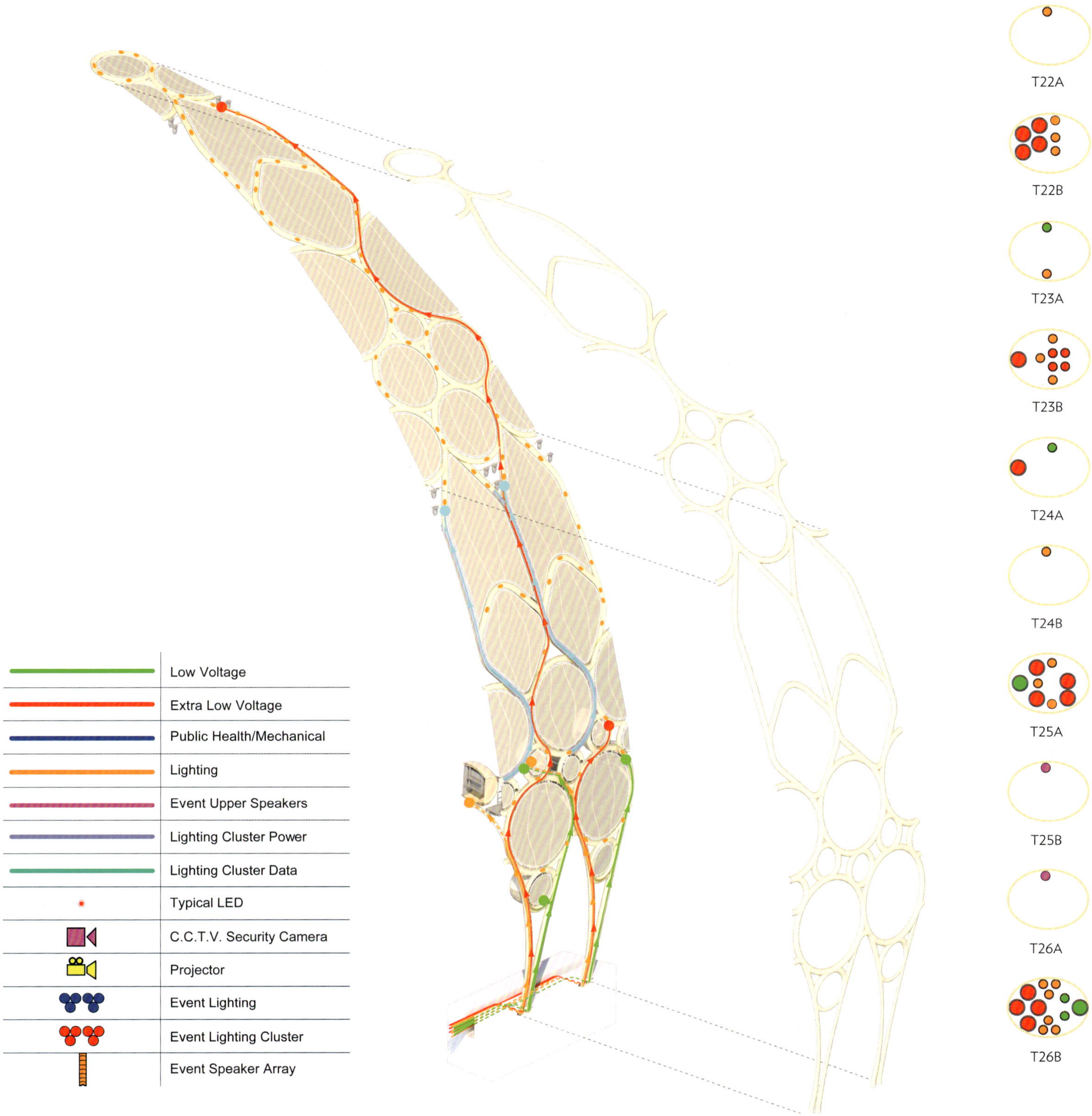

Low Voltage
Extra Low Voltage
Public Health/Mechanical
Lighting
Event Upper Speakers
Lighting Cluster Power
Lighting Cluster Data
Typical LED
C.C.T.V. Security Camera
Projector
Event Lighting
Event Lighting Cluster
Event Speaker Array
T22A
T22B
T23A
T23B
T24A
T24B
T25A
T25B
T26A
T26B

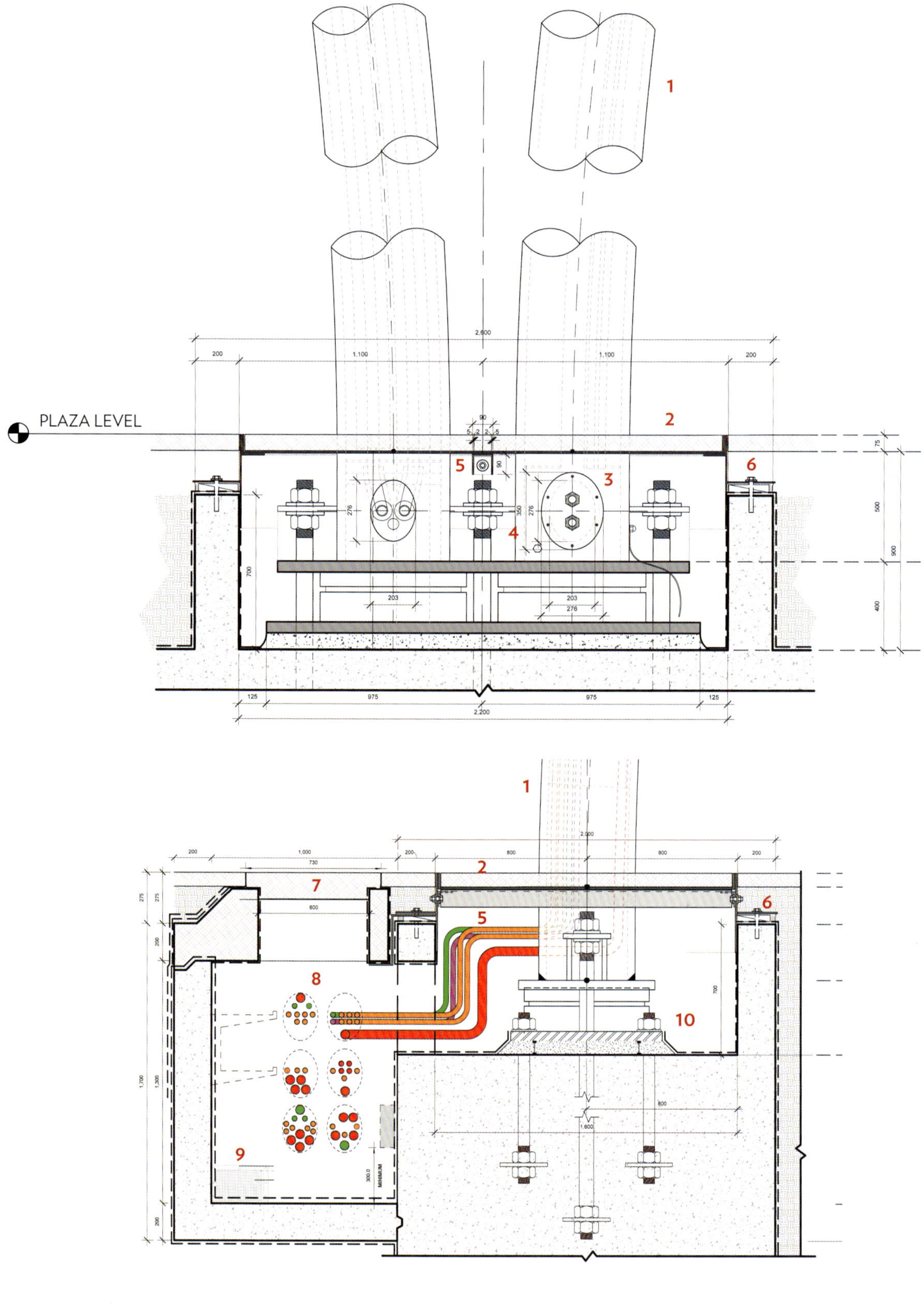

TRELLIS BASE + UTILITY TRENCH

1 TRELLIS STEEL STRUCTURE
2 REMOVABLE PAVER
3 ACCESS PANEL WITH CABLE GLANDS
4 DRAIN PLUG BOLT
5 REMOVABLE METAL CHANNEL SUPPORT
6 CONCRETE CURB WITH METAL STANDOFF
7 TRENCH ACCESS COVER PAVER
8 CONCRETE UTILITY TRENCH
9 SIDE-DRAIN
10 ANCHOR BOLT TO CONCRETE RING BEAM

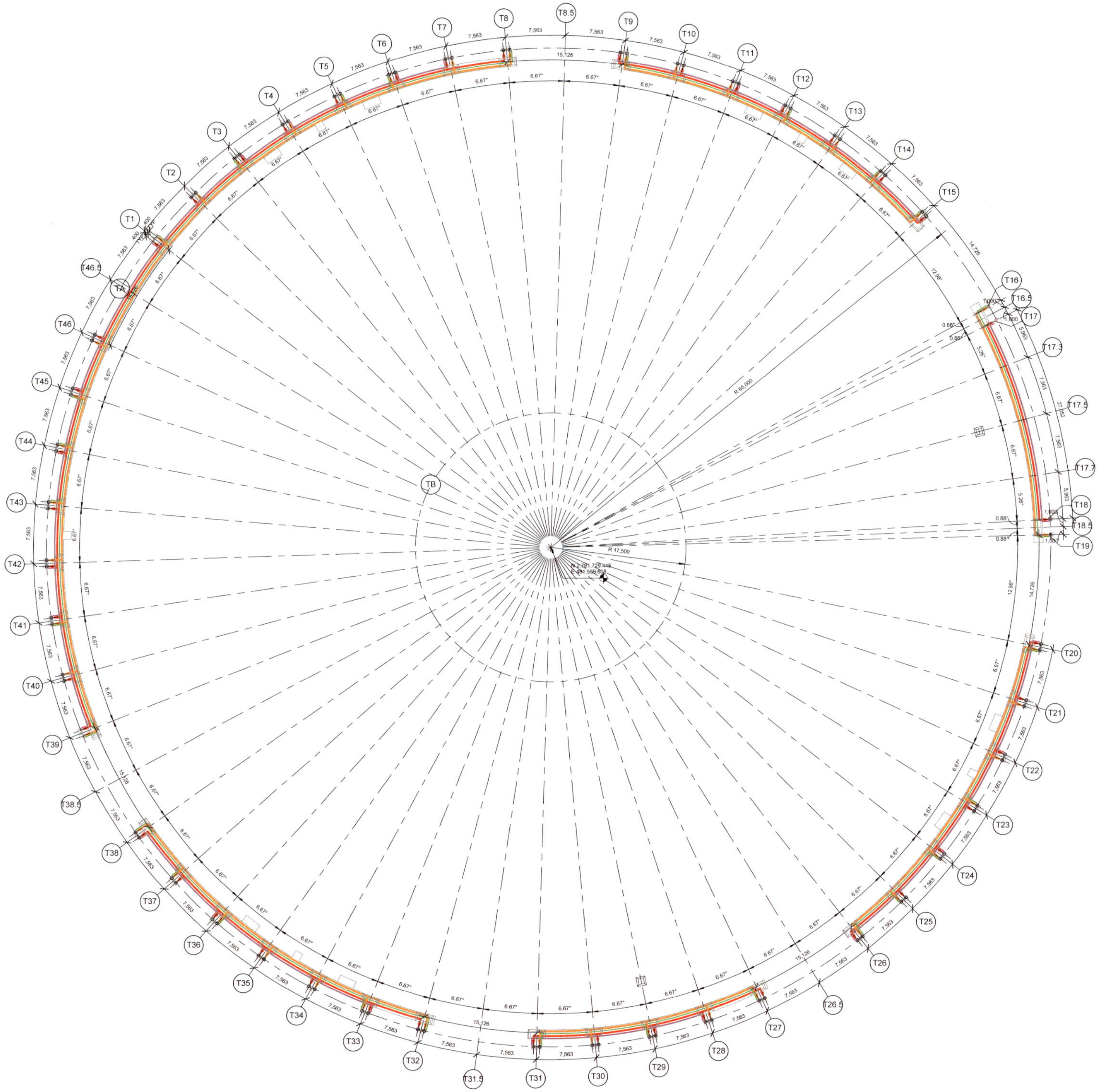
T1
T2
T3
T4
T5
T6
T7
T8
T8.5
T9
T10
T11
T12
T13
T14
T15
T16
T16.5
T17
T17.3
T17.5
T17.7
T18
T18.5
T19
T20
T21
T22
T23
T24
T25
T26
T26.5
T27
T28
T29
T30
T31
T31.5
T32
T33
T34
T35
T36
T37
T38
T38.5
T39
T40
T41
T42
T43
T44
T45
T46
T46.5
TA
TB
7,563
15,126
14,726
6.67°
12.98°
5.26°
0.88°
R 65,000
R 17,500

IMMERSIVE EXPERIENCE + PROJECTION MAPPING

Immersive experiences to date have been temporarily erected for celebrations, events, and festivals. Projection mapping has animated iconic facades around the world such as the Sydney Opera House, Empire State Building, and the Vatican with moving images since the early 2010s. HBO turned the New York Angel Orensanz Center into an immersive experience for the sixth season premiere of Game of Thrones in 2016. A temporary 120-foot geodesic dome immersive experience entertained festival goers at the Coachella Music + Art Festival in 2017. The technology and versatility of projection for immersive experiences was quickly evolving, yet a permanent exterior immersive dome concept such as Al Wasl Plaza had not been achieved.

In Al Wasl, the idea of a vibrant, transformative public garden was taking shape and guiding the overall design process. The concept of the shade structure was created to control and reduce direct solar radiation into the garden and enhance visitor comfort. At dusk, there was an opportunity to repurpose the shade structure. In this context, the idea of immersive experience emerged. The trellis provides an immense area of 25,380 sm, a projectable surface equal to over 35 typical IMAX screens. There was a clear opportunity to create an illusory environment that completely overtakes the senses.

An immersive experience of this scale, configuration and materials had never been conceived. Obscura Digital, since acquired by Madison Square Garden Companies, is a pioneer in immersive experience based in San Francisco. AS+GG engaged Obscura to collaborate on Al Wasl Plaza for their worldwide experience in projection mapping. This collaborative effort helped realize the immersive experience, determining the materiality of the screen, locating the projectors, and defining the technical equipment requirements. The placement of the projection equipment including its enclosure needed to efficiently and elegantly integrate into the functionality of the space.

The quality of a projection experience depends on the continuity of the projected surface, the light intensity, and the accuracy of the projection map. The steel structure and fabric receive projected light in a slightly differing manner, causing the viewer to experience subtleties in the definition of the architecture. The architects desired an overall continuous projection on the domed architecture, while maintaining the visibility of the bold geometry of the trellis. The voids between the panels and the structure made this more challenging, therefore the distance between the fabric panels and the structure was optimized as viewers are up to 130 meters from the projection.

The immersive experience in Al Wasl Plaza is a spectacle, evoking awe and astonishment. The integration of projection technology elevates the experience and delights visitors. Through diverse content, the veiled ceiling can transport the viewer into the deep sea, outer space, vast landscapes, and cultural experiences. The sloped configuration of the garden offers landscaped rooms for relaxation or observance of the spectacle above.
The buildings participate in the spectacle with front row seats with views into the venue. This vision redefines immersive experience by expanding the natural garden and civic space into a lively urban destination.

CONCEPTION OF THE PROJECTOR POD

Projection mapping and immersive experiences are most often temporary and event specific. Prioritizing ease of assembly and low cost, the equipment is usually mounted on scaffolding or similar transportable framework to satisfy the needs of the brief installation. In cases of permanent interior installations, projectors are typically housed in a control room integrated into the architectural layout. In Al Wasl Plaza, the concept for a trellis dome was presented to the client early in the competition. As the scale of the trellis solidified and the opportunity to create a permanent grand immersive experience became apparent, a new requirement emerged. The necessary amount of projection equipment to cover the trellis surface came with considerable spatial requirements which were undetermined at the time, but ultimately a total of 732 cubic meters.

Due to the nature of the technology, the projectors must be mounted in a calculated position for both height and angle in order to project across a space onto a surface. As the first permanent exterior immersive experience of this kind, Al Wasl Plaza did not fall into a previously tested application. Therefore, the design team had an ambitious charge; to locate and create a structure or enclosure for the equipment to sit on or within.

With excitement and anticipation for the array of events that could take place in this plaza, the Expo 2020 ceremonies team had already started to conceptualize nightly events in the space early in the design. Therefore, the projectors would need to be housed for the duration of Expo 2020 and not installed per event. It didn't take long for the architects to determine that the equipment would require a sealed enclosure, or enclosures, in response to the harsh Dubai climate. The delicate and costly equipment would need to be conditioned and sheltered from extreme heat, high humidity and dust particles. Simply put, it would require a room for protection and access for a specialist to tune and repair the equipment. However, the exterior plaza and trellis structure is not a typical enclosed building that projector control rooms could be easily integrated into.

The legacy of Al Wasl Plaza, or it's continued function as an important public space after Expo 2020, has always been a high priority for the client. It was clear that the client was making the decision to invest in the technology integration to expand the event capabilities of Al Wasl Plaza beyond the Expo 2020 event into the legacy to secure the space as an important public landmark. The direction was clear, and the architectural team proceeded to advance in the invention of capsule to enclose the equipment. The design of the AV enclosures developed through a series of options to identify the ideal configuration for the location, form and size while balancing technical requirements, access and integration into the plaza without obstruction of views. The enclosure went through a rigorous series of design studies, modeling, analysis and testing. All disciplines were involved beyond their typical scopes to invent the pod on a demanding schedule with a strict cost control process.

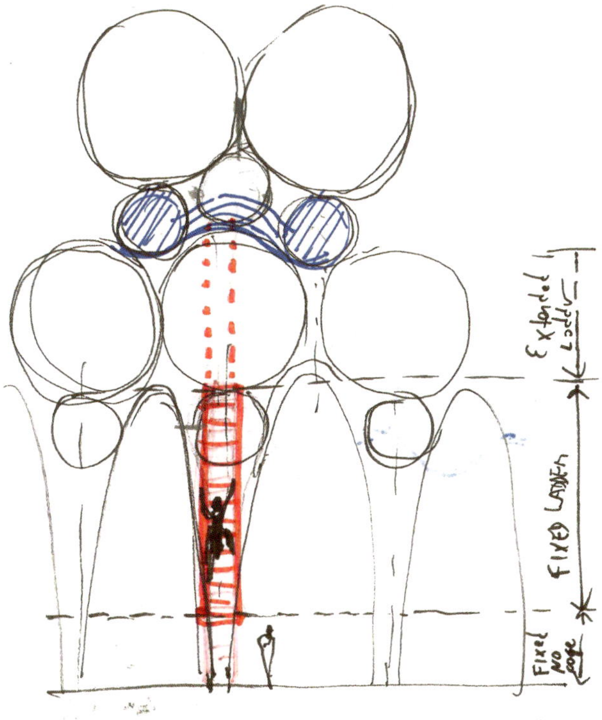
Extended Ladder
FIXED LADDER
Fixed no cage

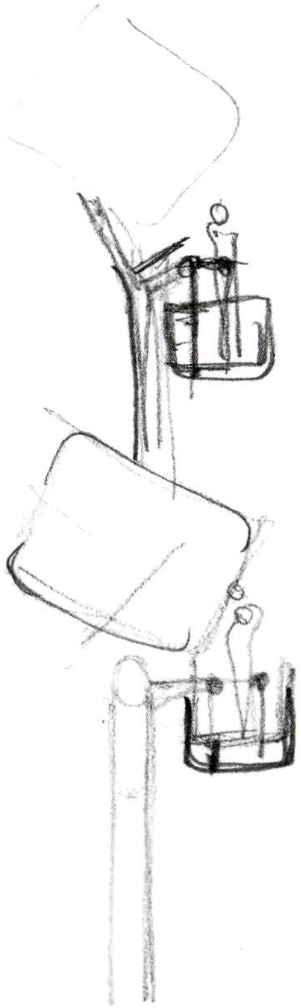

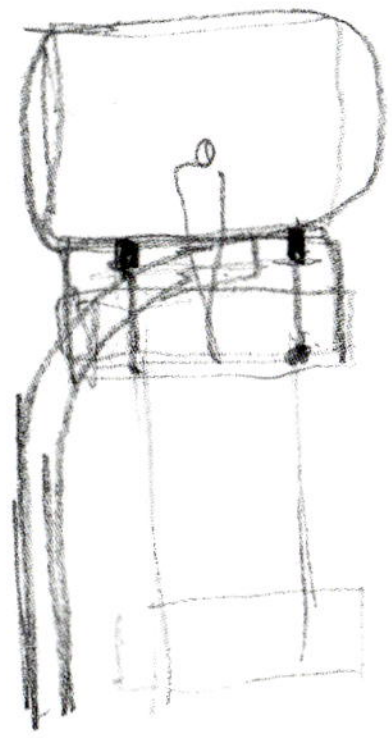

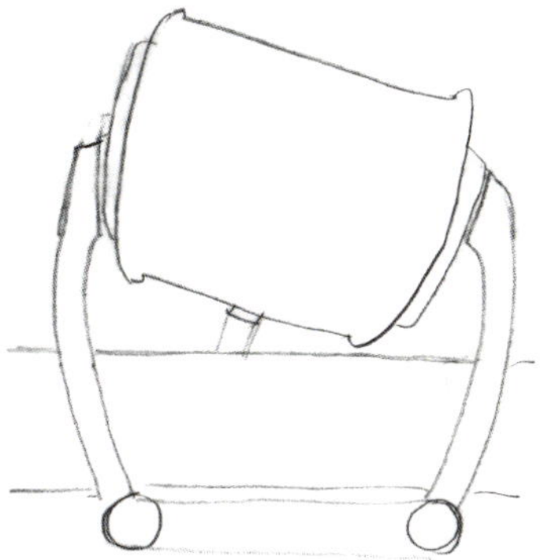

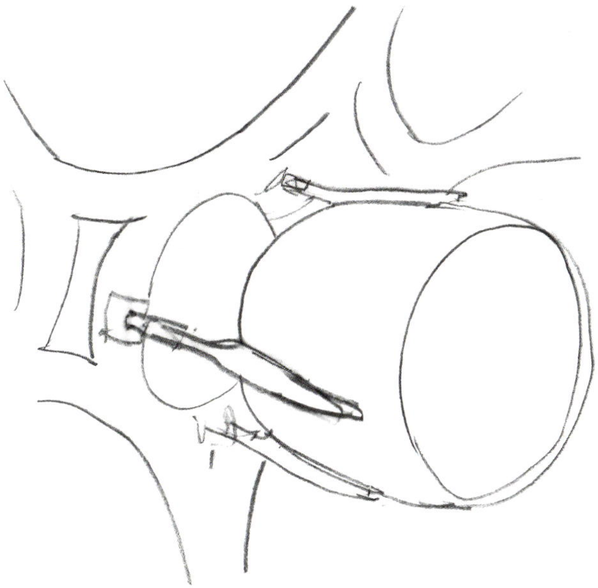

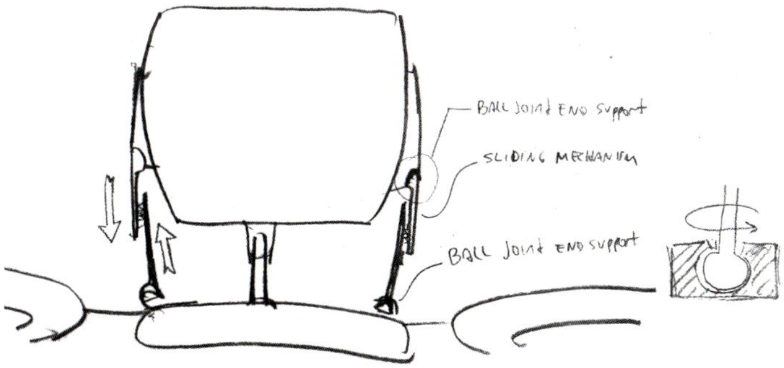
BALL Joint END Support
SLIDING MECHANISM
BALL Joint END Support

AV ENCLOSURE DESIGN PROCESS

The first design iteration and competition proposal placed the projection equipment in three locations near the center of the garden. The projectors were to project from the center outwards towards the trellis. Given the early stage of development, there was no need to assume a requirement for a permanent equipment enclosure. This idea followed the logic of most immersive projection experiences, which had temporary scaffolding housing the projectors to provide easy access. It was not until later when the shareholders agreed on the architects' holistic vision for the trellis that the full design of the immersive experience began.

The first scheme included four permanent enclosures containing 36 projectors each for a total of 144 projectors. Contrary to the competition proposal, it was identified that the projectors should be closer to the perimeter of the garden and project across the plaza. Placing enclosures in the garden allowed for the easy access and operations. This scheme, although technically efficient, impeded views and did not successfully integrate with the overall vision. Obscura Digital tested the mapping strategy for the immersive experience and determined that the angles of projectors allowed by the four enclosures could not provide enough coverage for the 360-degree dome. To achieve the full spectrum of projection, the projectors would need to be in a larger array. This led to the addition of two locations, while maintaining a total of 144 projectors, thus 24 projectors in each location.

Technically, six projectors work together to produce one optimized image. This is accomplished by designating a single projector as the primary, using it to establish the proper positioning and size of the image on the surface, and then aligning all other projectors to that master image. As a result, each set of six projectors is known as a channel of projection that receives an individual orientation to cover the entirety of the trellis. Projected light is brightest when it is either unobstructed or perpendicular to glass and it loses efficacy when at other angles. Therefore, the architecture developed the enclosures to contain each channel of projectors in a single pod that could be oriented at the required angles. The small pods were connected to a pole that allowed vertical access. It was more effective than the previous scheme and it reduced blocked views since the pods were elevated. However, the tower did not visually integrate with the overall garden aesthetic.

Next, to reduce the tower size, 11 slender posts were arrayed around the perimeter pedestrian pathway in line with the inner ring of palm trees. Atop each post were two pods. This option had advantages as it no longer interfered with the garden experience, however it was soon determined that this ring of palm trees would not be installed until Legacy deeming this scheme unfeasible for the Expo 2020.

The final studies placed the enclosures on the trellis, lifting the technology out of the garden and onto its canvas. The best way to geometrically integrate the enclosures with the adjacent trellis was to introduce a round pod. In this iteration 20 pods were placed on the lowest ring of the trellis to project onto the surfaces of the trellis above. This scheme successfully integrated the pods into the architecture and minimized blocked views.

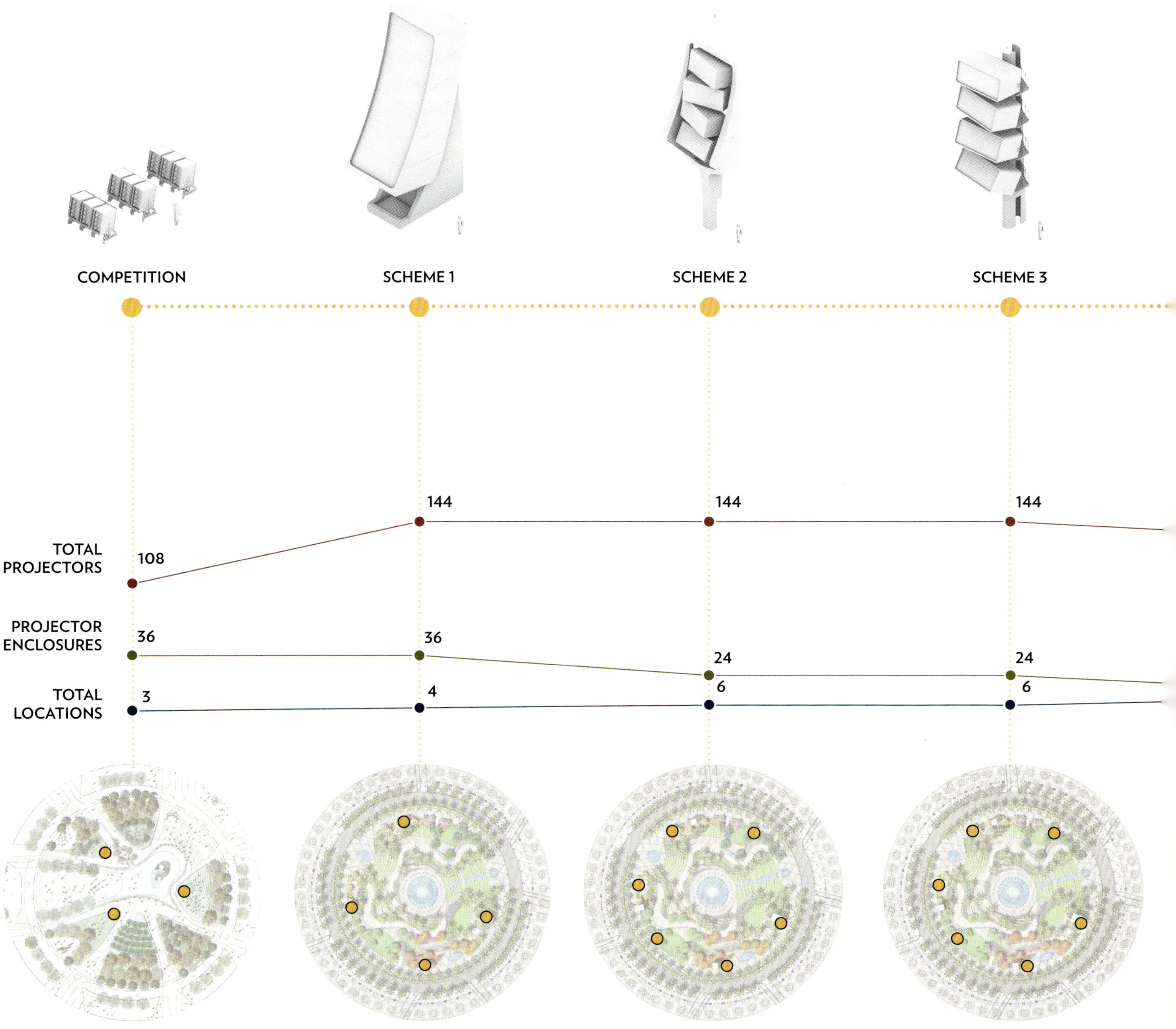
COMPETITION
SCHEME 1
SCHEME 2
SCHEME 3
TOTAL PROJECTORS
108
144
144
144
PROJECTOR ENCLOSURES
36
36
24
24
TOTAL LOCATIONS
3
4
6
6

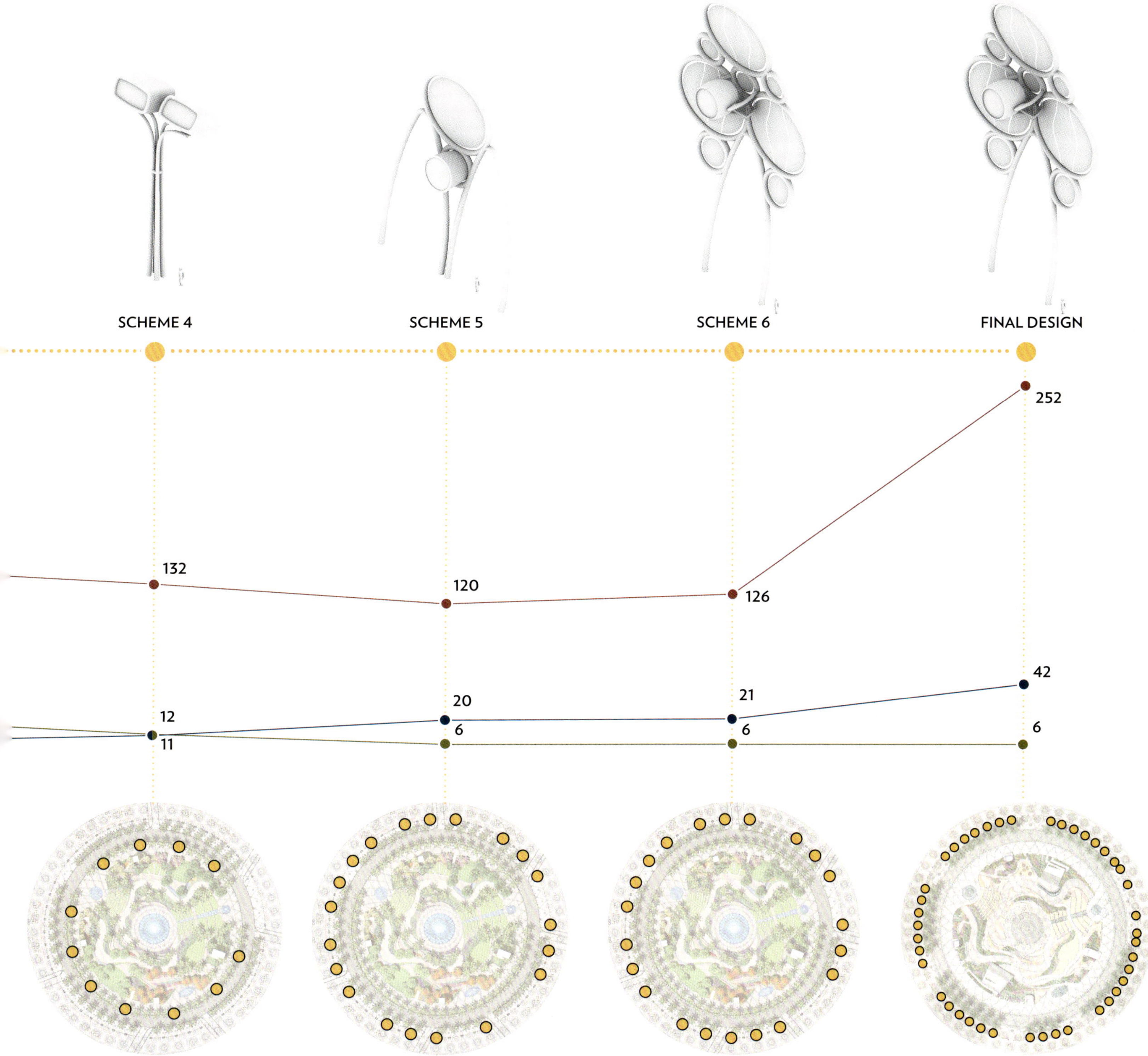
SCHEME 4
SCHEME 5
SCHEME 6
FINAL DESIGN
252
132
120
126
42
20
21
12
6
6
6
11

AV ENCLOSURE FINAL DESIGN

The final AV enclosure design, completed in early 2018, was a softly curved cylinder, similar in geometry to an aircraft engine nacelle. Flat, anti-reflective glass maximizes the intensity of the projected light. Mounted at an elevation of 19 meters, the placement in the trellis is the least disruptive location for the public at the garden level. In the design, 21 enclosures, housing six projectors each, were arranged in the trellis providing a light intensity of 100 lux.

The contract for the pods was awarded to Kinetica, a specialist fabricator located in Monterrey, Mexico. In late 2018, during the early stages of fabrication, the client requested an increase in light intensity to optimize the television broadcast images of the opening and closing ceremonies. It was also agreed that the lower boundary of the image be extended downward to a level about 8–meters below the pods themselves, thereby significantly increasing the surface area of the projected image. This matched the extent of the projected image tested in March 2018 on the full-scale mock-up.

To accomplish this significant request, a series of meetings were arranged in January 2019 at the AS+GG offices in Chicago. The meetings were attended by the full team including Expo and Expo events leadership, Expo AV integration consultant, Creative Technology, Expo event creative consultants AGB Events, PMC management, the trellis and projector pod fabricators, CRME and Kinetica, the projector manufacturer, Christie Digital, and the AS+GG design team consisting of Thornton Tomasetti, Hoare Lea, Threshold Design, and Obscura Digital, the structural, building services audio, and immersive experience consultants respectively. The objective of the multidisciplinary meeting was to find a way to triple the light intensity on the trellis making sure that the solution was technically and financially feasible within the original project schedule. Most importantly, this solution would need to integrate into the ongoing structural, architectural and MEP construction that was quickly advancing on site.

There were several challenging issues to resolve with the addition of the 21 AV enclosures. Since the original 21 pods were already being fabricated, any additional equipment was restricted to the pod size as designed. The structure of the trellis had to be analytically re-evaluated to ensure it could accommodate the resulting loads. Logistically, the equipment installation and operation doubled, requiring additional event coordination. The provision of additional power was perhaps the most critical change which required distribution from new infrastructure installed in an adjacent parcel as the physical capacity of Al Wasl Plaza had been reached. The void within the trellis structure had to be coordinated to accommodate the new conduit rising to the pods. Finally, the procurement of the current technology had to be made in time for the installation. All design and construction schedules were adjusted to accommodate the request, making the fast-track project even more challenging to complete.

The resulting final design has a total of 42 pods, enlarged somewhat to house six, high-output, laser projectors incorporating newly released technology. With a total of 252 projectors, the revised design can achieve approximately 255 lux light intensity on 25,380 sm of projected surface area.

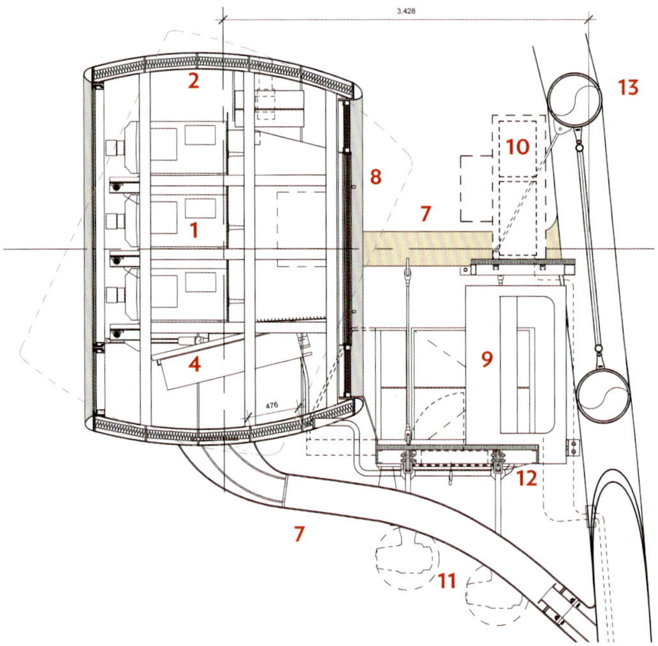

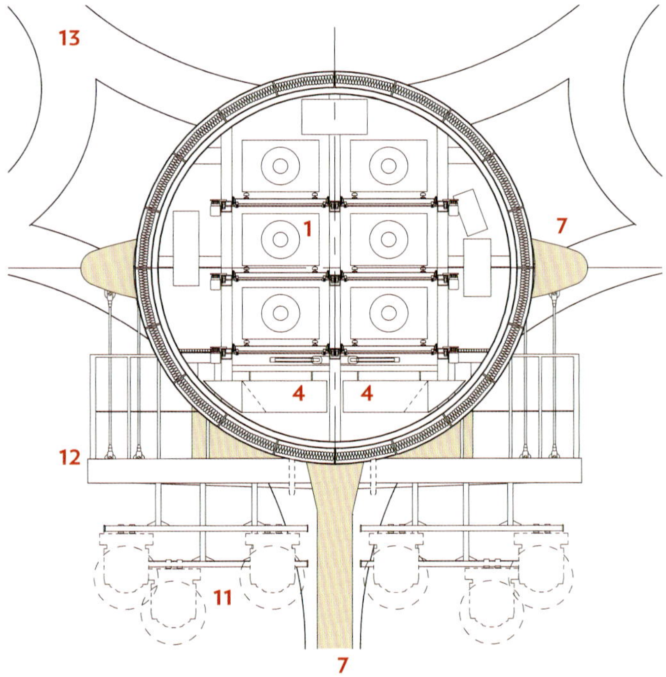

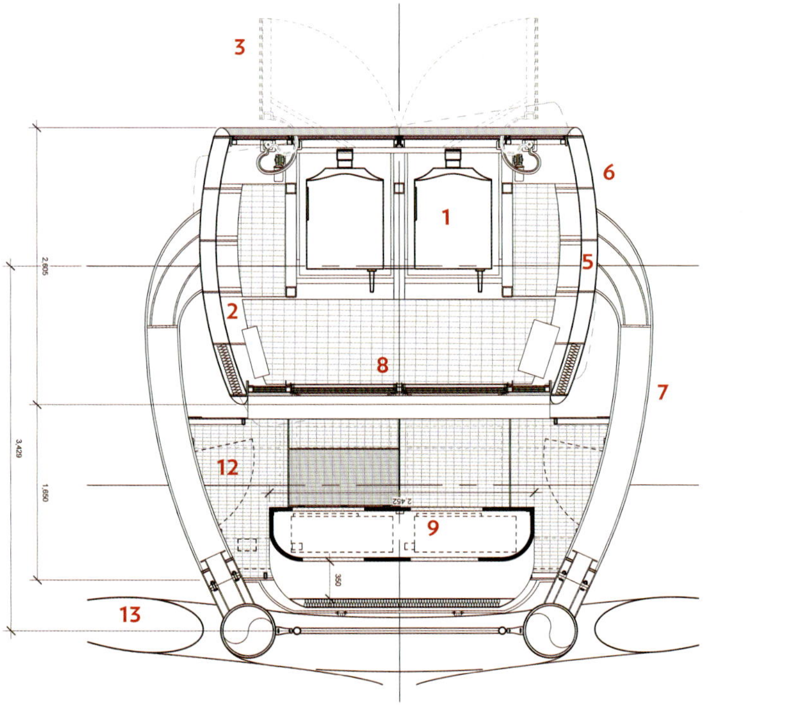

AV ENCLOSURE

1 PROJECTOR ARRAY
2 MONOCOQUE ALUMINUM RIB SHELL
3 MECHANICALLY OPERATED FRONT DOOR ASSEMBLY
4 FAN COIL UNIT
5 PROJECTOR POD ARM CONNECTION
6 INTERIOR AND EXTERIOR DOUBLE CURVED ALUMINUM SKIN
7 STEEL SUPPORT ARM
8 ALUMINUM DOOR ASSEMBLY
9 ALUMINUM CONDENSER ENCLOSURE
10 EVENT LIGHTING POWER AND DATA RACKS
11 EVENT LIGHTING SUSPENSION SYSTEM
12 STEEL WORK PLATFORM
13 TRELLIS STEEL STRUCTURE

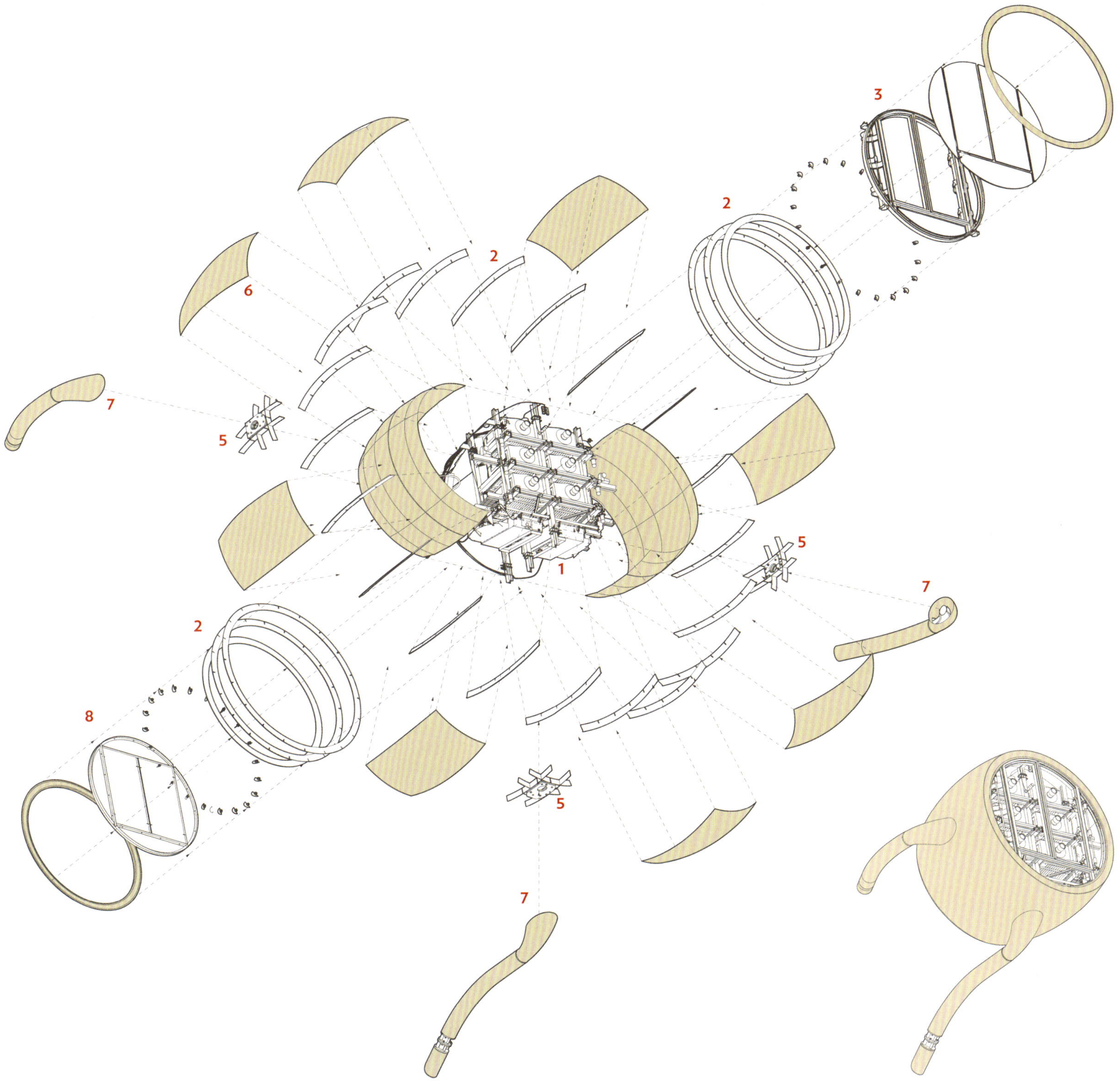

3
2
2
6
7
5
2
5
1
7
2
8
5
7

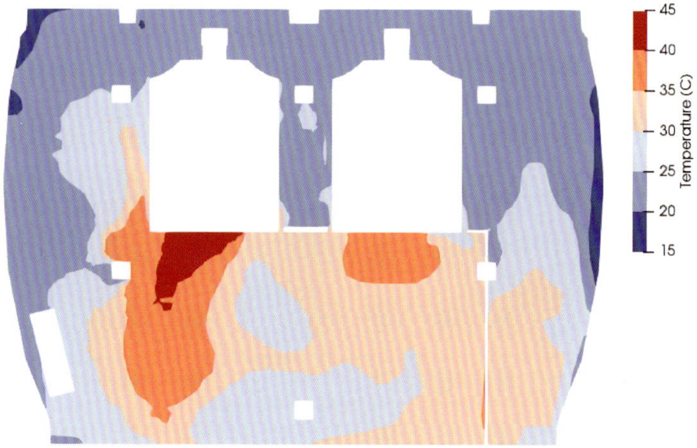

TEMPERATURE

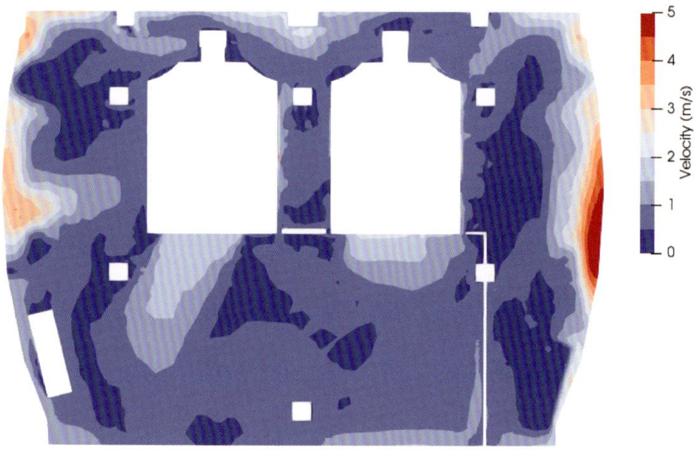

VELOCITY

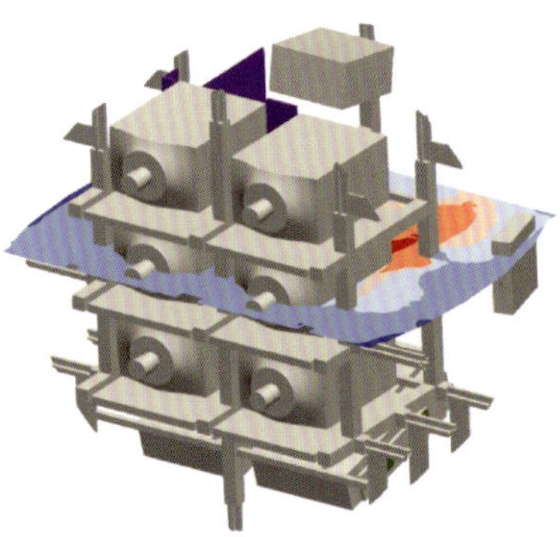

AV ENCLOSURE CFD ANALYSIS

As the trellis is nearly fully enclosed from a wind sail standpoint, wind loads were determined through use of a High Frequency Pressure Integration (HFPI) wind tunnel test performed by Rowan Williams Davies + Irwin Inc. (RWDI) at their laboratories in Ontario, Canada. The trellis was tested for two configurations: the full Expo build-out and a configuration without the adjacent five buildings and utilized the locally mandated wind speed of 45 m/sec as the basis of testing. The five adjacent buildings tend to shield the trellis, although some deleterious funneling of wind between the buildings onto the trellis was detected from the testing. However, overall test results indicated a significant reduction in the peak negative design pressures observed at the apex of the dome when compared to codified references for wind pressure gradients on closed spherical surfaces. This reduction is attributed to the vented regions of the center oculus and openings at the base of the structure and the design of the trellis was able to take advantage of these reductions to achieve a slenderer and more elegant structural framework.

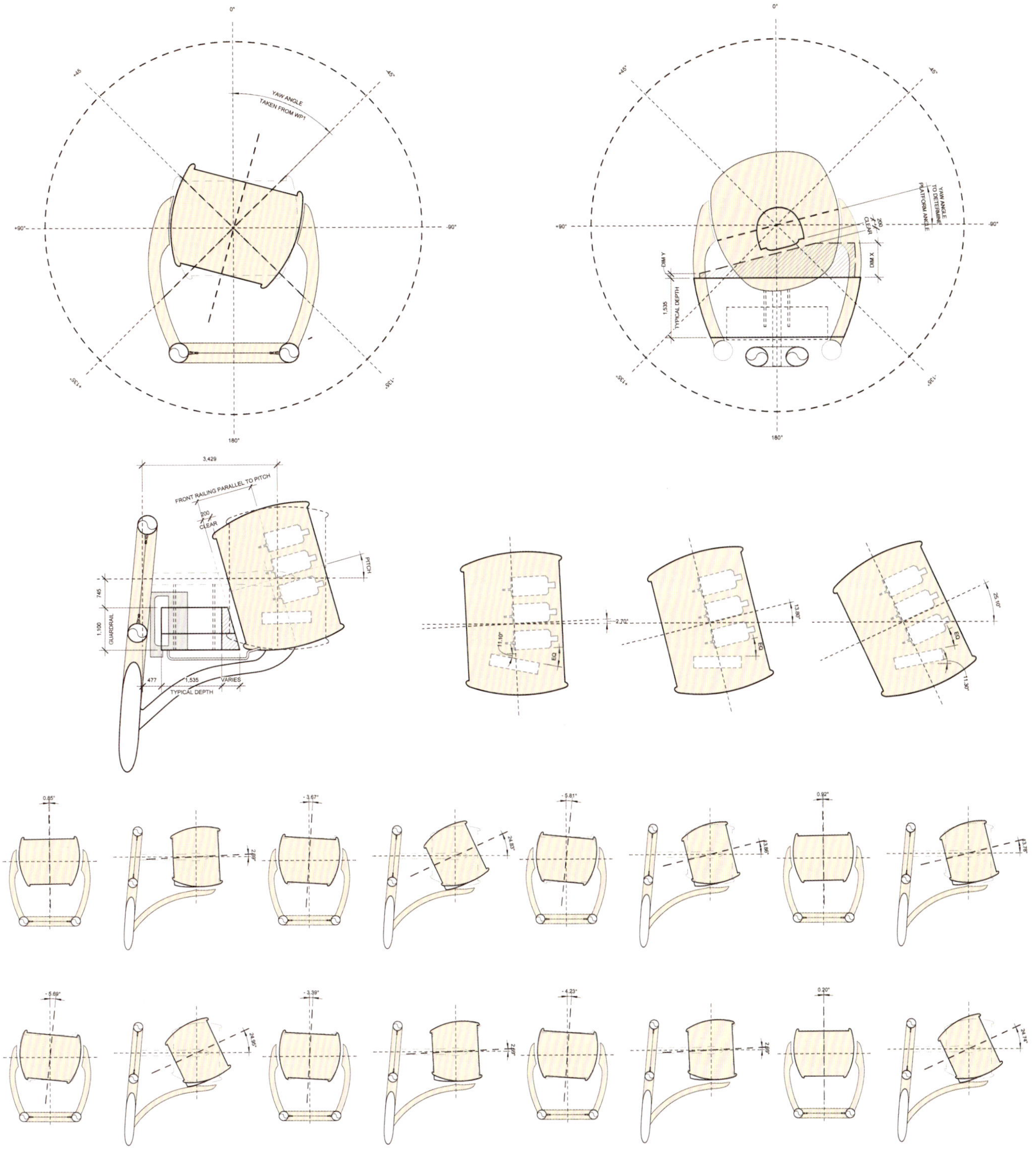
0°
YAW ANGLE
TAKEN FROM WP1
+90°
-90°
180°
YAW ANGLE
TO DETERMINE
PLATFORM ANGLE
200
CLEAR
DIM X
DIM Y
1,535
TYPICAL DEPTH
3,429
FRONT RAILING PARALLEL TO PITCH
PITCH
745
1,100
GUARDRAIL
477
1,535
VARIES
TYPICAL DEPTH
2.70°
13.80°
25.10°
EQ
11.30°

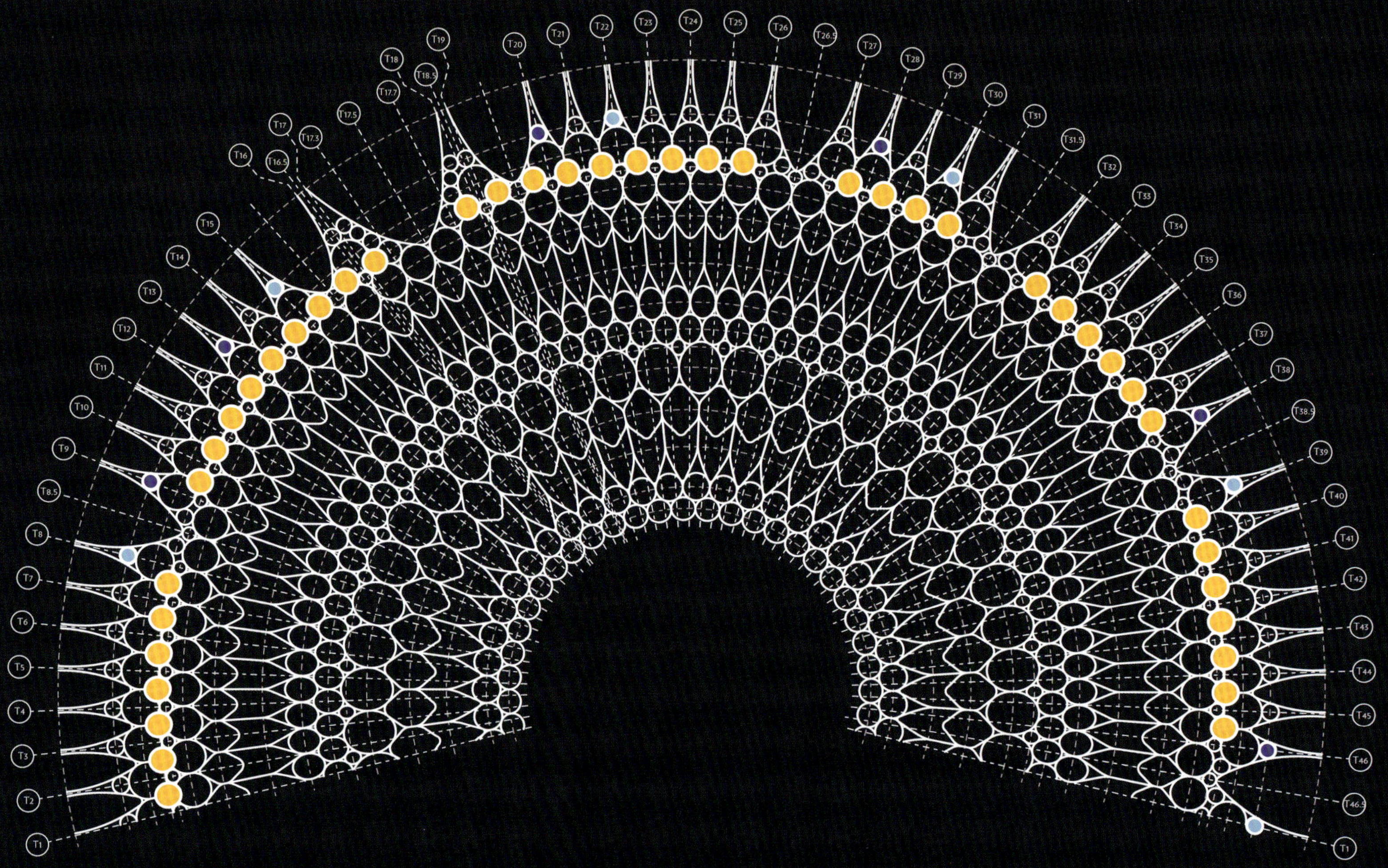

IMMERSIVE EXPERIENCE CONTENT DELIVERY SYSTEM

360 Immersive content enables visual experiences that are not possible using a flat screen. Everywhere the viewer looks is an extension of an immersive environment. The viewer is no longer looking into a window but is instead centralized within a world. The Al Wasl immersive system is designed to combine spherical imagery and rectangular imagery as experienced at the cinema. By using specialized software, the imagery is calibrated to the exact form of the architectural surface. The virtual program mimics the real surface that it is projecting onto, resulting in a precision mapping of controllable light on the complex 3D geometry. Convergence is the process of aligning a group of projectors together, pixel for pixel, to increase brightness and build redundancy into the projection system. This is necessary to achieve the desired brightness of the projection at a large scale. The Al Wasl design uses an array of 42 pods which house six projectors each. The images from all six of the projectors converge to create one bright image on the opposite side of the trellis, this collective image is called a channel. The channels are angled to cover three rings of the trellis as shown in the diagrams.

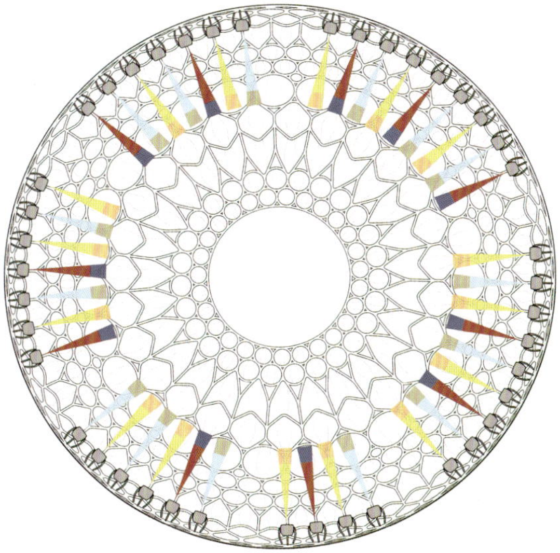

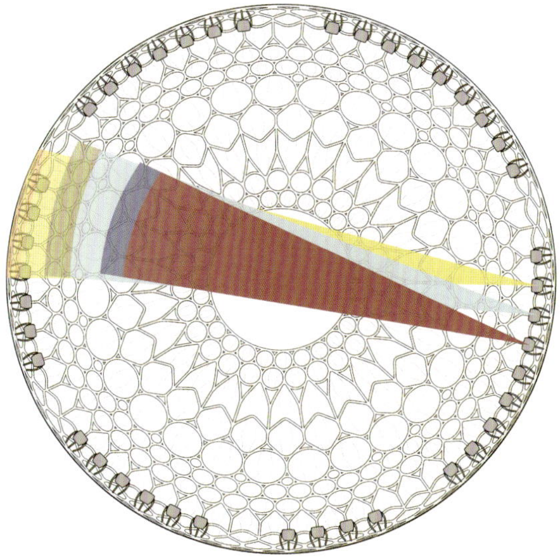

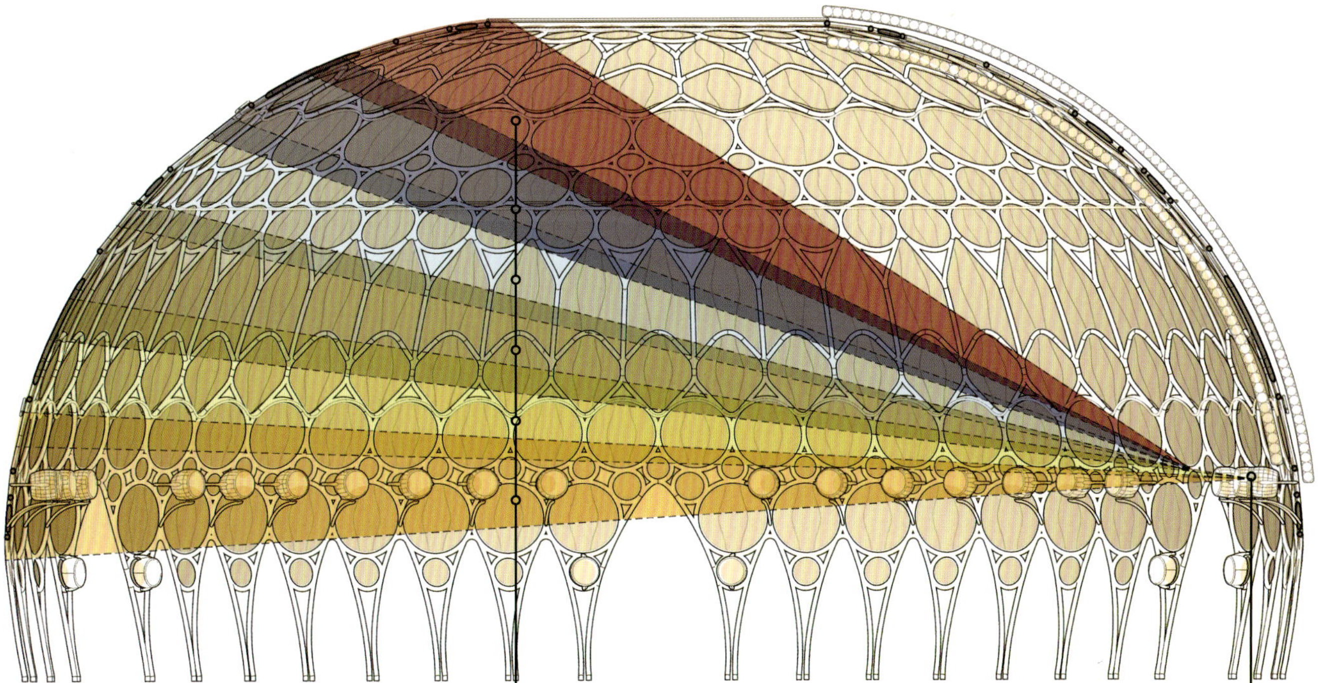

There are six rings of projection.
Each projector pods is calibrated to one of
the zones to provide full coverage.

42 Projector Pods contain
a total of 252 projectors

TRELLIS MOCK-UP

Architectural mock-ups are typically fabricated in the late stages of the design for the architect, client, and contractor to review aesthetic and construction quality. For Al Wasl Plaza, the mock-up was also required to prove that this new blend of technology and architecture was feasible. The mock-up needed to demonstrate that Al Wasl would achieve its intent as the world's largest, exterior, 360–degree immersive projection experience in the world.

Prior to steelwork tender, Expo commissioned the construction of a full-scale visual and installation mock-up of a portion of a typical lower section of the trellis. The 25–meter-tall structure was fabricated and installed in December 2017 at the Expo site office by a specialist steel fabricator Waagner Biro. Although large in nominal terms, the mock-up represented only 1.3% of the overall trellis structure, a nod to the significant scale of the full structure. The trellis steelwork is designated as Architectural Exposed Structural Steel (AESS) based on American Institute of Steel Construction (AISC) specified requirements for various categories of quality according to the visual proximity of the steelwork in relation to observers the ground plane or in the proximity of the adjacent buildings.

The mock-up also included the complete multi-coat steel paint system, fabric panel installation, routing of electrical and plumbing services, and several different approaches to the welded steel joints. On initial completion, the mock-up was used to establish the final design direction with respect to paint color and sheen, fabric types and seam locations and the finish to the welded steel joints. Once established and the adjustments were agreed on by the design team and client, the mock-up was modified and became the benchmark standard that the trellis tenderer would be required to meet. As a result of the tendering process and based on meeting the standard established by the mock-up; the Italian specialist steel fabricator Chamoli Redmond Middle East (CRME) was awarded the contract for the trellis.

Having established the design and materiality of the components of the trellis, the trellis mock-up was then used in confirming the feasibility, viability, and quality of the projected images on its surface. It was therefore determined that to confirm materiality, technology and content a full-size field test would be necessary.

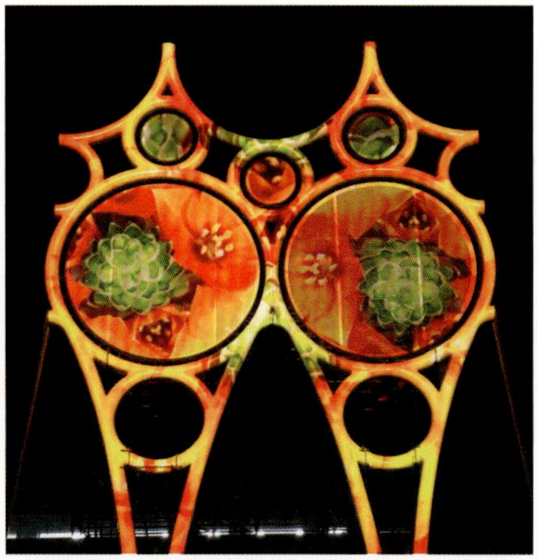

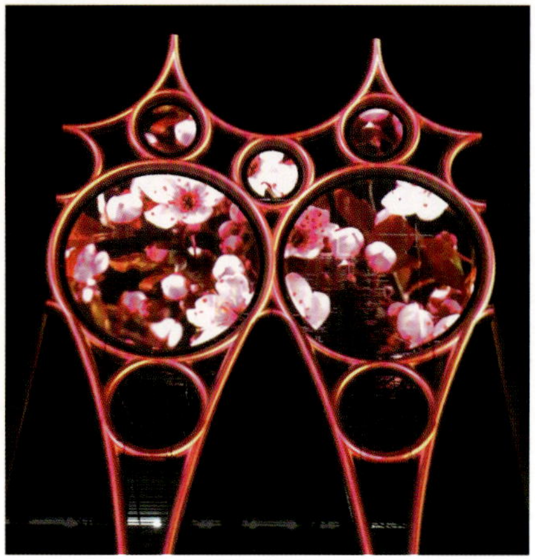

TRELLIS PROJECTION TEST

Several technical questions needed to be answered by this test: Was the perforated fabric and steel structure able to successfully receive the projected images? Was the projected light intensity adequate? Were the seams on the fabric a noticeable distraction? Was the projected content visible from both sides as intended? Was the viewer able to capture a single continuous experience on the designed structure? To answer these questions, six projectors were installed 130 meters from the mock-up to simulate the trellis diameter. A set of speakers were also set up on site to provide audio content for the test to mimic the immersive experience. AS+GG's immersive experience consultant Obscura Digital, created the content used for projection and conducted the testing. The mock-up and projection test were highly successful. The Expo 2020 Dubai leaders shared their excitement and confidence with the design team knowing that they would be able to deliver this highly anticipated vision to Dubai and the world. Her Excellency Reem Al Hashimi, Managing Director for Expo 2020 Dubai, noted the experience was "spiritual" and would be a legacy for the United Arab Emirates.

AL WASL PLAZA AUDIO SYSTEM

Al Wasl Plaza and its surrounding buildings is a unique environment regarding audio and video systems. The plaza is a welcoming space that people can experience on an intimate level, yet it accommodates up to ten thousand people for spectacle events. The distinct zones of the garden unite to transform into one large singular immersive experience through well-planned infrastructure and creative design solutions. The impact of the music, voice, and sounds enhance and support life in the public space.

A system of high-performance loudspeakers integrated into the trellis structure provides high-impact sound playback to accompany video projection shows and other spectacle events. The initial design of this loudspeaker system, comprised of 6 six-element, L-Acoustics K2 line arrays and, 6 four-element L-Acoustics KS28 subwoofer arrays, mounted on the trellis to broadcast inward from the perimeter of the trellis to blanket the garden with high fidelity sound. Each of the loudspeaker and subwoofer arrays is processed as a separate channel to minimize phase interaction and to allow sound designers to create sweeping immersive sound effects. The K2 and KS28 arrays hang from the trellis structure, suspended in trellis openings 12 meters above ground level. The K2 arrays are angled and splayed to cover from the inside of the ring road to the center of the plaza.

While robust, the K2 and KS28 loudspeaker elements require protection from environmental forces including excessive UV radiation, dust, and humidity to ensure consistent performance and longevity. Each loudspeaker and subwoofer array are surrounded in a protective housing, fully enclosed on the back and acoustically transparent in front directing sound towards the garden. The fabric at the front of the enclosure is backed with acoustically transparent foam to capture dust particles to prevent damage to the loudspeaker components while allowing sound energy to pass through. The side and back panels of the enclosures are solid GFRC panels to shield the buildings surrounding the plaza from back-radiated sound from the loudspeaker system.

The cable for each loudspeaker or subwoofer runs down the leg of the trellis where it drops below ground level into the nearest AV equipment room in the lower level. AV equipment rooms are distributed through the lower level to minimize the lengths of the cable runs. AV equipment rooms in the lower level of the plaza house the sensitive equipment that powers the audio and video experience above. A single centralized AV equipment room serves as the primary hub for AV systems and includes a control center for all permanent audio and video systems including the projection. A network of fiber optic lines connects the centralized AV Equipment Room with three remote AV rooms distributed around the perimeter of the lower level.

In July 2019, Expo leadership asked that the design team enhance the audio aspect of the immersive experience. It was therefore agreed to incorporate a 27–channel system, consisting of 27 speaker arrays mounted on the trellis approximately 34–meters above the ground. Each array consists of 16 L-Acoustics KIVA II speakers. With the addition of these speaker arrays, it was agreed to eliminate the K2 line arrays of the initial design. Their speaker enclosures remain installed on the trellis, should further enhancements be desired in the future.

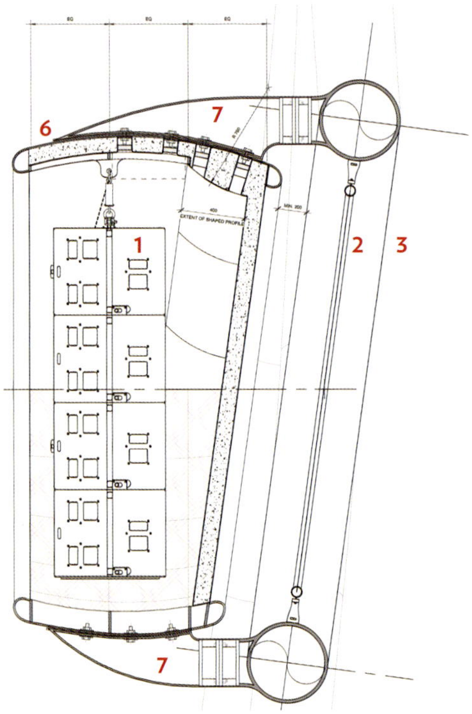

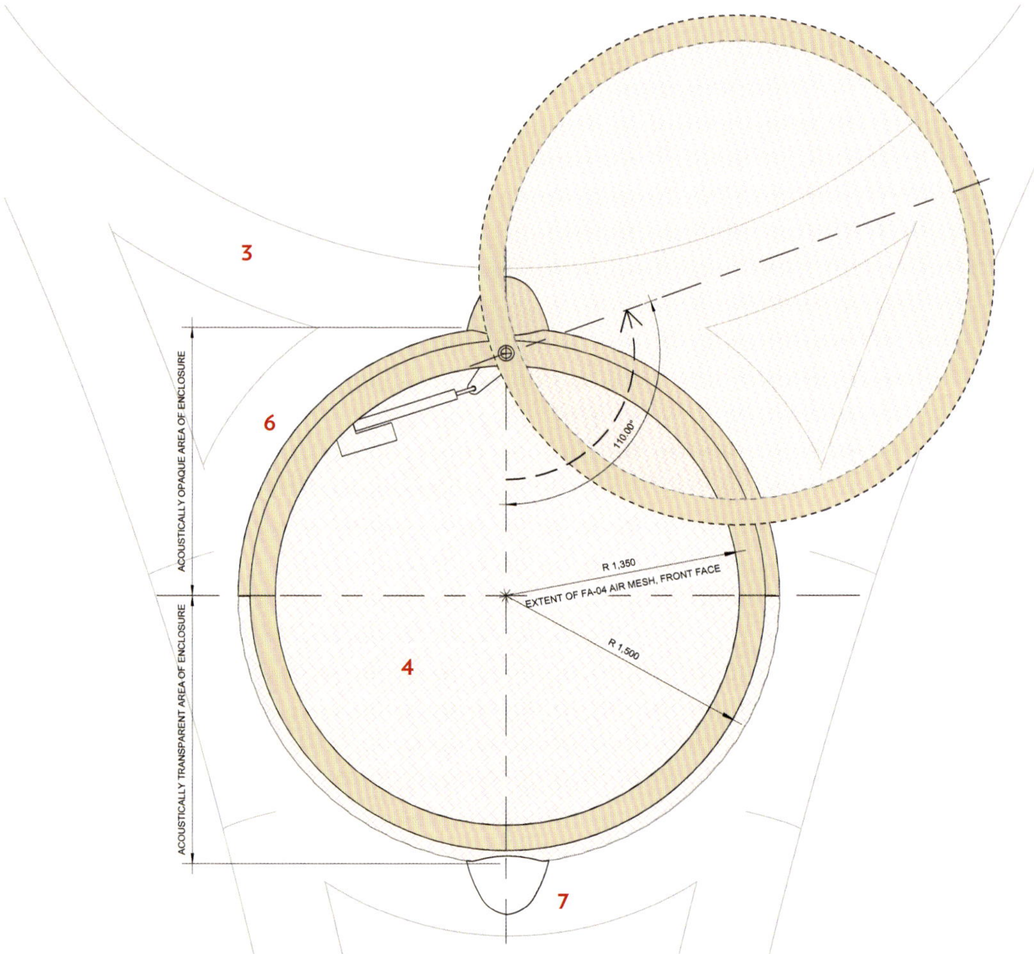

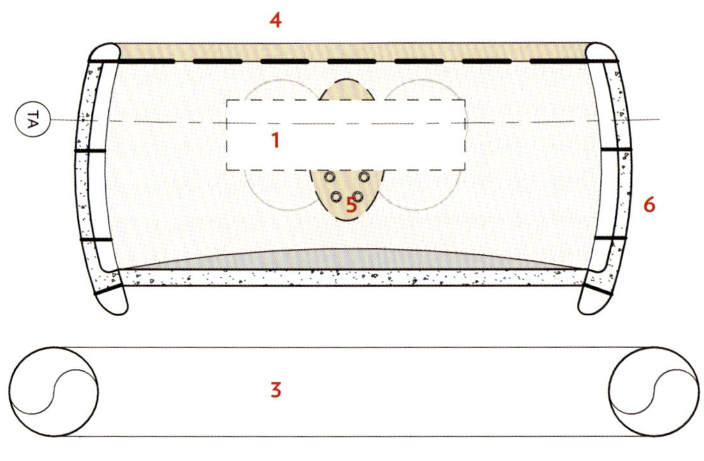

SPEAKER ENCLOSURE

1 SPEAKER
2 PTFE FIBERGLASS MESH
3 TRELLIS STEEL STRUCTURE
4 ACOUSTIC AIR MESH
5 SIDE AIR MESH
6 GFRC WITH ALUMINUM SKIN
7 SUPPORT PYLON
8 STEEL RIBBED STRUCTURE
9 SAFETY ELEMENTS

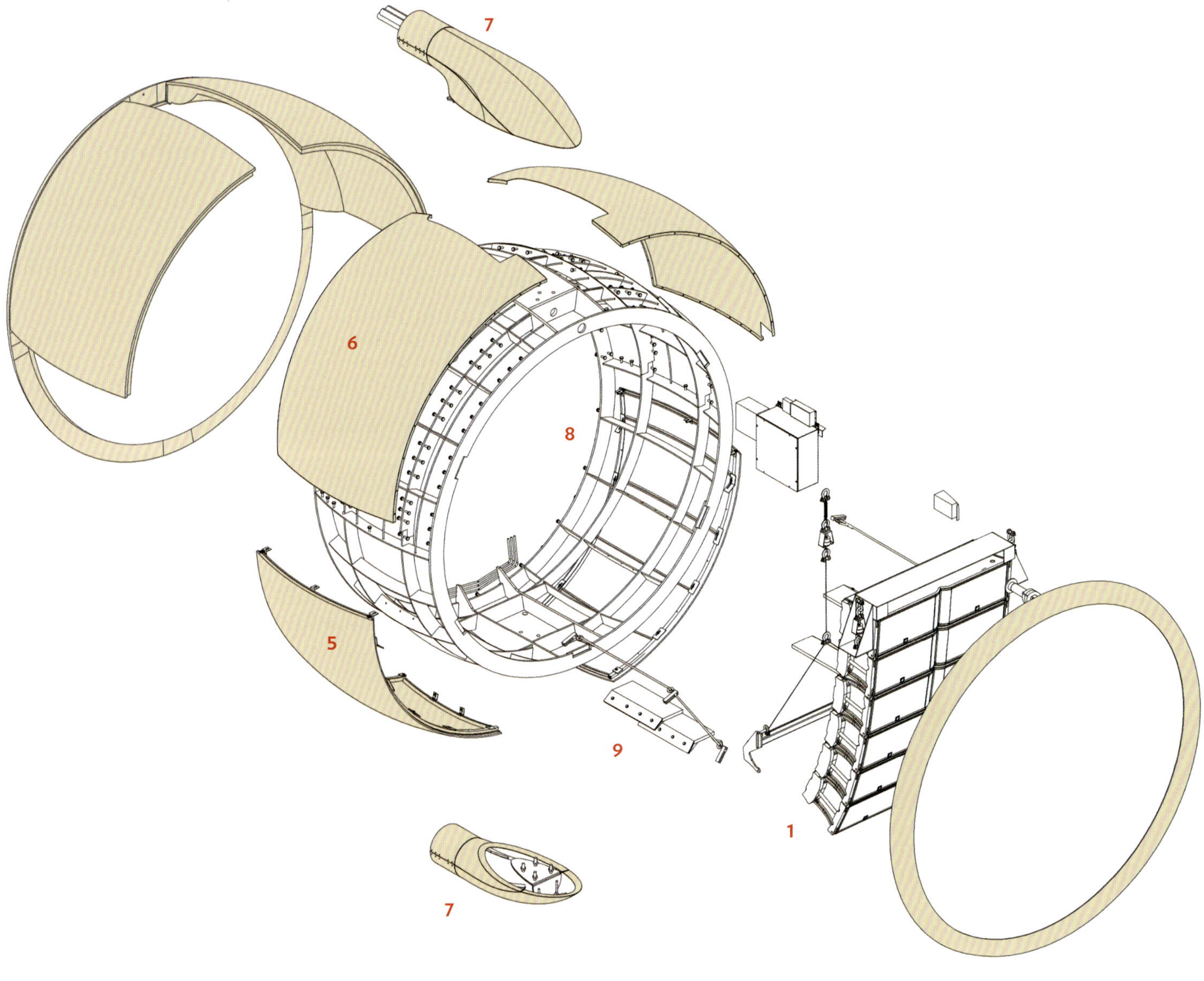
7
6
8
4
5
9
1
7

TRELLIS MAINTENANCE ACCESS SYSTEM

The Al Wasl Plaza trellis and its projection and audio equipment represent an investment of hundreds of millions of dirhams. As the figurative and literal centerpiece of Expo 2020 and the post-expo legacy development, there are high expectations that it not only performs magnificently but that it is also in pristine condition. To fulfill these expectations, the design team knew from the beginning that a comprehensive maintenance access system would be required for the functionality and appearance of the structure.

The basis of design defined by the Expo 2020 client directed the design team to eliminate any permanently fixed ladders, bridges or extensive catwalks while providing a safe and adequate means of maintenance to the trellis structure, fabric, services, and AV enclosures. It was the priority of the design team to integrate the access system seamlessly into the complex geometry of the trellis, without compromising the sinuous forms of the logo-inspired design.

Technically, access is required to every aspect of the structure. The inside and outside surface of every trellis structural pipe member and fabric panel, from grade to the oculus, must be able to be physically reached by a worker for routine maintenance and cleaning. All permanent devices including light fixtures, speakers, security cameras, and the internal containment servicing these devices require access. Temporary event-specific devices such as banners, lighting, or speakers also require access and cannot be mounted in locations that inhibit the movement of the gantry system. Of high importance is the forty-two AV enclosures and their associated work platforms, which must be accessed for cleaning, maintenance, projector calibration, repair, and replacement.

Therefore, in designing a comprehensive maintenance access system appropriate to meet the objectives noted above. The design team needed to address multiple challenges including aesthetics, functionality, and safety in the design of the comprehensive maintenance access system to address the objectives. Furthermore, given this unique structure and equipment installed the team had to conceptualize the means and methods to be applied in maintaining every element of the trellis to design the equipment required to facilitate each.

The primary inner and outer gantry systems cover most of the trellis, from the highest archway at 22m above ground to the top oculus at 65m above ground. It was not viable to extend this motorized gantry to the ground due to the challenge of spanning the grand arches at the base. The mobile aerial work platforms and/or scissors lifts are used to cover the lowest portion of the trellis, including the exterior surface of the forty-two AV enclosures. These mobile machines also provide access for cleaning crews and maintenance specialists to the gantries.

TRELLIS ACCESS GANTRY SYSTEM

1 TRACK 1
2 TRACK 2
3 TRACK 3
4 TRACK 4
5 INNER GANTRY
6 OUTER GANTRY

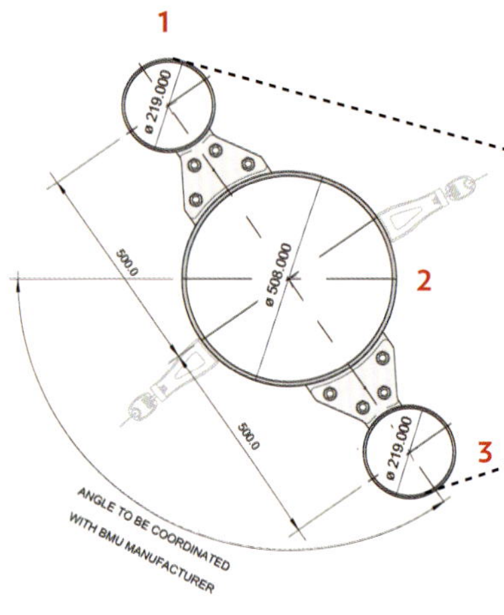

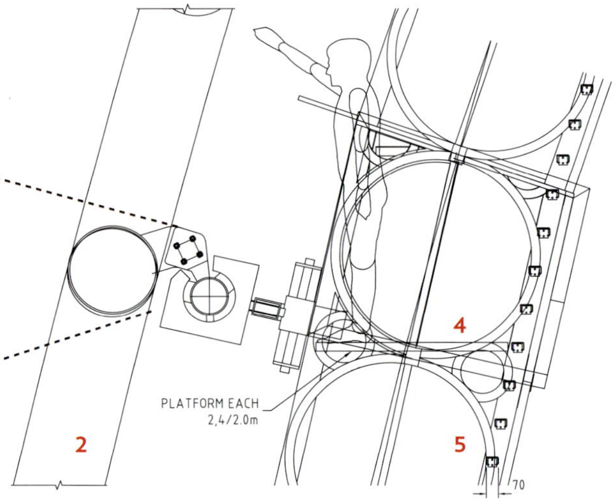

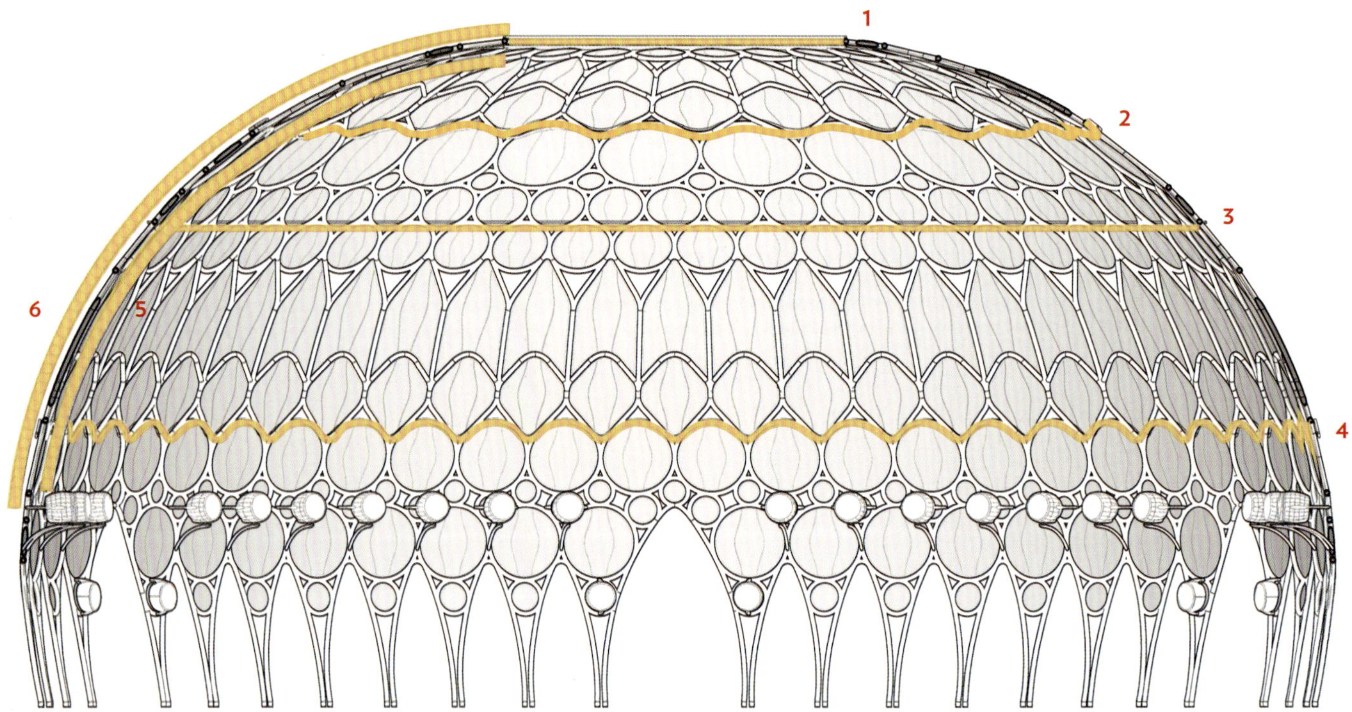

AV ENCLOSURE ACCESS, OPERATION + MAINTENANCE

Without a precedent for the design of an AV (projector) enclosure, more commonly called the projector pod, the design and engineering team was on a fast-track schedule to literally invent it. Not only did it need to be designed to accommodate the six projectors, but questions as to how it would be fabricated, installed, operated, and maintained needed to be addressed. AS+GG led a team of consultants, engineers, and fabricators from around the world, working with the client to ensure procurement was possible in time for the Expo event.

Each of the 42 AV enclosures contain six high performance laser projectors, model D4K40-RGB, manufactured by Christie Digital Systems USA. Each projector can produce 40,000 lumens of brightness and requires 4 kilowatts of power, which in turn produces 13,650 BTU's of heat. Therefore, given that the ambient environment in Dubai is hot and humid, the projectors must be contained in a cooled, environmentally stable environment. Therefore, each AV enclosure houses two fan coil cooling units in addition to the projectors. Each AV enclosure contains associated electrical distribution boards and control equipment to assist in the functionality of the projectors and cooling system. The interior of the enclosures is air-tight to reduce dust infiltration and maximize the efficiency of the cooling system.

Directly behind each AV enclosure, and suspended from its support arms, is a work platform. In addition to providing a walkway for AV maintenance specialists; each work platform houses the air-cooled condensers that provide refrigerant to the fan coil units as well as power and control distribution boards for the AV enclosures and performance lighting. The work platform provides direct access to the AV enclosures rear access doors. Once the doors are removed and placed in storage shoes fixed to the work platform floor grating, the specialist technicians can access, inspect, maintain, and effect repairs to the equipment therein.

The inner face of the AV enclosure is fully glazed with a set of doors. The glazing is necessary to allow the projection of the images across the plaza towards the far side of the trellis, and the doors are required to allow access to the projectors for installation, inspection, maintenance, and replacement if necessary. The specialist technicians will utilize a mobile scissors lift to gain access to this end of the AV Enclosure for frequent cleaning of the glass as well as the projector maintenance.

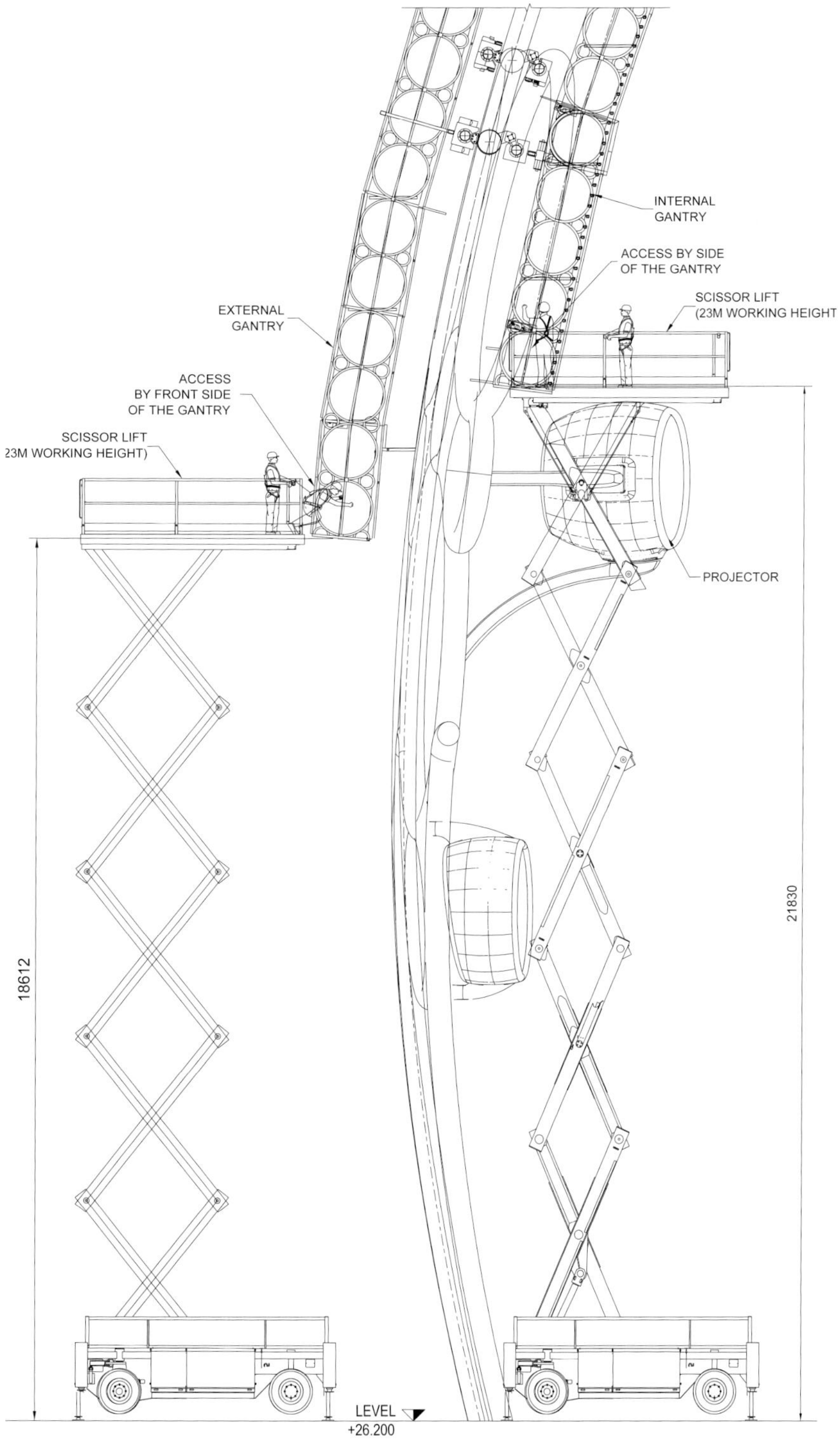

PARTIAL SECTION OF EXTERNAL + INTERNAL GANTRY ACCESS

THE SPACE BETWEEN

The experience within the trellis evokes awe at a grand scale looking toward the sky. From another perspective, the buildings surrounding Al Wasl were designed to engage in an equally important visual experience, a unique elevated perspective analogous to upper galleries of a theater. The intimacy of the space between the buildings and trellis was a critical part of the envisioned Al Wasl experience. The relationship between the steel structure, fabric panels and glass facade had to be balanced architecturally and technically for fire and life safety. To achieve the design intent and target costs, the steel structure and building exterior walls needed to be free of fire proofing and fire rating, respectively and the fabric needed to be transparent enough to allow views into the garden. This overall architectural concept was approved by the client but testing and authority approval was required for the project to be considered feasible for advancement.

Building codes require minimum separation distances and fire-rating requirements to minimize the hazard due to the possibility of fire transferring from one structure to another. In the case of construction in Dubai, a minimum nine-meter separation is required for structures without fire-rated exterior wall. That being the case, achieving a close relationship between the buildings and the trellis was a unique challenge. The intimacy was achieved by stepping the face of each building to follow the shape of the trellis. The delicacy of the trellis was achieved by using the smallest reasonable diameter of architectural exposed, painted, structural steel pipe, without conventional fire protection or cladding.

Given that this unique typology did not fit a standard category within the applicable codes; AS+GG involved a series of experts including Jensen Hughes as FLS consultants, TT structural engineers, and eConstruct, the local architect with the Dubai municipal and Civil Defense authorities, at a very early stage in the design. The team worked to optimize the materiality, minimize the separation distance, and achieve the desired aesthetics, while maintaining the requisite level of safety deemed necessary by the local authorities. Working with the local authorities it was determined that Al Wasl would be subject to a performance-based fire and life safety analysis. The local authorities stipulated, and the design team agreed that a Fire Dynamic Simulation (FDS), a digital fire model to represent a set of scenarios, would be created to test fire scenarios within the building and outside the building.

Jensen Hughes performed the FDS which demonstrated that a fire event inside the building, even if uncontrolled and with flames breaking out of the facade at the designed four-meter separation, will not raise the temperature of the exposed steel trellis to the point that it would cause instability. The second FDS simulated a fire at the base of the trellis in the roadway.

This series of performance-based simulations and analyses allowed the design team to confirm the materiality of the exposed structural steel and non-fire rated curtain wall system, reduce the offset distance to four meters to achieve the desired aesthetic effect while maintaining the necessary safety for the public. This approval was a milestone in the project and allowed the design to progress in further detail

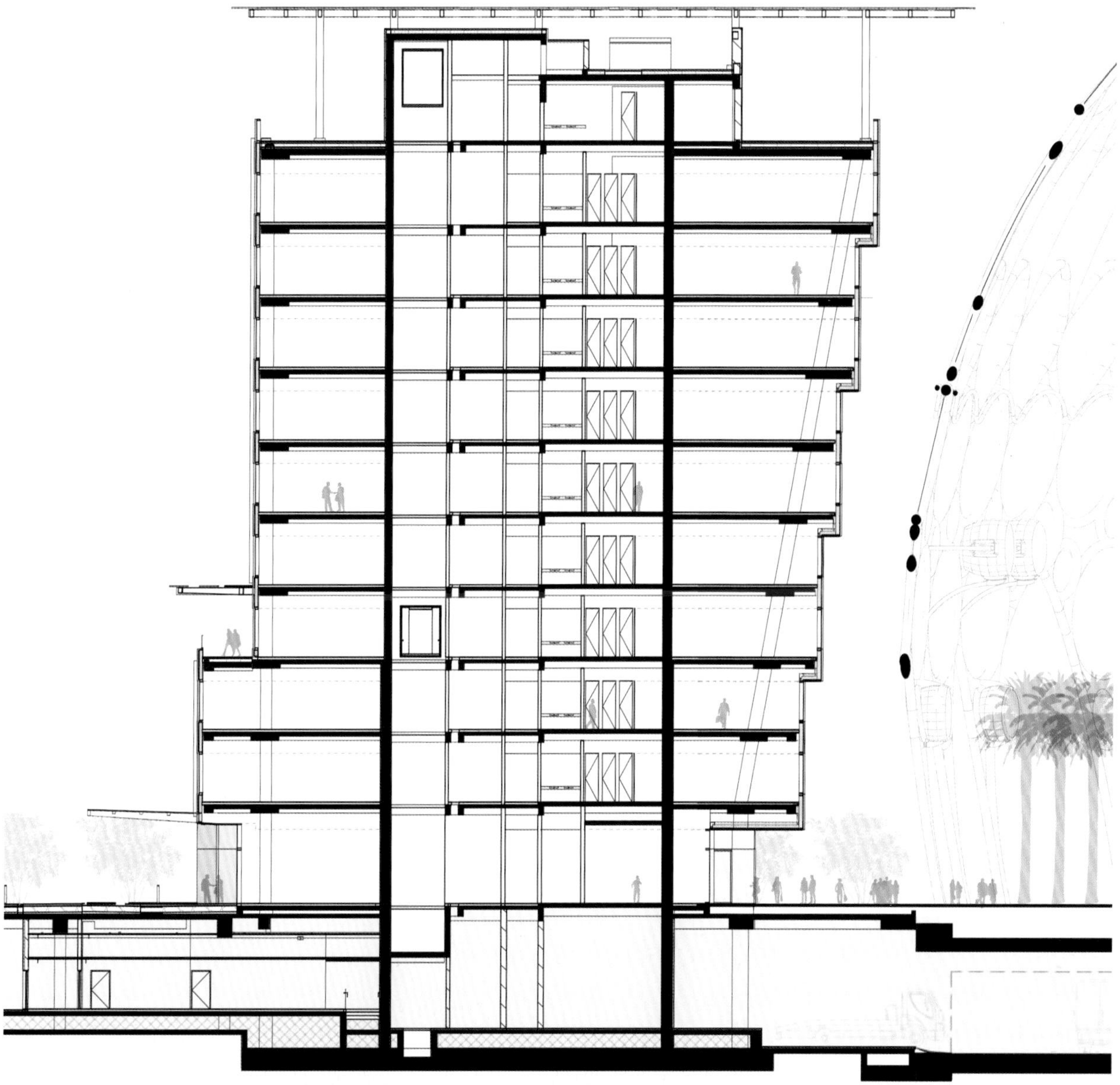

OFFICE

As the frame of Al Wasl Plaza's urban room, the office buildings are integral to their context and cannot be observed in isolation. The unparalleled experience of Al Wasl is rooted in the interconnected nature of the public space, semi-public hotels, and semi-private tenant office buildings. The building programs and spatial sequence complement each other to form the ring in the center of the district. At the close of Expo 2020, the office buildings will anchor the overall district attracting corporate tenants to Al Wasl Plaza, thus expanding the innovation and economic development in the area. The opportunity to design an integrated public amenity of such grand physical scale, global impact and visibility during the expo event, and strong legacy impact for the vitality of the district is rare. The office buildings represent an opportunity for forward thinking, connectivity, innovation, and knowledge sharing.

This section explores the office design which was developed with full integration with its adjacent context: the trellis, garden, hotels, public realm, and edge of the adjacent district. Simultaneous development of these parcels created interesting design opportunities and technical challenges. The constructed form and architectural expression of the office buildings integrates into the architectural language of Al Wasl. This is the story of Al Wasl through the lens of the office buildings. It highlights the layout, exterior wall, interiors, and sustainability achievements. The cooling for the office buildings is provided by a chiller plant in the thematic district, which uses a high proportion of renewable electricity provided by the Dubai Electricity and Water Authority (DEWA). These buildings will be the first in Dubai to collect and treat rainwater, condensate, grey water, and treated wastewater to be used in a reclaimed water system for the use of toilet flushing, eliminating the use of fresh water for toilet flushing. This is estimated to reduce total building potable water consumption by 73%.

OFFICE DESIGN

The uses, floor areas, and building heights of the six parcel sites surrounding Al Wasl Plaza were defined by AS+GG in their 2016 legacy master plan. The objective of the master plan was to provide suitable accommodations and facilities that maximize investment and activate the central parcels after the Expo. The comprehensive legacy master plan design identified office, retail, and hotel programs to complement the functions within the legacy souk districts and maintain a central focus for the overall development. Residential buildings had been considered as an extension of the mixed-use souk districts. However, residential use, being less active and more private, would not easily coexist with the active immersive experience venue. Therefore, offices and hotels are more appropriate uses for this public location. Office use is especially important for the legacy use being that it will have the ability to attract corporate tenants who desire larger building scale, which is not available elsewhere within the core of the Expo 2020 district.

The office and hotel buildings have a unique relationship to the central public space. Due to the concentric geometry, the parcels surrounding the central circle terminate with a narrow edge along Al Wasl Plaza. These properties expand outwards in varying wedge shapes between the roads towards the districts. A simple extrusion of the given parcels would have been ineffective to fully define the central space. With large gaps between the building forms, this direction was not able to define an urban room with a strong edge. Furthermore, these narrow facades facing the central garden missed the opportunity to optimize the views towards the public plaza.

To enhance the relationships between the narrow facades and the public space, AS+GG studied tilting the buildings inward to create a sense of intimacy. This action created performative benefits by self-shading the facades and the public space below to enhance comfort in the hot Dubai climate. Next, a simple study model tested an idea to flip the upper portion of the building mass creating a wider facade facing Al Wasl Plaza while maintaining the podium form at grade. This experimental move was not obvious at first as it required extending over the master plan property lines into the public space. It broke several guidelines established by the original master plan but achieved the desired effect. The circular site felt contained, achieving an implied spherical enclosure, focused on the Al Wasl Plaza, as the design team intended.

This arrangement was unprecedented, thus the premium associated with the design and structural complexity had to be understood and managed for the project to proceed. The design placed additional floor area with larger leasable floor plates at the top of each building and created more building facade with premium views of the garden. This signature group of buildings and public garden amenity will serve as a magnet of growth in the legacy development of Dubai South City. The benefits of this massing extend beyond achieving a defined room for the central public space; the additional height and leasable area increase the Expo's return on investment in the overall Al Wasl development. The final three building designs are nearly identical and were designed in the same architectural language as the two hotels, creating an architecturally cohesive centerpiece.

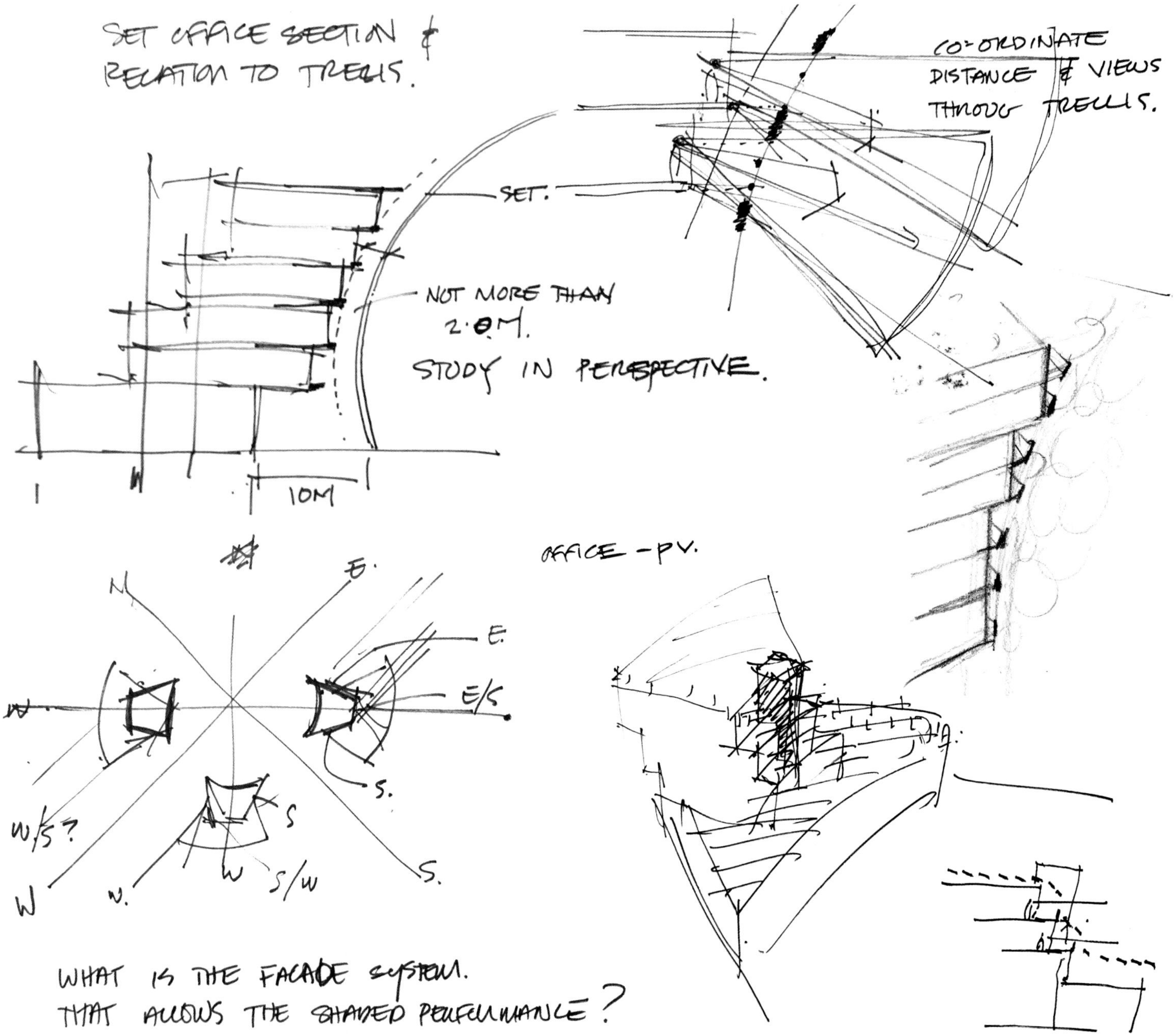
SET OFFICE SECTION & RELATION TO TRELLIS.
CO-ORDINATE DISTANCE & VIEWS THROUG TRELLIS.
SET.
NOT MORE THAN 2.0M.
STUDY IN PERSPECTIVE.
10M
OFFICE - PV.
N
E.
E.
E/S
S.
S
S.
W/S?
W
N.
W
S/W
WHAT IS THE FACADE SYSTEM.
THAT ALLOWS THE SHADED PERFORMANCE?

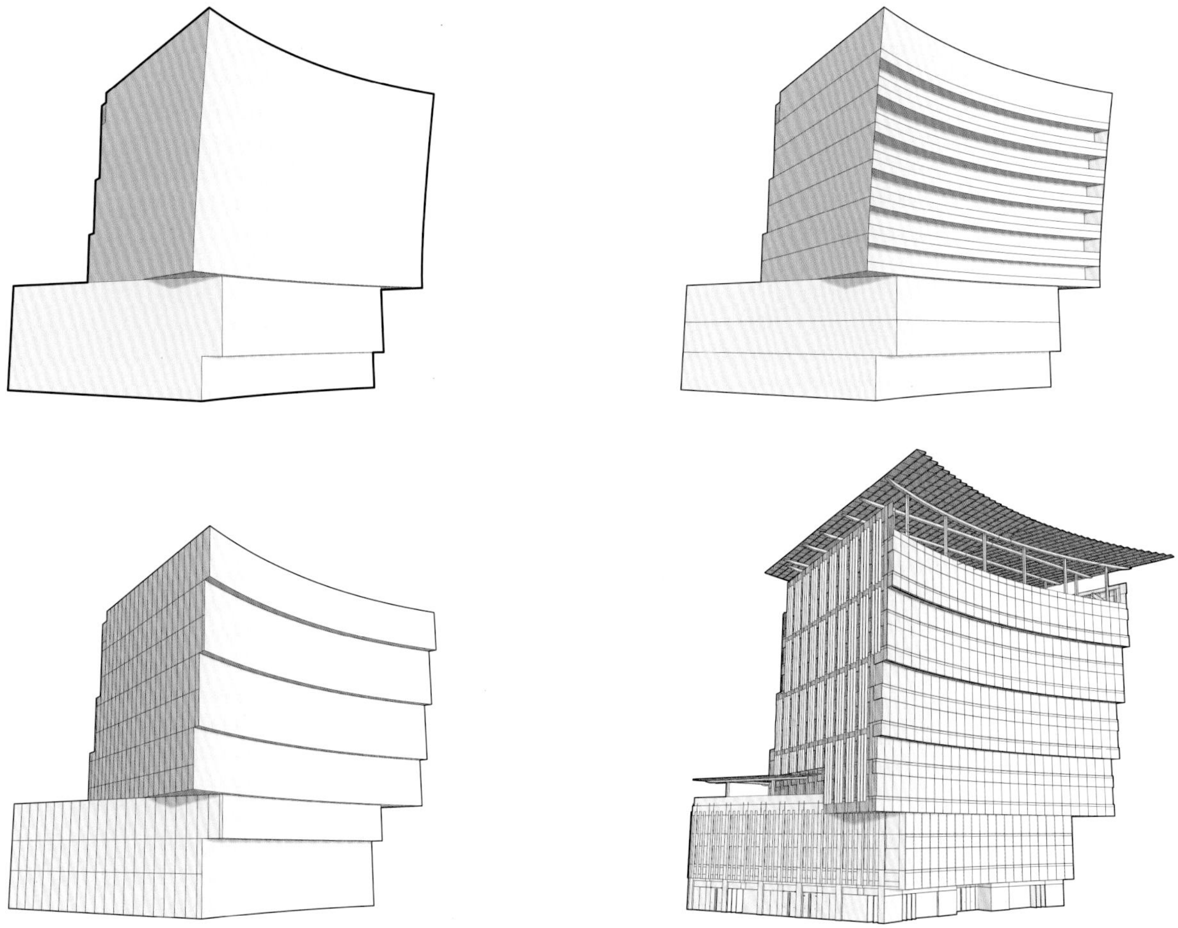

OFFICE MASSING DEVELOPMENT

Due to the fast-track nature of the project, priority was placed on optimizing the office building form to set the ground level and typical floor plans to expedite basement and foundation design. Facing Al Wasl Plaza, the office buildings have prime interior space that act as a theater gallery to the events in the plaza below. The design of this inner wall began with a double-curved facade that closely followed the form of the trellis. While clearly responding to the trellis form, the facade and layout complexity was not justifiable. A design was also proposed that included balconies facing Al Wasl on each level as a premium user amenity. It was deemed an unnecessary additional cost, leading to a single rooftop terrace. The final design offsets the curvature of the trellis into a stepped single-curved facade. Each of the five stepped volumes contains two levels, the sectional profile closely following the trellis. Opposite the trellis, the massing steps down to the scale of the thematic districts. Along the concourse streets, the tower flies over the podium to capture views of Al Wasl Plaza. This unusual stepped cantilevered configuration required an innovative structural solution as well as a significant amount of coordination between the design consultants.

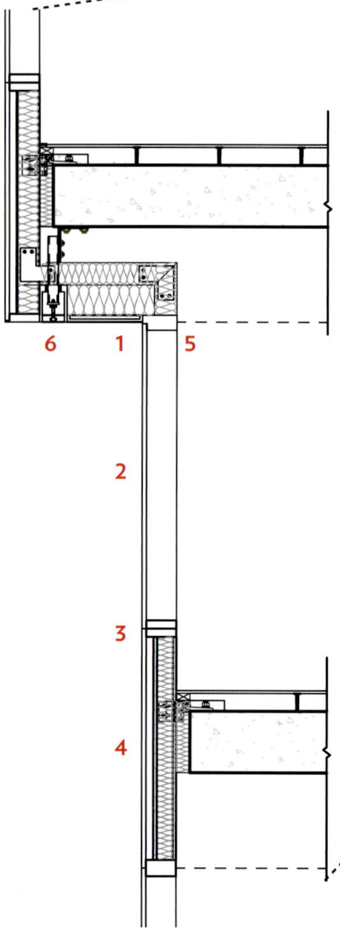

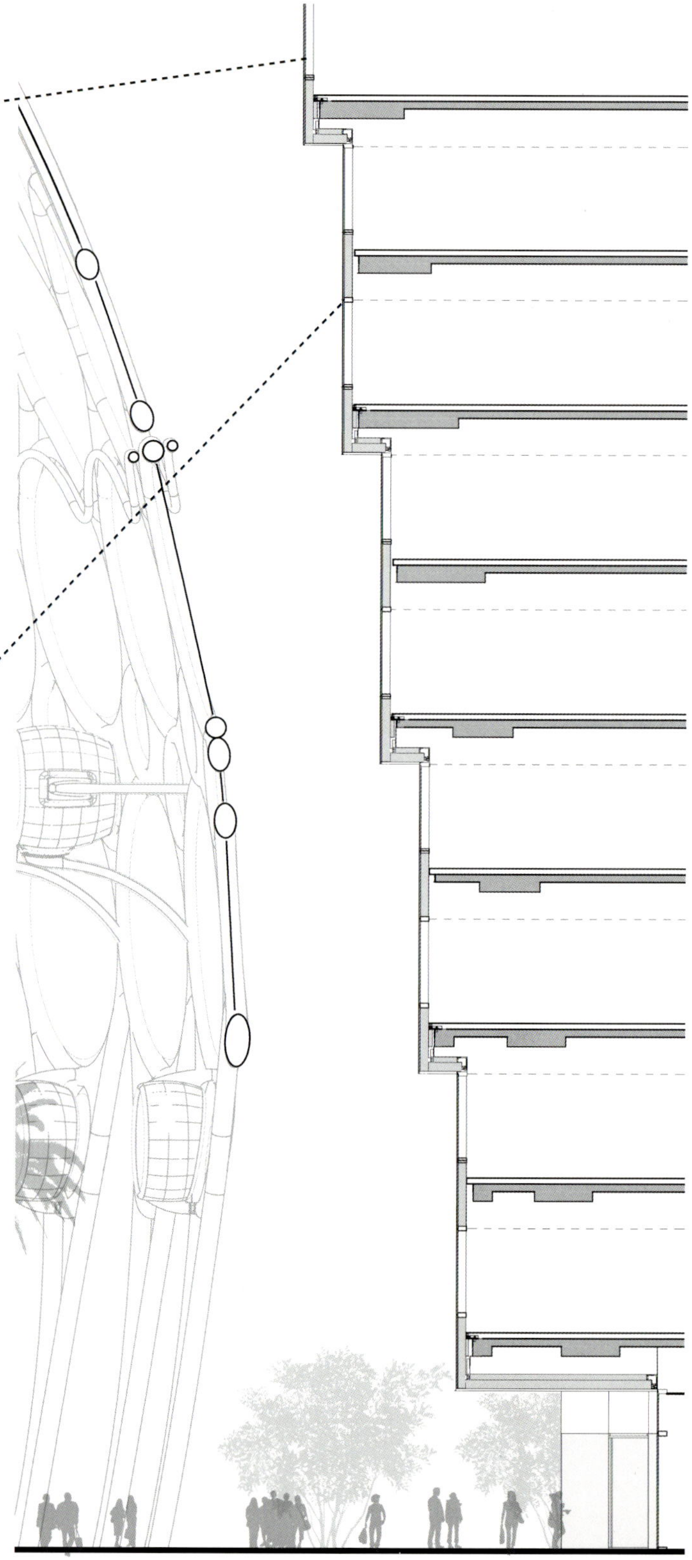

1 PERFORATED SHEET ALUMINUM FOR EVENT ACOUSTICS
2 CLEAR VISION INSULATED GLASS
3 STACK JOINT
4 SINGLE GLAZED PAINTED SHADOWBOX
5 ALUMINUM MULLION
6 FACADE ACCESS MONORAIL, SUPPORTED FROM FLOOR SLAB

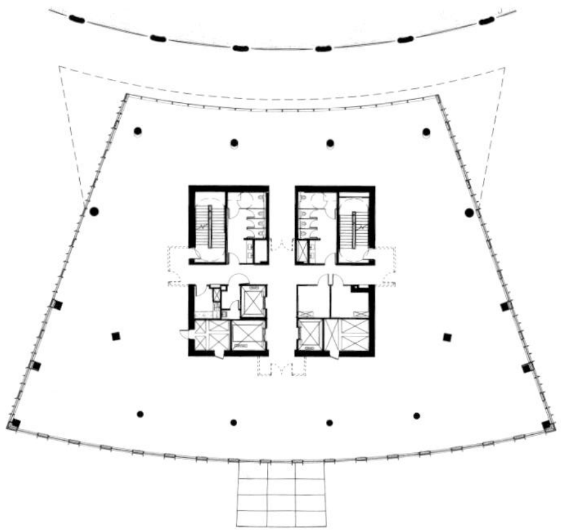

LEVEL 1

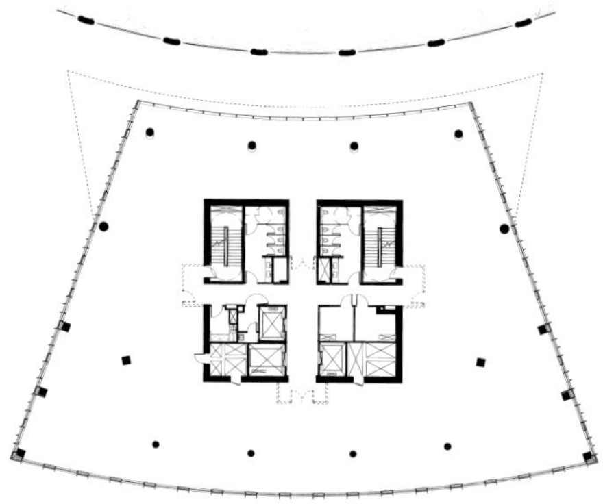

LEVEL 2

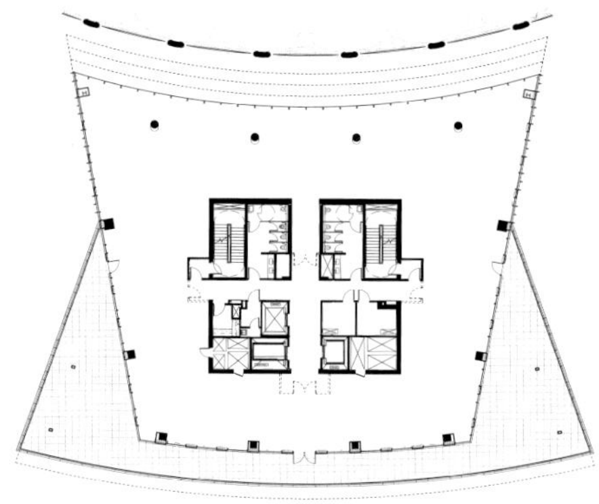

LEVEL 3

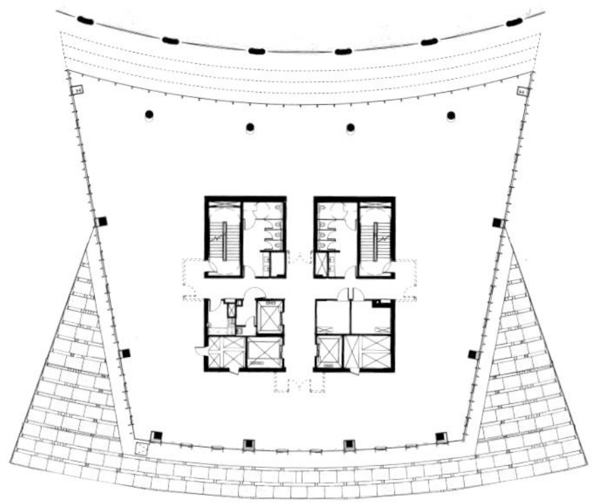

LEVEL 4

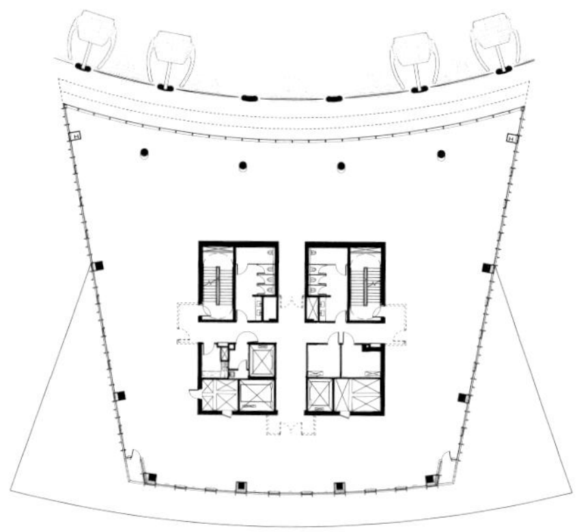

LEVEL 5

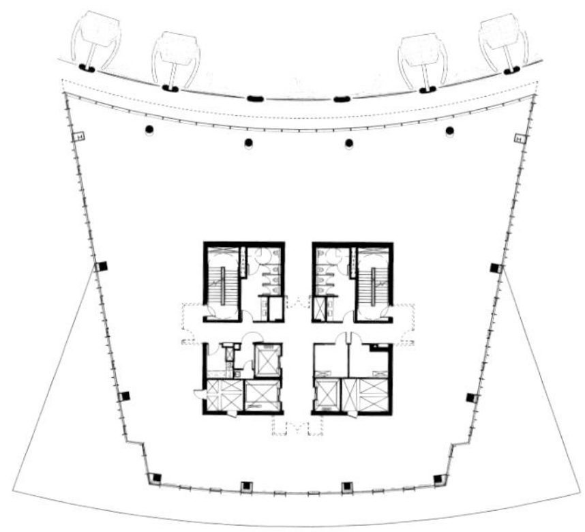

LEVEL 6

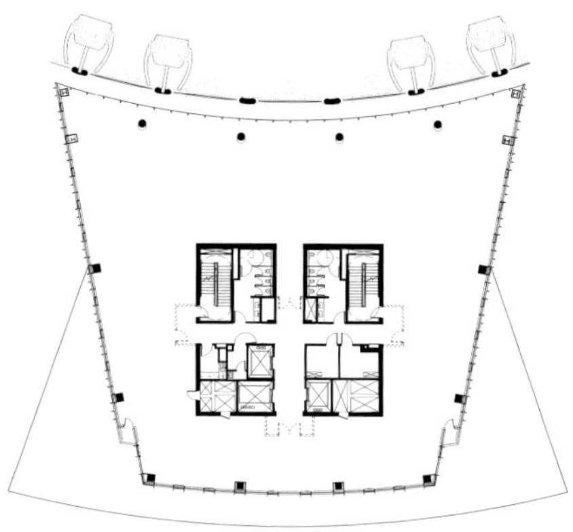

LEVEL 7

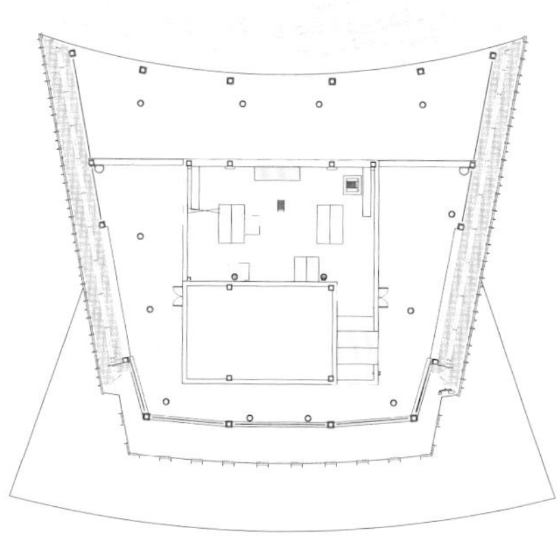

ROOFDECK

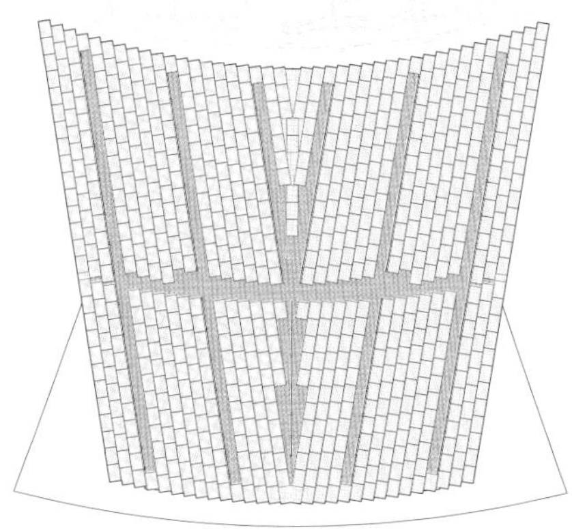

ROOFTOP

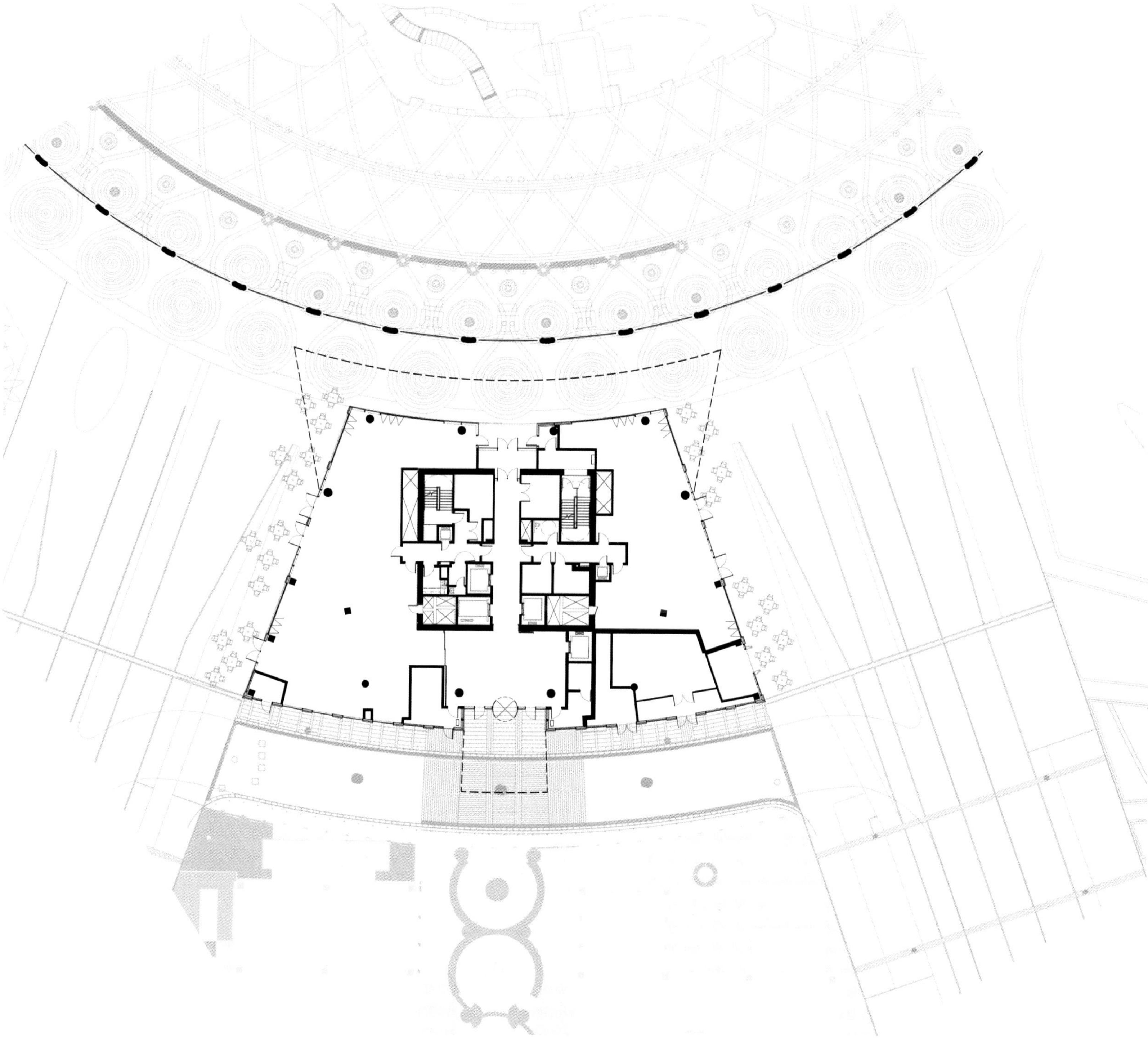

GROUND LEVEL

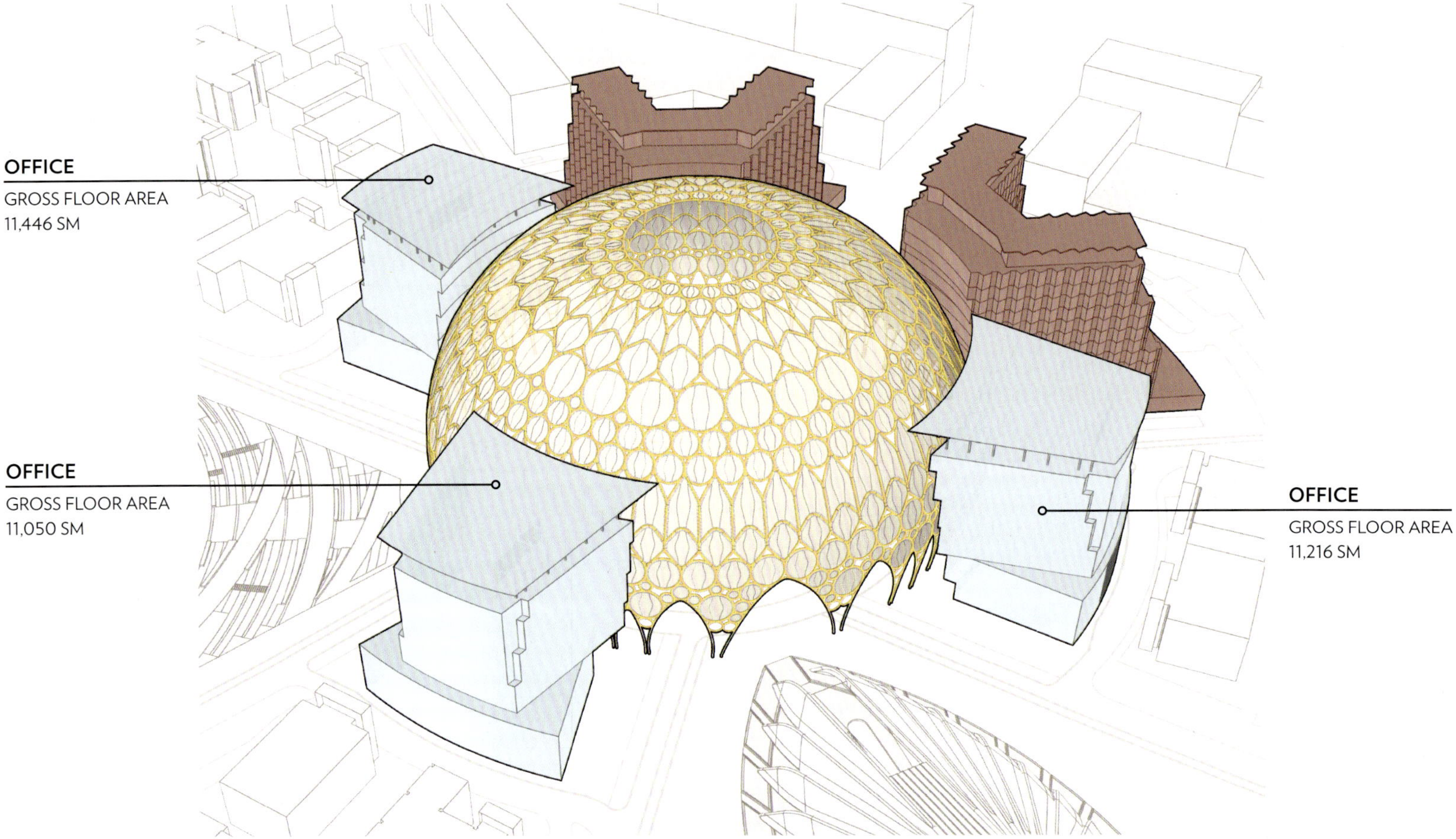

OFFICE EXPO TO LEGACY TRANSITION

The office buildings are vital components of Al Wasl Plaza, which would not be complete without its physical framework or the activation of the program within the center of the legacy district. The buildings function for both Expo event and legacy market-driven functions. As a result, the core and shell are designed for flexibility and a range of functions. During Expo 2020, the buildings provide event support such as a media center and corporate hospitality. Another objective of the design was to simplify the transition between event and legacy minimizing demolition and new construction. Speed of transition, sustainability in reducing waste and ability to adapt to new functions were key priorities. Office tenants will occupy the buildings following the close of Expo 2020, tailoring each office suite to their needs. As most of the legacy construction in the district will be from the ground up, the minimal transition period for the Al Wasl buildings is critical to spearhead the development of the new district from the center outward.

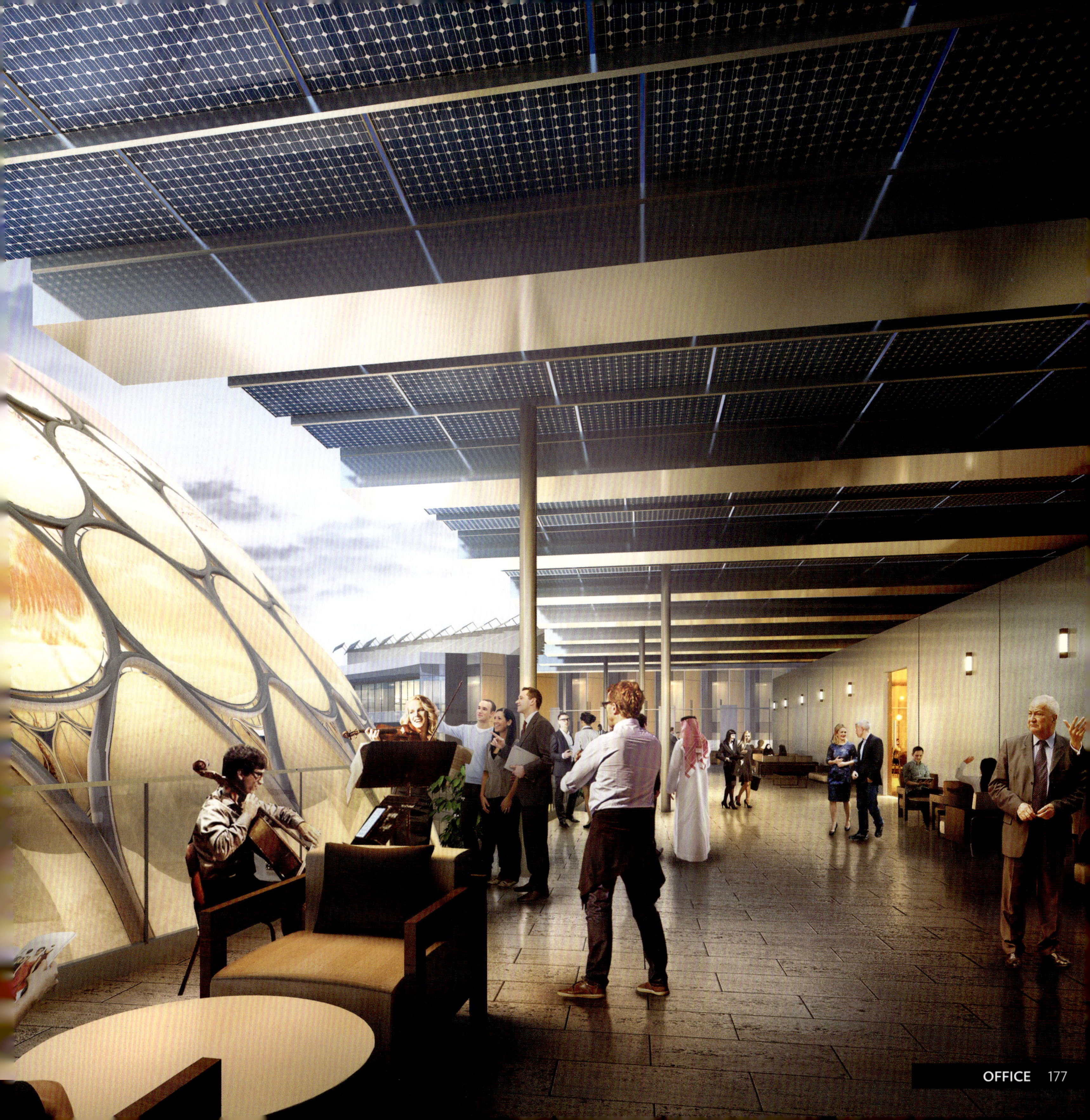

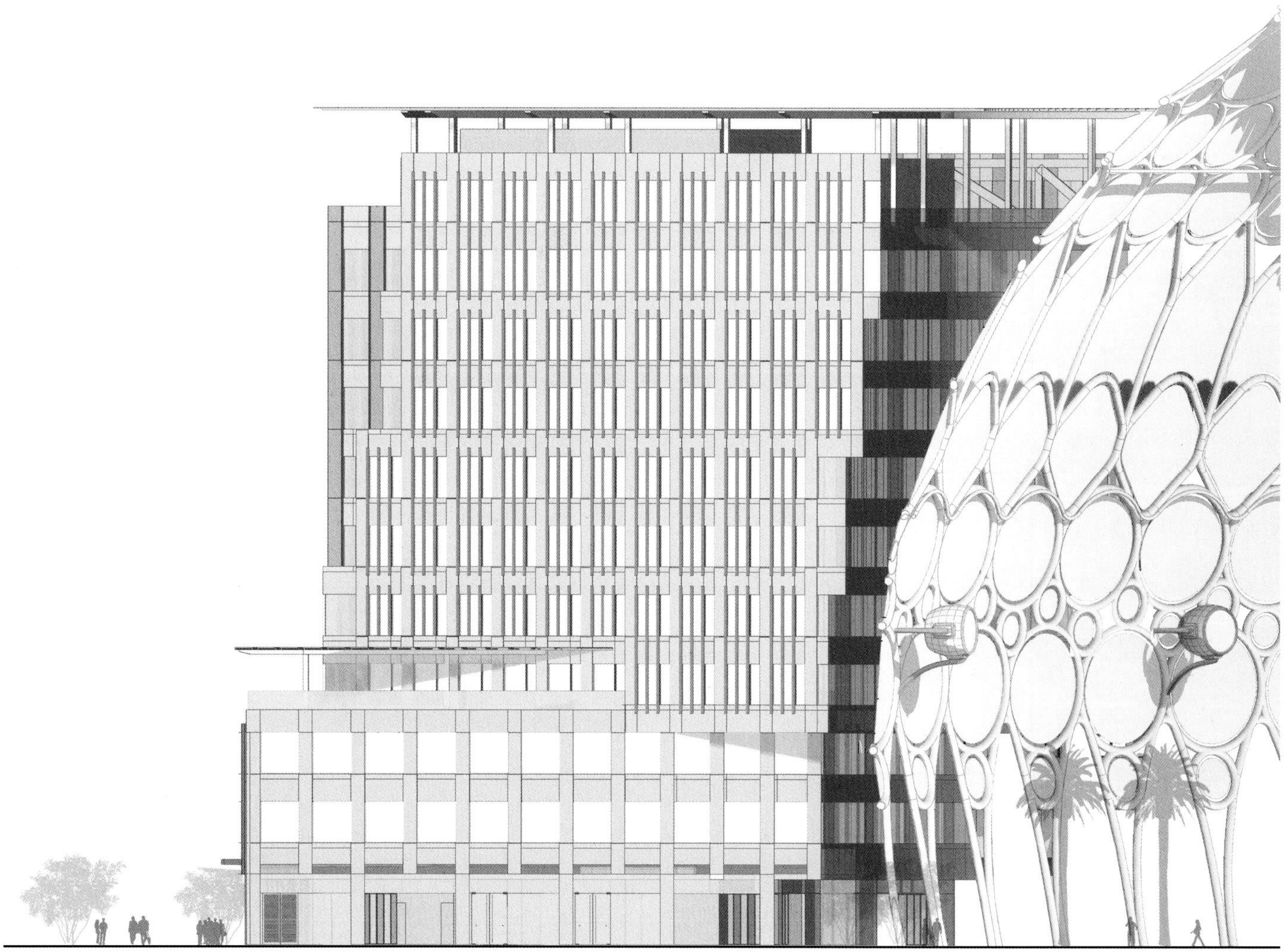

OFFICE ELEVATION

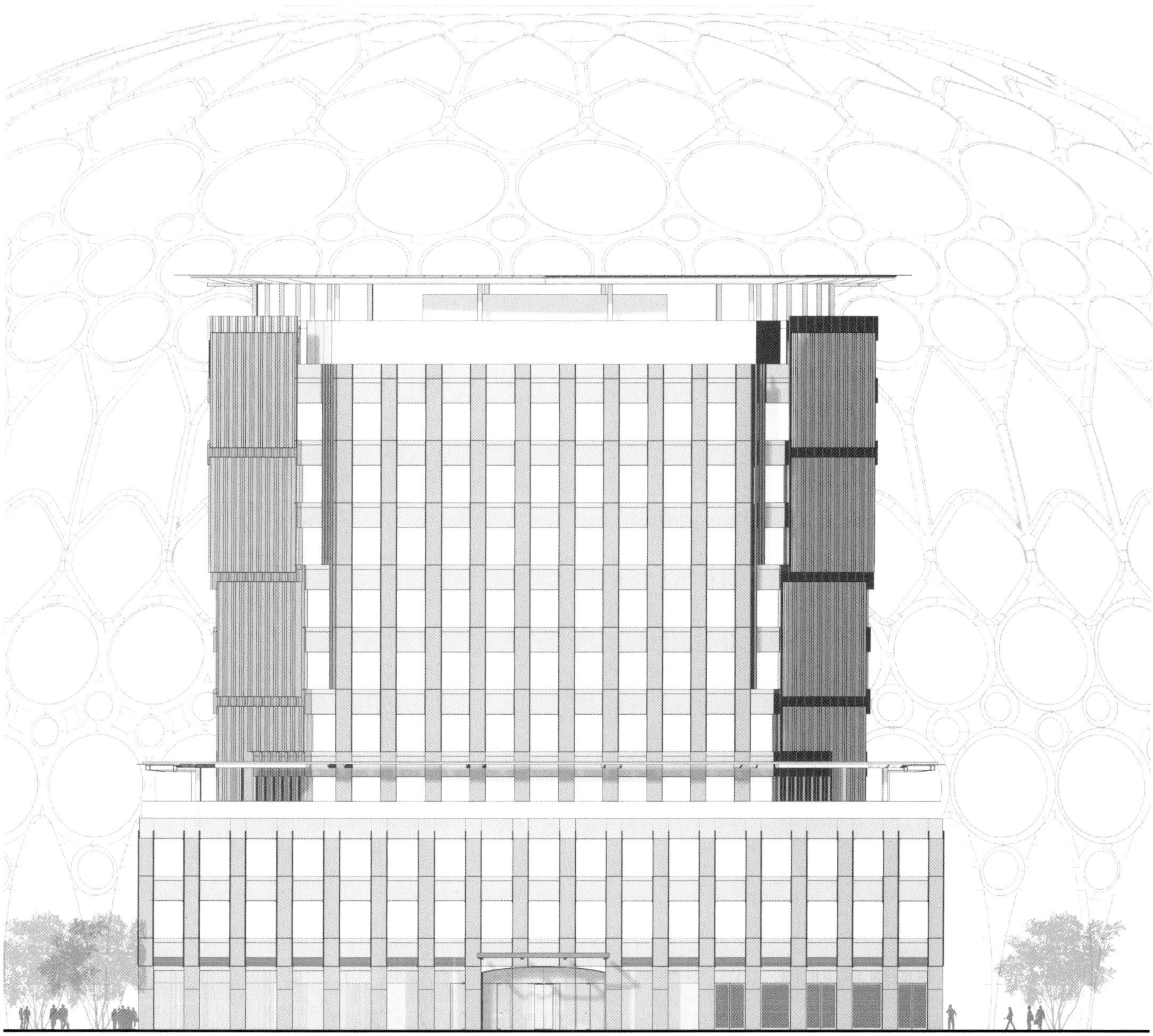

OFFICE ELEVATION

1 EXTRUDED ALUMINUM FIN
2 HIGH PERFORMANCE COATING
3 ALUMINUM CONNECTION
4 TYPICAL GLAZING PANEL
5 TYPICAL SPANDREL PANEL

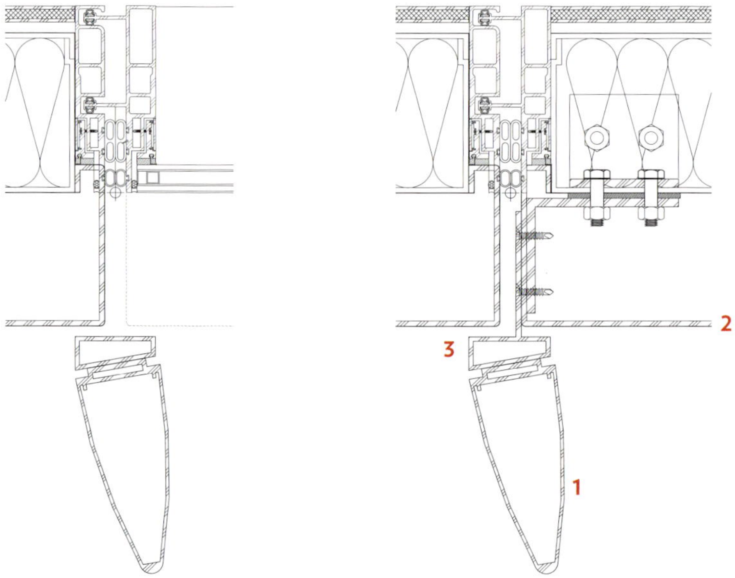

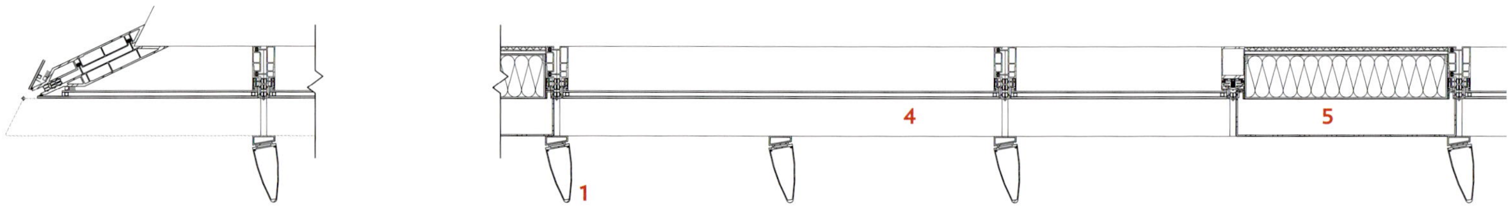

OFFICE EXTERIOR WALL

The exterior wall responds to three distinct conditions. Facing Al Wasl, a full glass facade steps inward following the curvature of the trellis, self-shading both the interior space and the public plaza below. A continuous faceted vision and spandrel glass system provides uninterrupted views of the trellis and garden. The soffit between each step is clad with an acoustic-backed perforated aluminum panel to minimize sound reflections into the central plaza. This stepped facade presented technical challenges to incorporate a continuous rail to ensure 100% coverage of the facade access system. Along the promenades, solar heat gain reduction is essential while balancing interior daylight. This wall is an aluminum-clad punched window wall system with a vision glass ratio of 50%. Vertical fins enhance the performance and provide a vertical aesthetic. Facing the district, the facades are also a punched window system with a vision glass ratio of 50% and shallow vertical fins framing the glazing. The original design included horizontal panels with building integrated photovoltaics to generate renewable energy. Those photovoltaic panels have been installed in trellis configurations above the roof and Level 3 terraces. The ground level exterior wall is an operable glass system for retail and cafes along the boulevard.

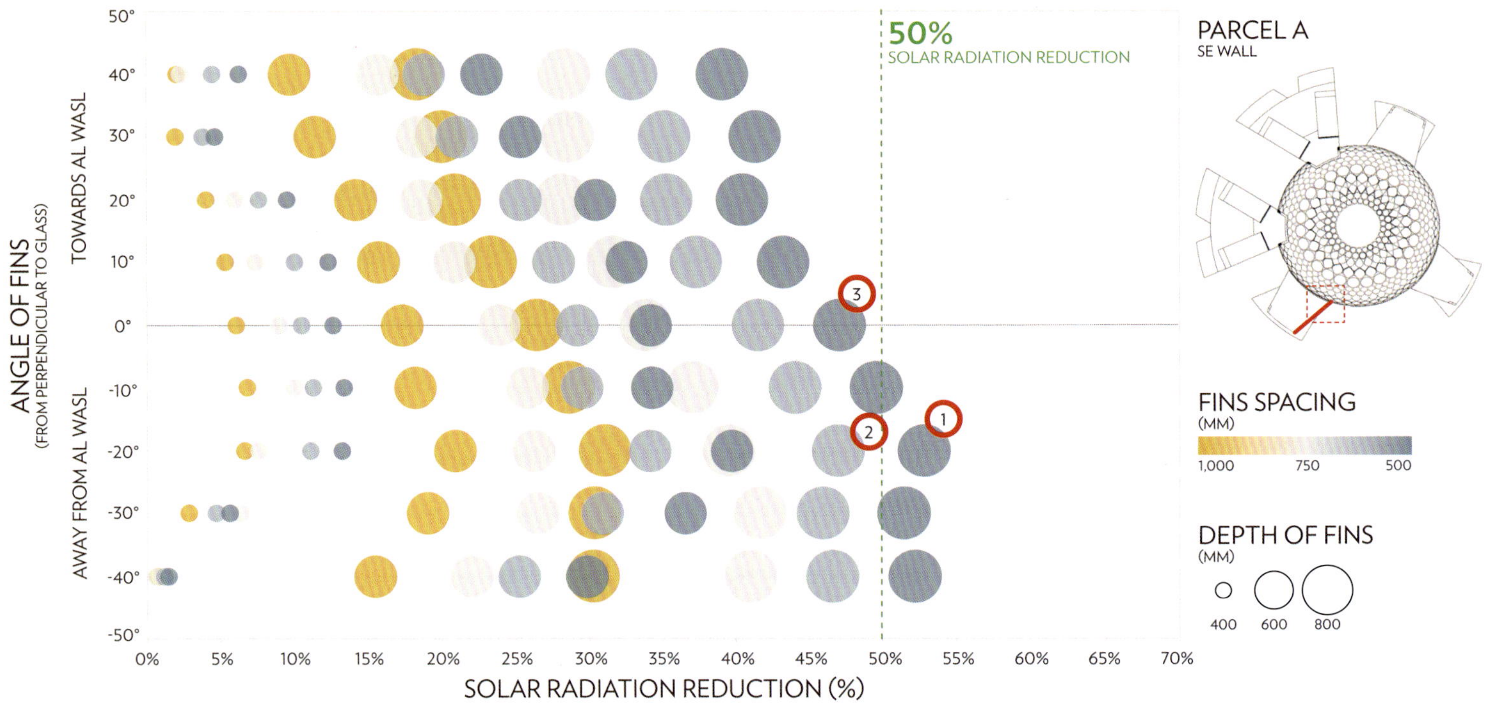

1
OPTION
53%
SOLAR RADIATION REDUCTION

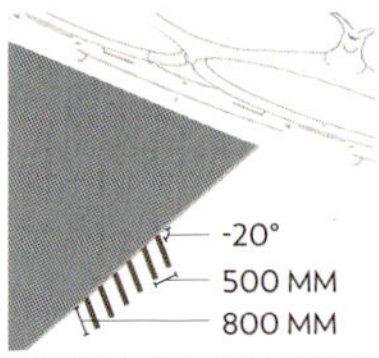

2
OPTION
47%
SOLAR RADIATION REDUCTION

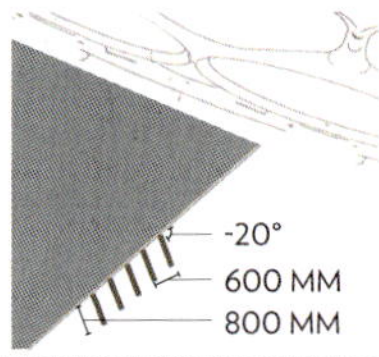

3
OPTION
47%
SOLAR RADIATION REDUCTION

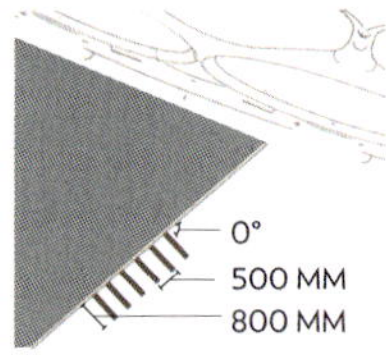

OFFICE SHADING ANALYSIS

The provision of exterior sun control and shading devices, which increase energy efficiency, reduce solar heat gain, and reduce interior glare was a priority in the design of the office buildings. These passive, long-term energy reduction strategies are studied during the design development for optimal orientations. In comparison to a horizontal system, vertical fins were chosen for the facades perpendicular to Al Wasl Plaza to limit sand and dust accumulation, minimizing required maintenance. An iterative analysis was performed to optimize the effectiveness of the fins, determining the best angle of rotation on each of the different wall orientations. To streamline the procurement process, the angle was limited to three variables: zero degrees or perpendicular to the glass and a 30-degree rotation in the positive and negative directions. Angles up to 50 degrees performed better in reducing solar impact, however a maximum rotation of 30 degrees was determined not to block views from the interior space. A fin spacing of 750 mm and depth of 200 mm was the ultimate configuration when considering cost and procurement impacts of the various options.

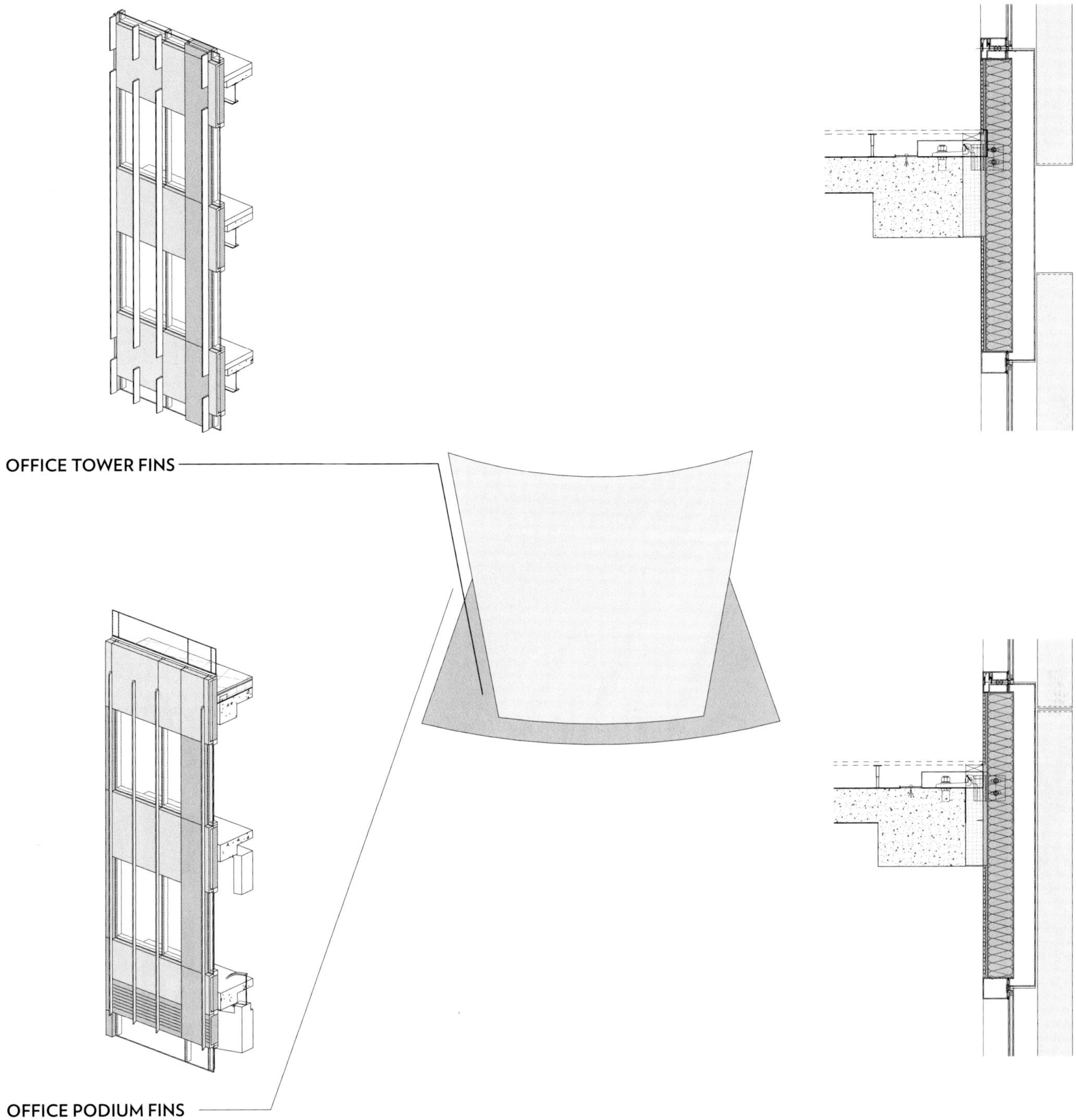
OFFICE TOWER FINS
OFFICE PODIUM FINS

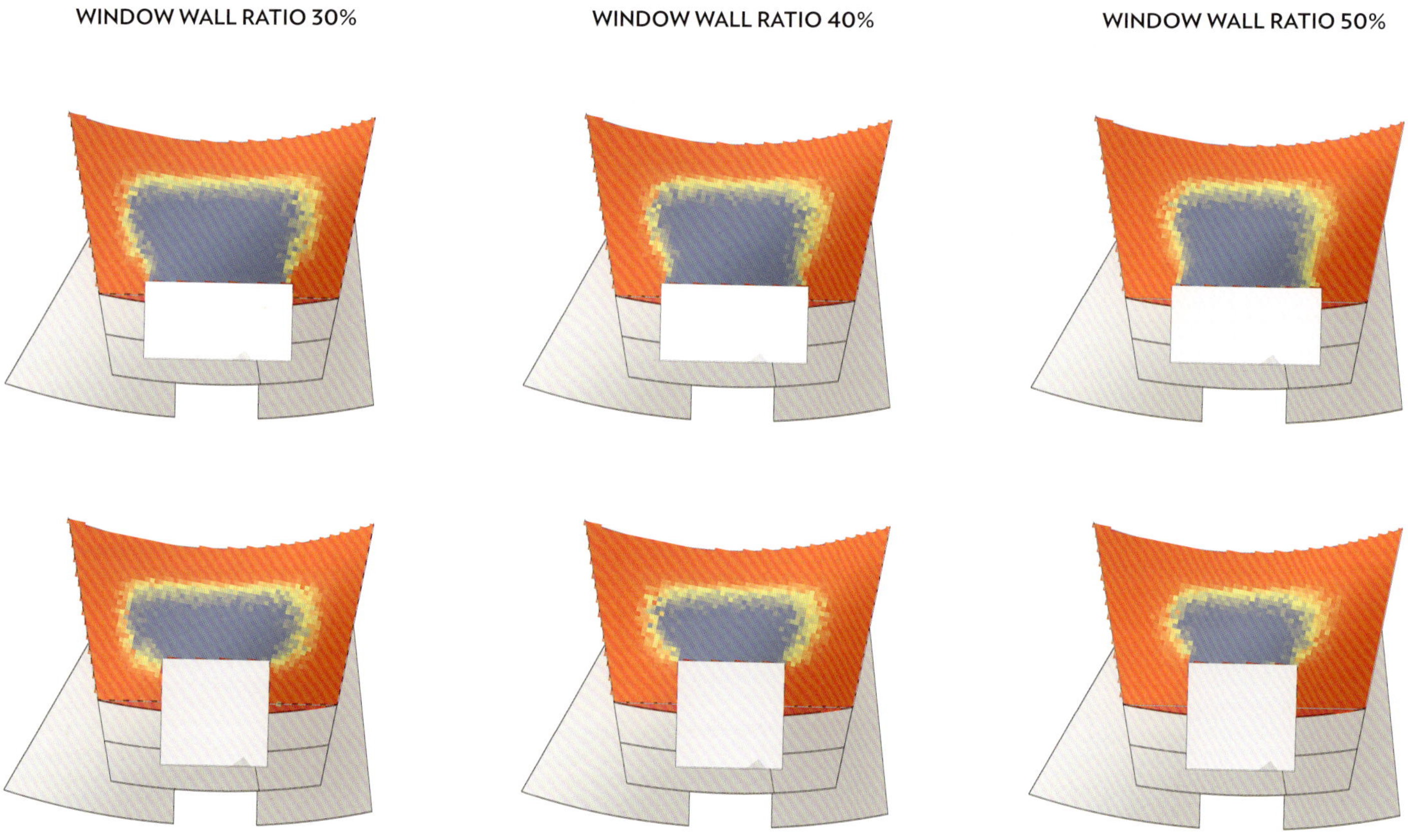

BUILDING DAYLIGHT ANALYSIS

Enhancing user comfort and experience are paramount in a long-term sustainable strategy. Maximizing daylight is a passive strategy that has the potential to impact the wellbeing of users and significantly reduce carbon emissions for the life of the building without necessarily adding cost or materials. To be effective, daylight simulations must be an integral part of the early design while developing the overall building geometry, exterior wall articulation, and floor plans. Exterior wall orientation, vision glass ratio, depth and shape of the wall system, and sun shading devices all have a direct impact on the amount and quality of daylight that reaches the interior spaces. The design must allow for adjustment to these variables when to achieve target daylight levels. For the office buildings, the overall geometry and the placement of the building core was confirmed by digitally testing the daylight to achieve the LEED requirements for daylight in the office space.

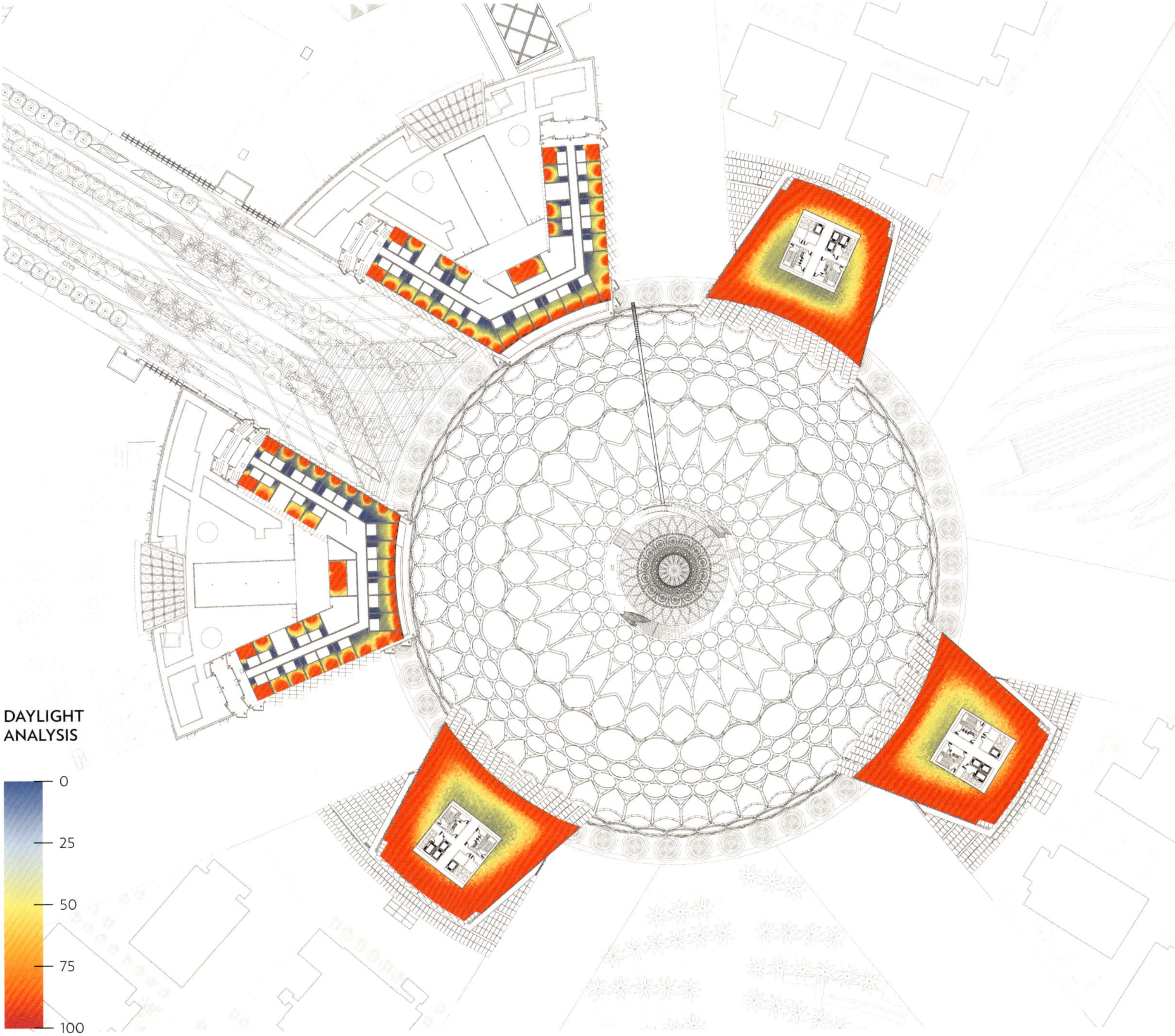
DAYLIGHT
ANALYSIS
0
25
50
75
100

PHOTOVOLTAIC SYSTEM

Dubai has a hot desert climate near the Tropic of Cancer with an average of over eight hours of sunlight per day, year-round. This natural resource presents an immense opportunity to harness solar energy. AS+GG created an ambitious sustainability plan for Al Wasl Plaza with a high target of achieving X amount of renewable energy for the office and hotel buildings. To maximize the energy generation, the designers studied photovoltaic (PV) area, orientation, and panel distribution on the building roofs. A flat orientation outperforms angled configurations due to the exposed site condition with high direct solar radiation, and it is also preferred for maintenance. The first design iteration limited the PVs to cover only the rooftop mechanical areas, however this quickly expanded to shade the rooftop amenity areas to increase user comfort and energy generation. A secondary PV canopy shades the amenity areas on level 3. Additionally, building integrated photovoltaics (BIPVs) are integrated as a shading device on the office district facades and on the office drop-off canopies. As constructed, a total of X sm of photovoltaic panels provides X energy for the buildings.

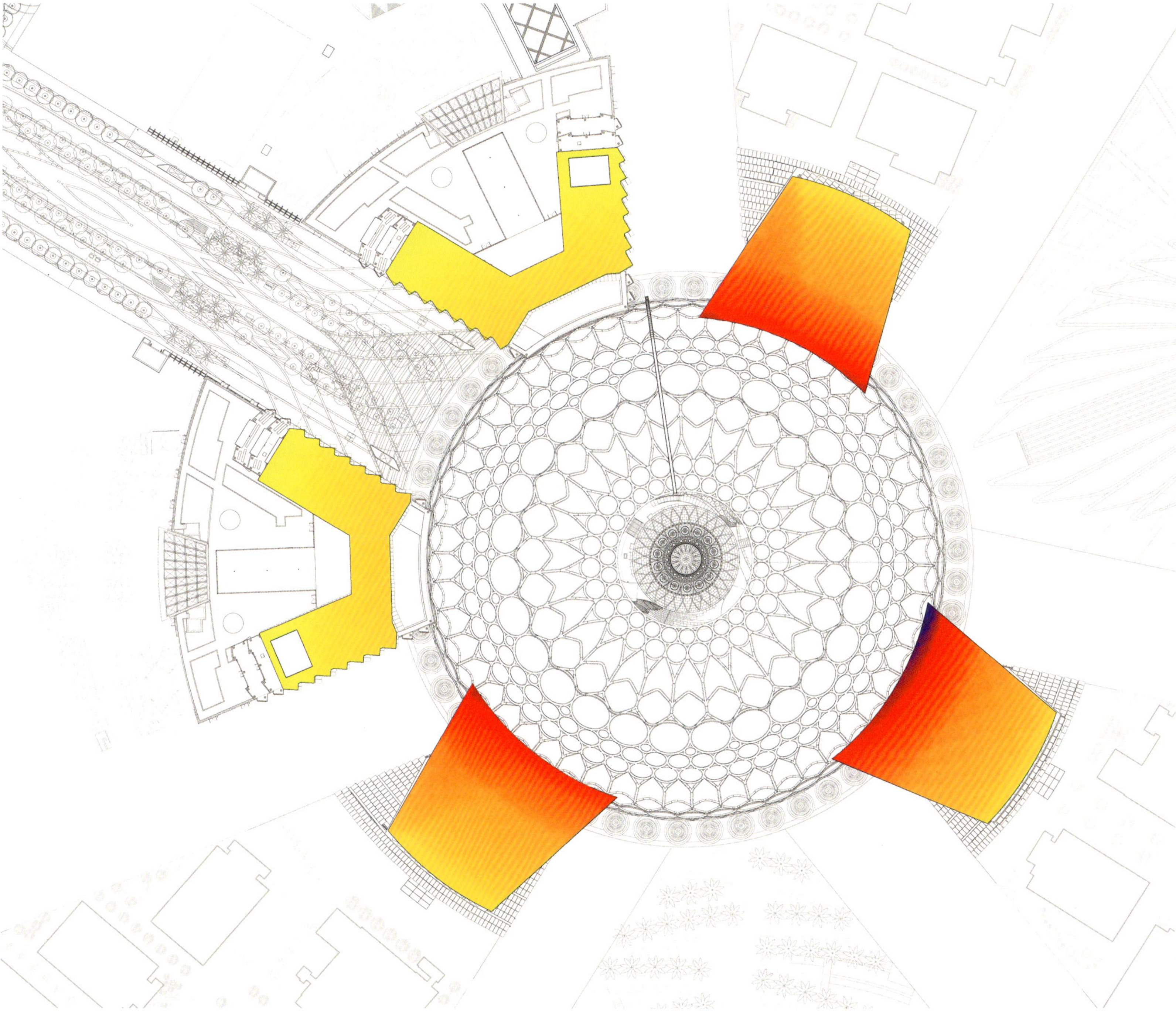

smartfoo

ood
PATRIZIA
PATRIZIA

HOTEL

World Expos have visitors flowing through the attractions during the day with operations and maintenance occurring at night in preparation for the next activities. As a result, hotels are not typically located within expo sites because of the inconvenience to guests, due to this nighttime activity, related access restrictions and security concerns.

However, for Expo 2020, Expo leadership identified the early inclusion of the Al Wasl hotels in the legacy master plan as an opportunity to support and complement tourism in accord with the Dubai Exhibition Center (DEC) programming. The two hotel structures frame the primary gateway to Al Wasl at the east terminus of the Arrivals Plaza, the major pedestrian boulevard connecting the Expo 2020 Metro and the central plaza. They are vital components in the ecosystem of Al Wasl, activating the inner ring as their lobbies and cafés extend into the plaza below the trellis.

Since the expo event precedes the legacy, the classification of the hotels was not determined until late into the design process. Dubai has a well-deserved reputation for luxury. However, it was determined by the Expo that the legacy hotels be developed as three-star business hotels, suitable for the surrounding development of Dubai South City. This target helped identify the amenities and overall requirements. In designing the hotels, the AS+GG team needed to resolve the dichotomy of an economical hotel in a high-profile location.

Sited at the center the Expo 2020, guests from around the world expect high quality. The hotel designs therefore focused on creating an experiential value, capitalizing on their intimate relationship to the trellis and its evening immersive events. Each hotel lobby creates a direct path from drop-off to Al Wasl Plaza and each room's balconies are oriented with views of the trellis. The rooftop pool deck also offers unparalleled views of the trellis crown.

Given these unique qualities, economical but with high expectations Expo leadership attracted well-known hotel operators with a reasonable entry cost and an offer of a unique location reinforced by exceptional architectural design that would enhance the value of their brands.

HOTEL DESIGN

At 13 stories, with approximately 300 rooms in each, the hotels are the tallest buildings in the district. Their height serves an important role in the enclosure of Al Wasl Plaza. AS+GG's vision to create an urban room with an active perimeter required constructing the full surrounding enclosure before opening day of the Expo. However, Expo 2020 had a set of spatial criteria to be housed in the hotel parcels for the event that would not necessarily translate into the legacy plan. The challenge was that the legacy hotel area was much larger and of a different configuration than the event spatial requirements. To justify this up-front capital expenditure, it was imperative to confirm the program requirements for the event and legacy to determine a streamlined transition strategy.

The extent and sequencing of the hotel construction had several factors. The initial investment, construction schedule, architectural design, and experiential contribution to the Al Wasl Plaza enclosure were considered. To separate the Expo and legacy program and costs, the client suggested a phased approach early in the design. In response, AS+GG proposed constructing the podium in time for the event with a temporary tower structure framing Al Wasl Plaza. After the completion of the event, a hotel operator would replace the temporary tower with a permanent hotel atop the podium. This idea reduced the initial capital expenditure but could not achieve a unified architectural expression, nor would it have met sustainability goals with an intent for minimal construction transition for the hotel occupancy. It was also technically challenging as the podium structure would need to account for future loads of an undefined building above.

Alternatively, the expo program could be constructed in line with Al Wasl Plaza, with the hotel constructed after the event. This option would allow the future hotel operator flexibility to develop in the open plot behind the expo building. However, this idea did not advance as it could not provide a vibrant enclosure adjacent to the trellis as intended. It would have also limited the level of activity at street level since hotel lobbies with restaurants can create vibrant atmospheres throughout the day. The client was committed to the overall vision for Al Wasl Plaza for both the Expo event and the longevity of the district.

After these explorations, Expo 2020 agreed that construction of the complete hotel enclosure in advance of opening day was the most viable option to achieve a unified architectural expression for Al Wasl, meet sustainability goals, and provide flexibility within the space for the event. This decision had a series of positive impacts on the legacy of the project. First, it allocated Expo funds to achieve the architectural intent for Al Wasl Plaza under the same leadership and control process. Second, it significantly reduced the time needed to convert the Expo use to the permanent legacy use, allowing the overall site to open for business shortly after the Expo closing.

Given the ambitious schedule to meet the fixed opening date, it was necessary to advance the design without a hotel operator. To proceed on the core and shell, without full interior fit-out and finishes, a prototype hotel program was developed by Meraas/North 25. This program was based on similar projects but made significant assumptions to provide a functional hotel building that would easily adapt to the needs of a yet to be appointed operator.

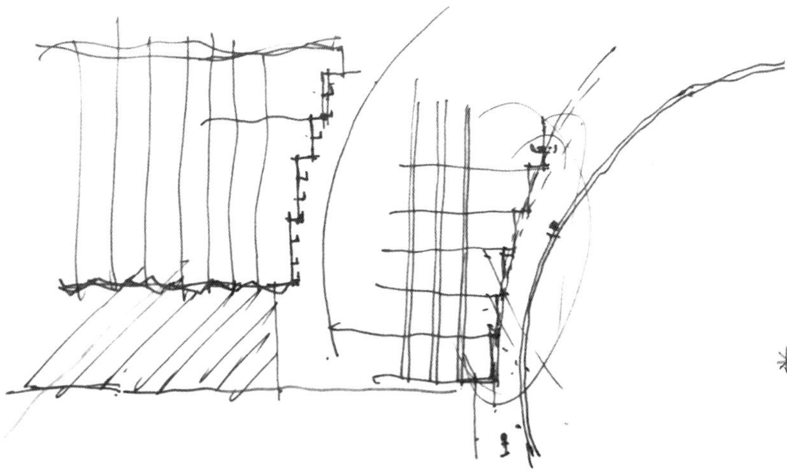

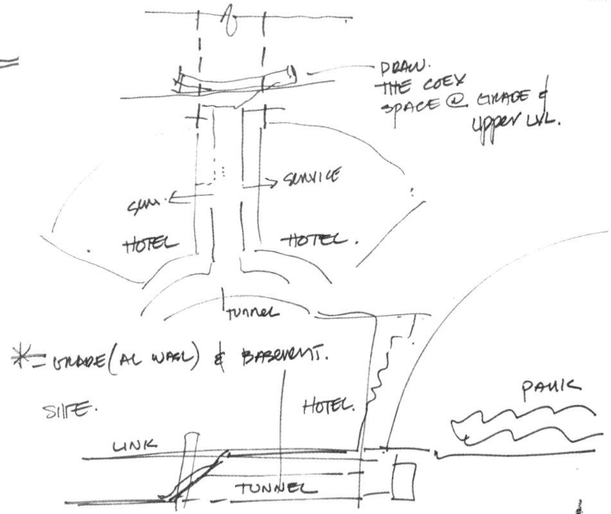
DRAW.
THE COEX
SPACE @ GRADE &
UPPER LVL.
SERVICE
HOTEL
HOTEL.
TUNNEL
*= GRADE (AL WALL) & BASEMENT.
SITE.
HOTEL.
PARK
LINK
TUNNEL

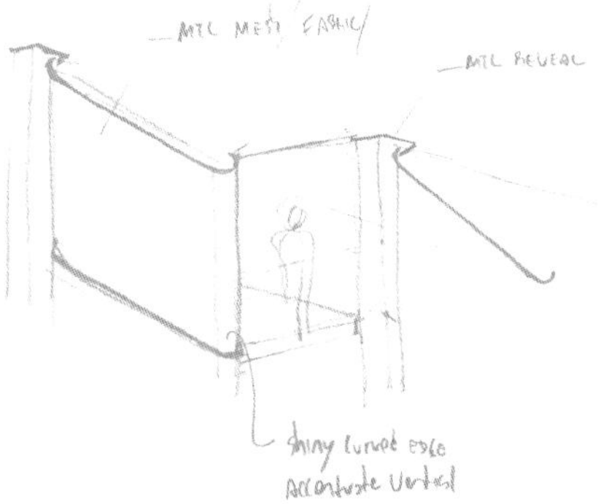
MTL MESH FABRIC
MTL REVEAL
shiny curved edge
Accentuate Vertical

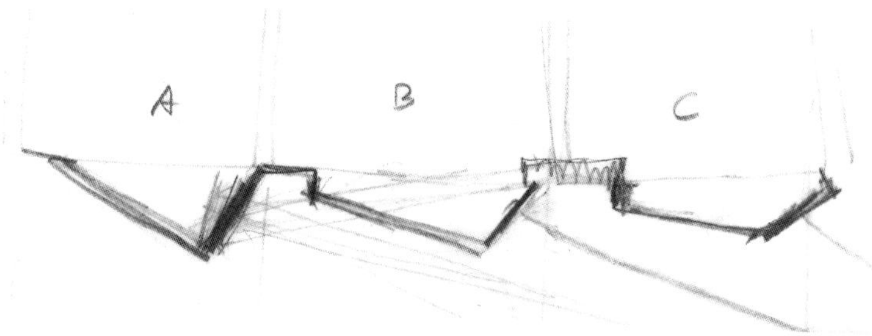
A
B
C

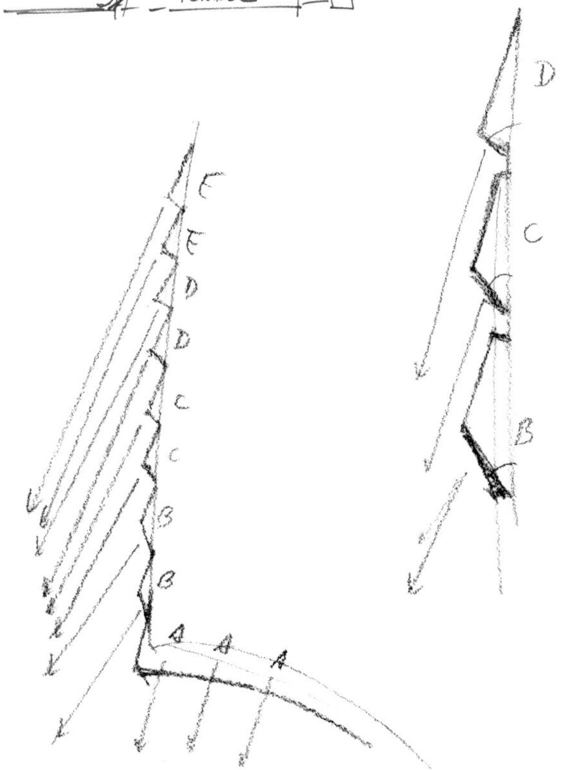
E
E
D
D
C
C
B
B
A
A
A
D
C
B

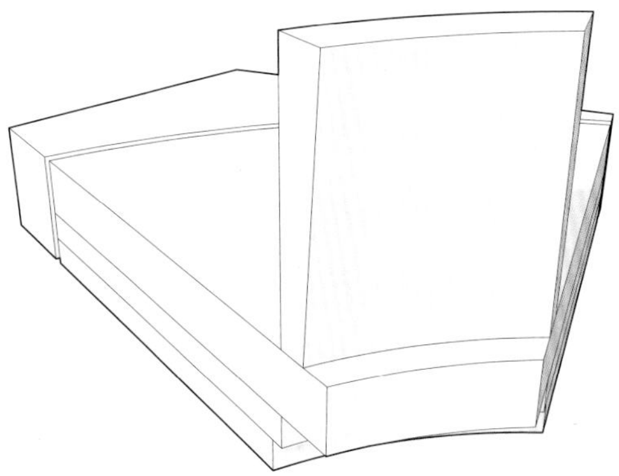

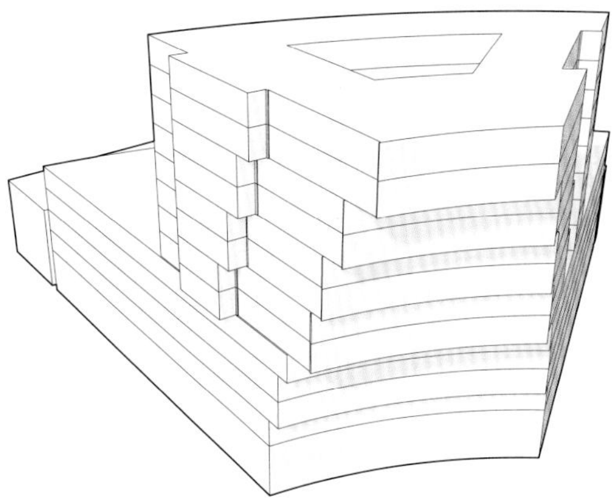

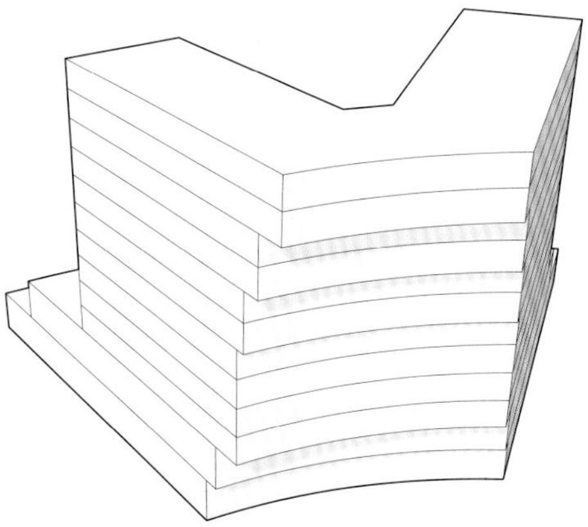

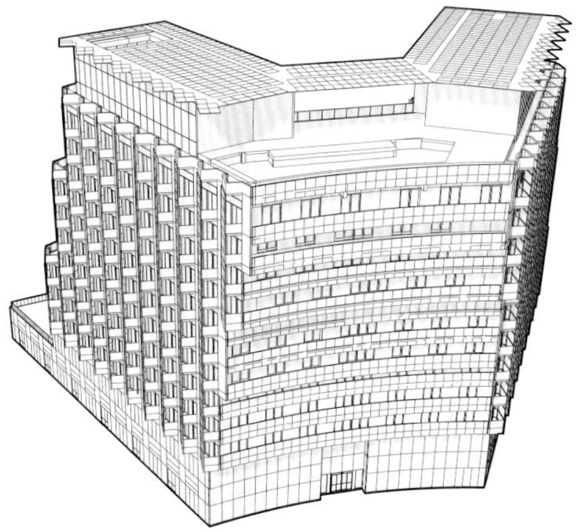

HOTEL MASSING STUDIES

Facing Al Wasl Plaza, the hotels fan outward in a wide-V arrangement with a double loaded corridor of hotel rooms. The outward expansion of the massing optimizes the number of hotel rooms with views towards Al Wasl Plaza and opposite, the district. Several massing arrangements were considered including a courtyard configuration, but the chosen arrangement provides the district-facing rooms optimal daylight. In parallel with the office building design, the inner wall facing Al Wasl was tested as a double-curved facade to closely follow the form of the trellis. While clearly responding to the dome-like shape of the trellis, the height of the buildings coupled with the complex form was not economically feasible. The final design offsets the curvature of the trellis into a stepped single-curved facade with balconies. Each of the five stepped volumes contains two or three levels, the sectional profile closely following the trellis. Opposite the trellis, the massing steps down to the scale of the thematic districts. The podium and tower rooftops are occupiable providing guests unforgettable experiences and views.

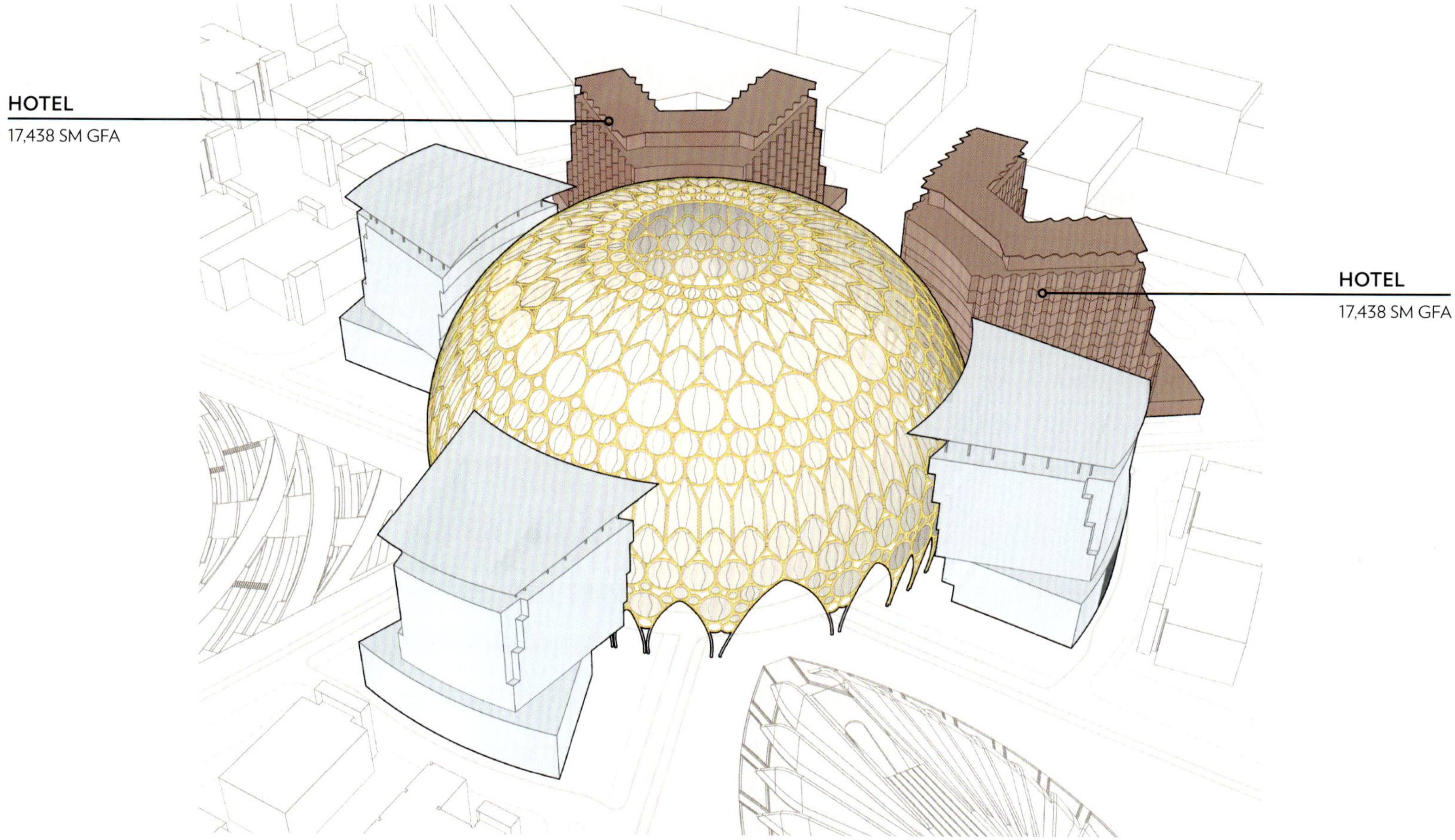

HOTEL EXPO TO LEGACY TRANSITION

Hotel management typically oversees the design to achieve brand standards, but this was not the case for Al Wasl. The hotel buildings were critical to activating Al Wasl Plaza and the District 2020 legacy development. Therefore, the architecture needed to compliment the Al Wasl experience and support the needs of the potential operator while controlling cost and minimizing post-event construction. To achieve this, the room layouts and back of house distribution were designed to allow hotel operations to run efficiently regardless of final hotel classification. Exceptional experiences were provided with hotel room balconies, a roof terrace and pool, and ground level public areas. Expo leadership was successful in engaging Emaar Hospitality group, as the operator for the south hotel. Construction of the north building was well underway when the Dubai Engineering Office was retained to design the fit-out so that it could be occupied during Expo 2020 by UAE Government and Royalty. Dubbed the Leadership Pavilion, it was re-programed and fit-out to suit the needs of this group and is discussed in more detail in the following chapter.

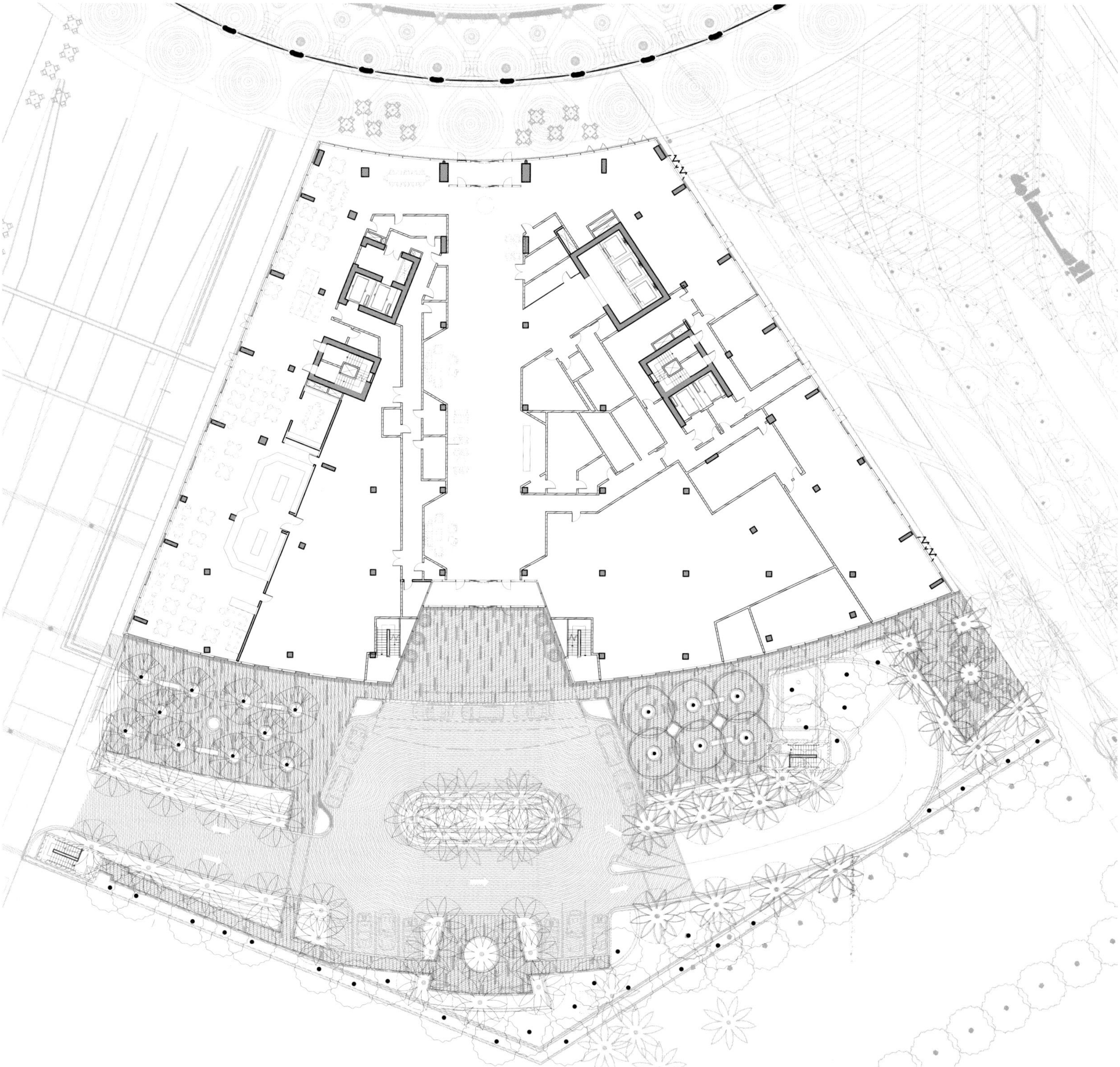

HOTEL GROUND LEVEL

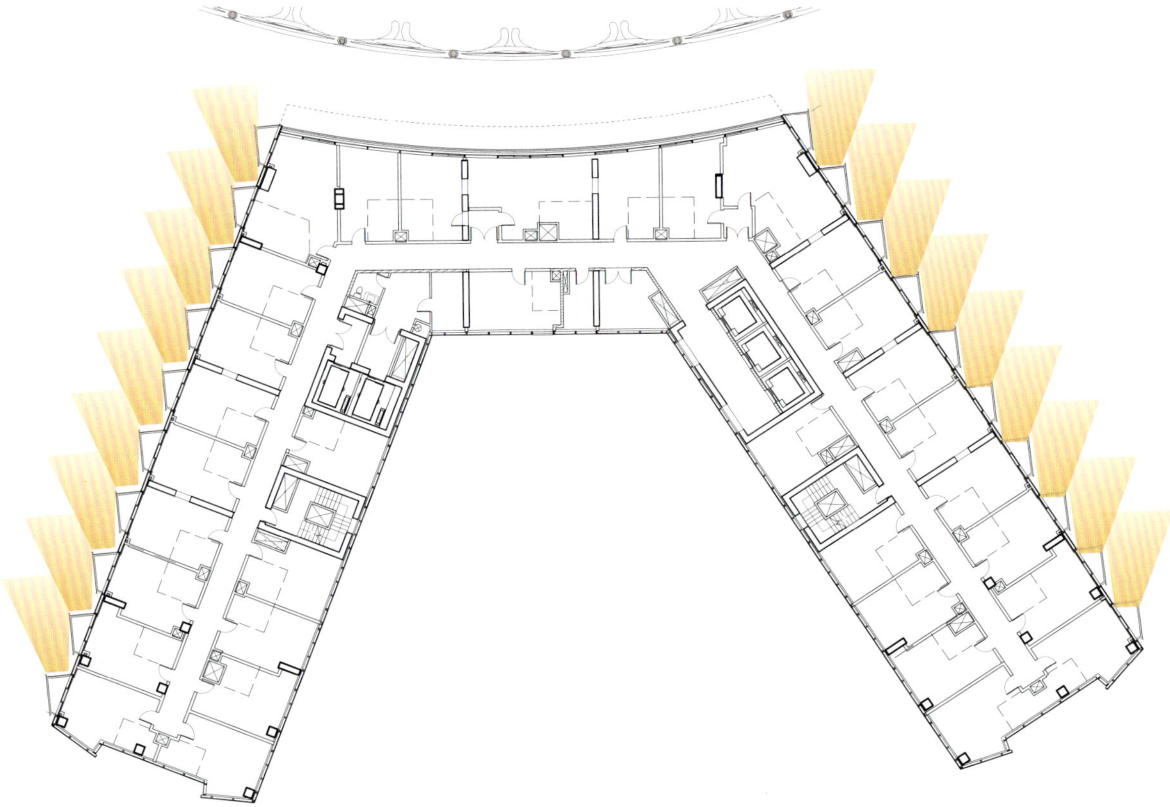

HOTEL ROOM BALCONIES

The hotel layout allows guests to directly engage with Al Wasl Plaza, creating a unique guest experience. Rooms along the inner plaza have direct views of the plaza with balconies extending the rooms into the space between the trellis. Along the sides at the concourse roads, angled balconies extend outward to capture direct views of Al Wasl Plaza. Expanded aluminum panels on the balconies minimize direct solar radiation, provide a privacy screen for the occupant, and give an overall vertical aesthetic to the facade. Occupant comfort was carefully considered in the hotel design. Sliding glass balcony doors provide guests with the option of natural ventilation. Guests have the choice to view the projection shows or close a curtain to block out any undesired light when privacy is preferred. Simultaneously, it was important that light from the hotel rooms does not spill out of the buildings negatively impacting the projection experience. Achieving a balance of views toward the trellis, occupant privacy, and reduction of competing light from the buildings was achieved through controlled shades on the building interior.

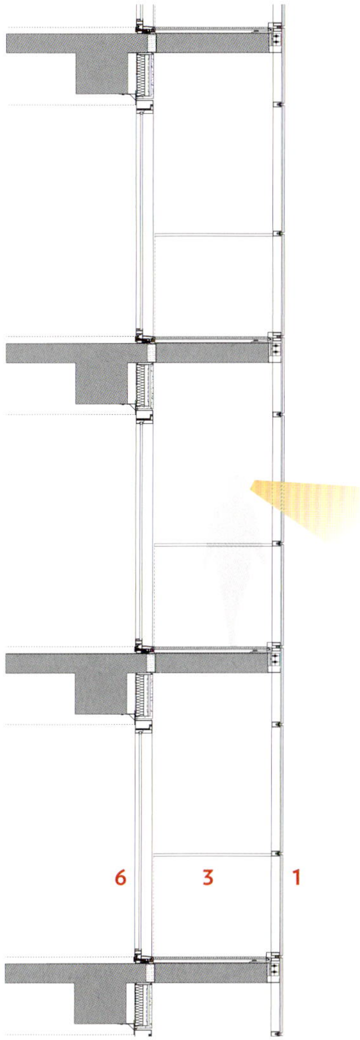

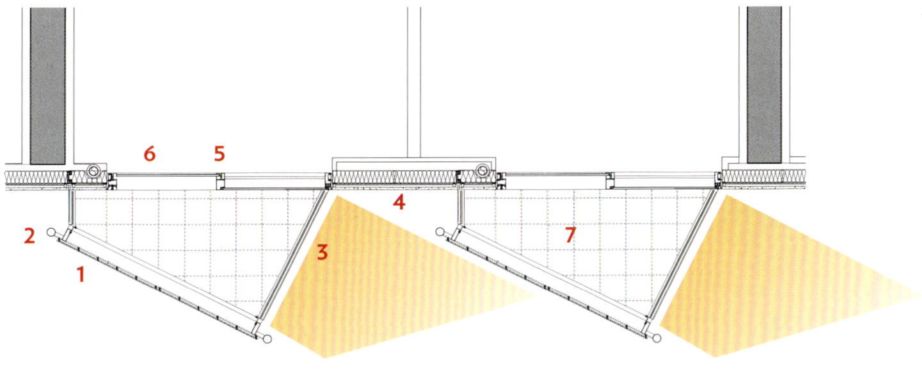

1 EXPANDED METAL MESH PANEL
2 ALUMINUM EXTRUSION
3 SAFETY GLASS
4 WALL PANEL
5 MULLION W/ PVDF COATING
6 CLEAR VISION GLASS
7 BALCONY FLOOR FINISH

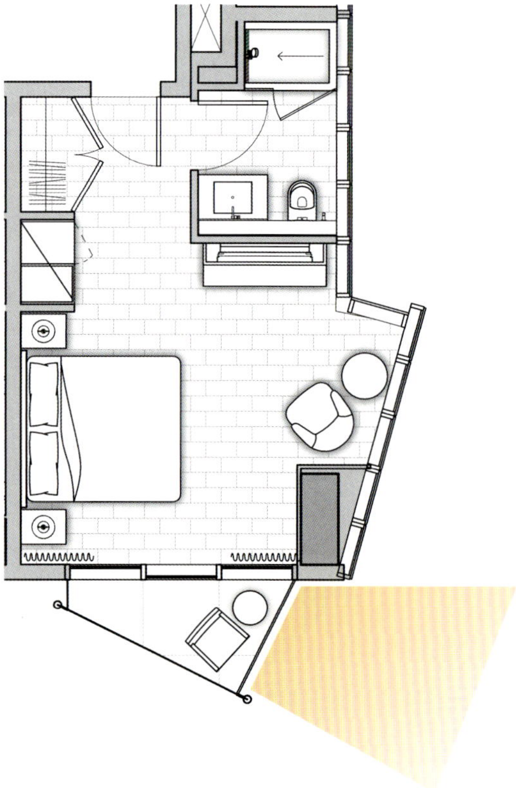

STANDARD ROOM, 27 SM

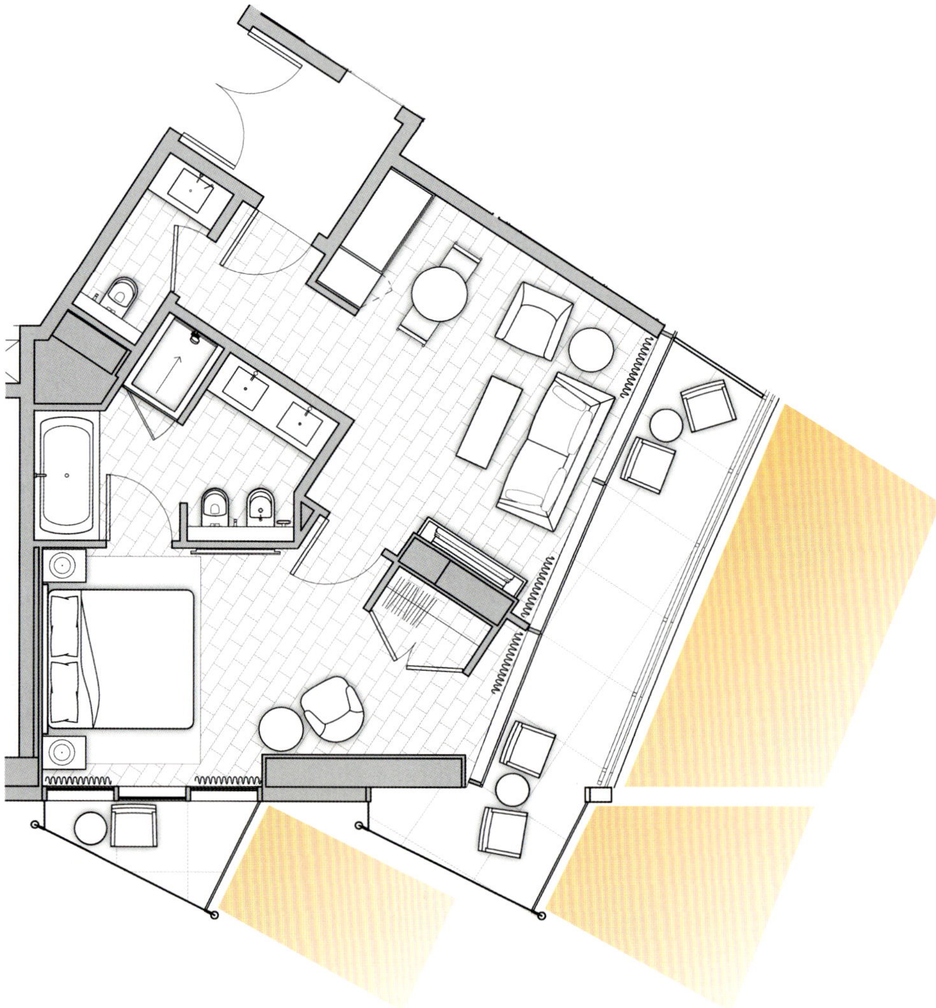

EXECUTIVE SUITE, 54 SM

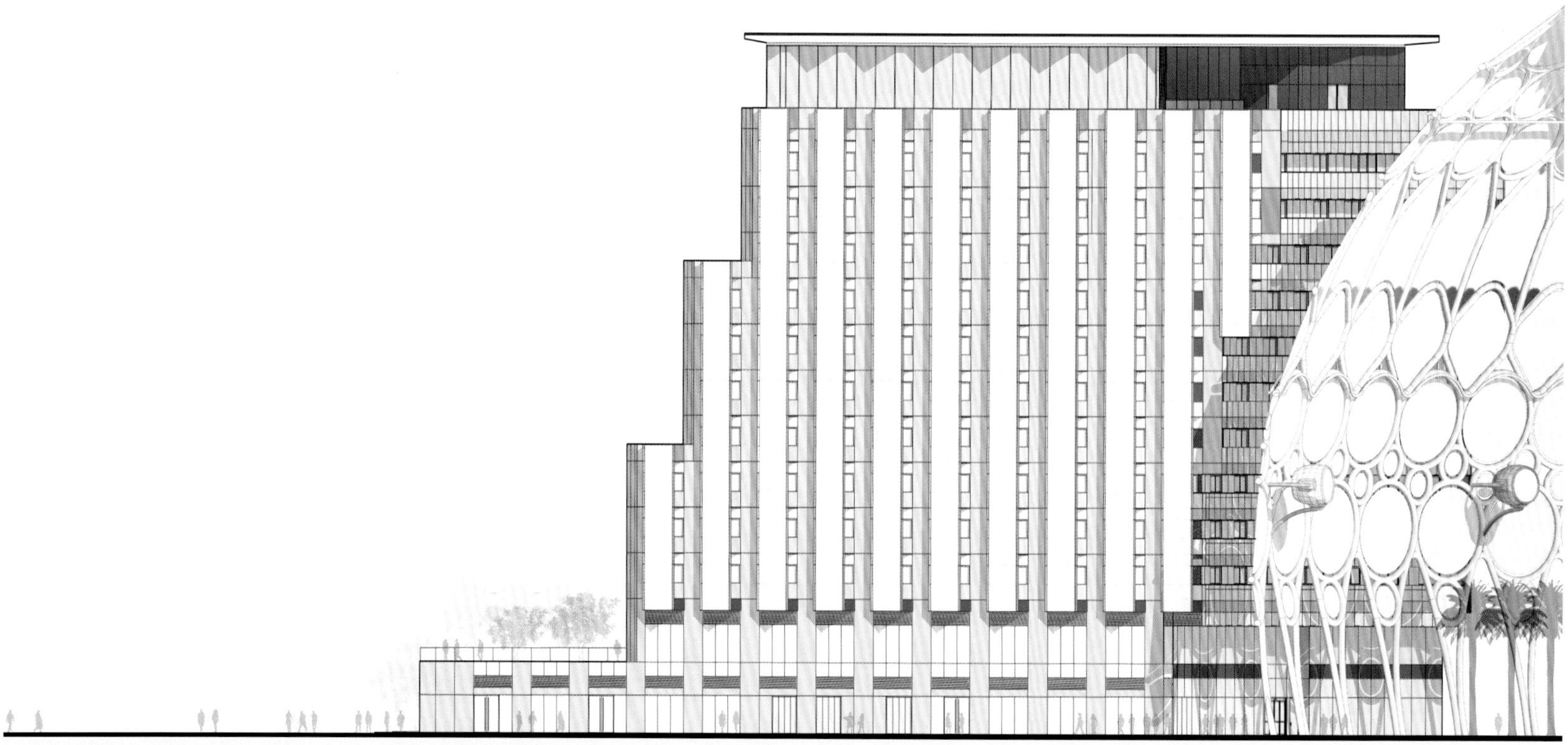

HOTEL ELEVATION

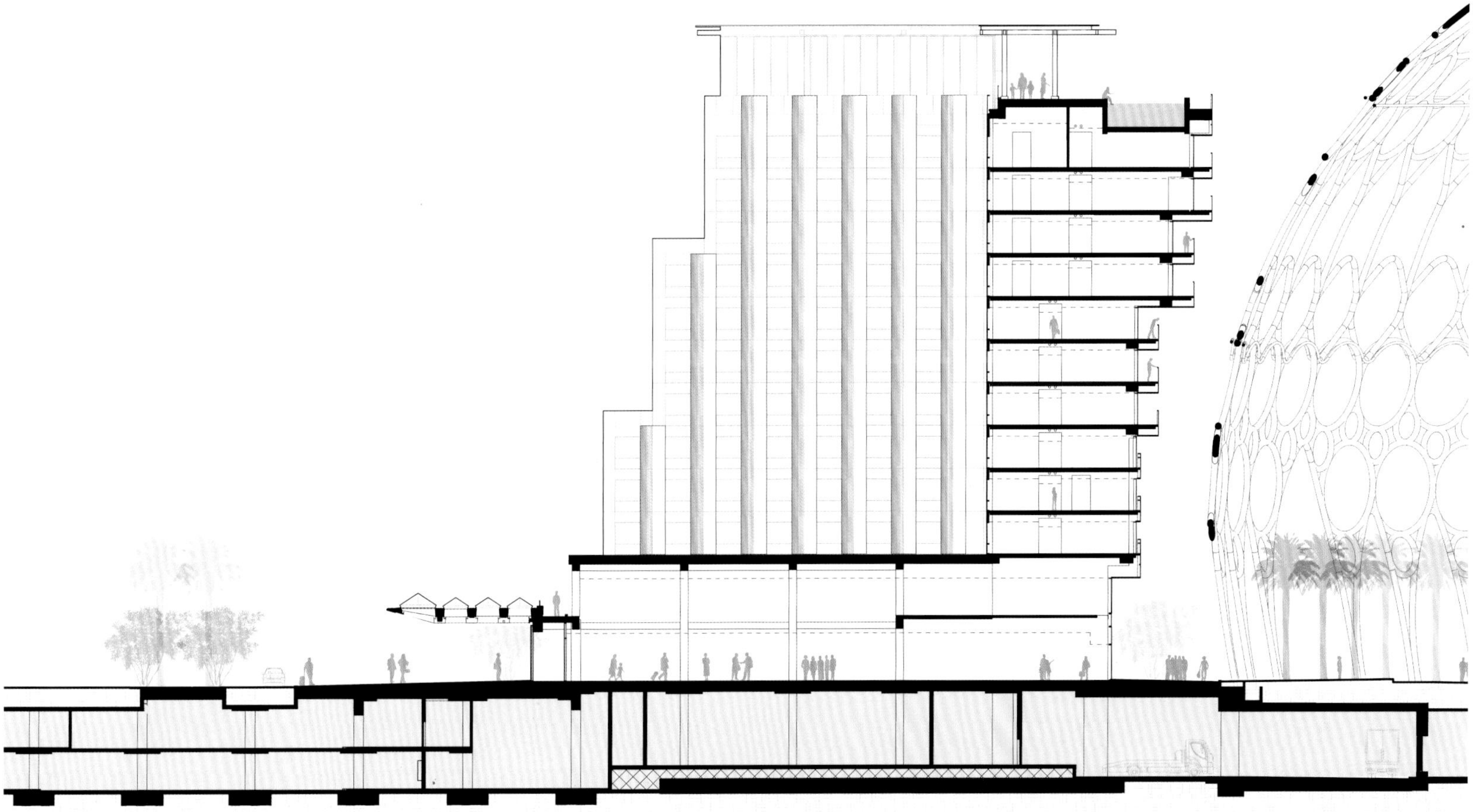

HOTEL SECTION

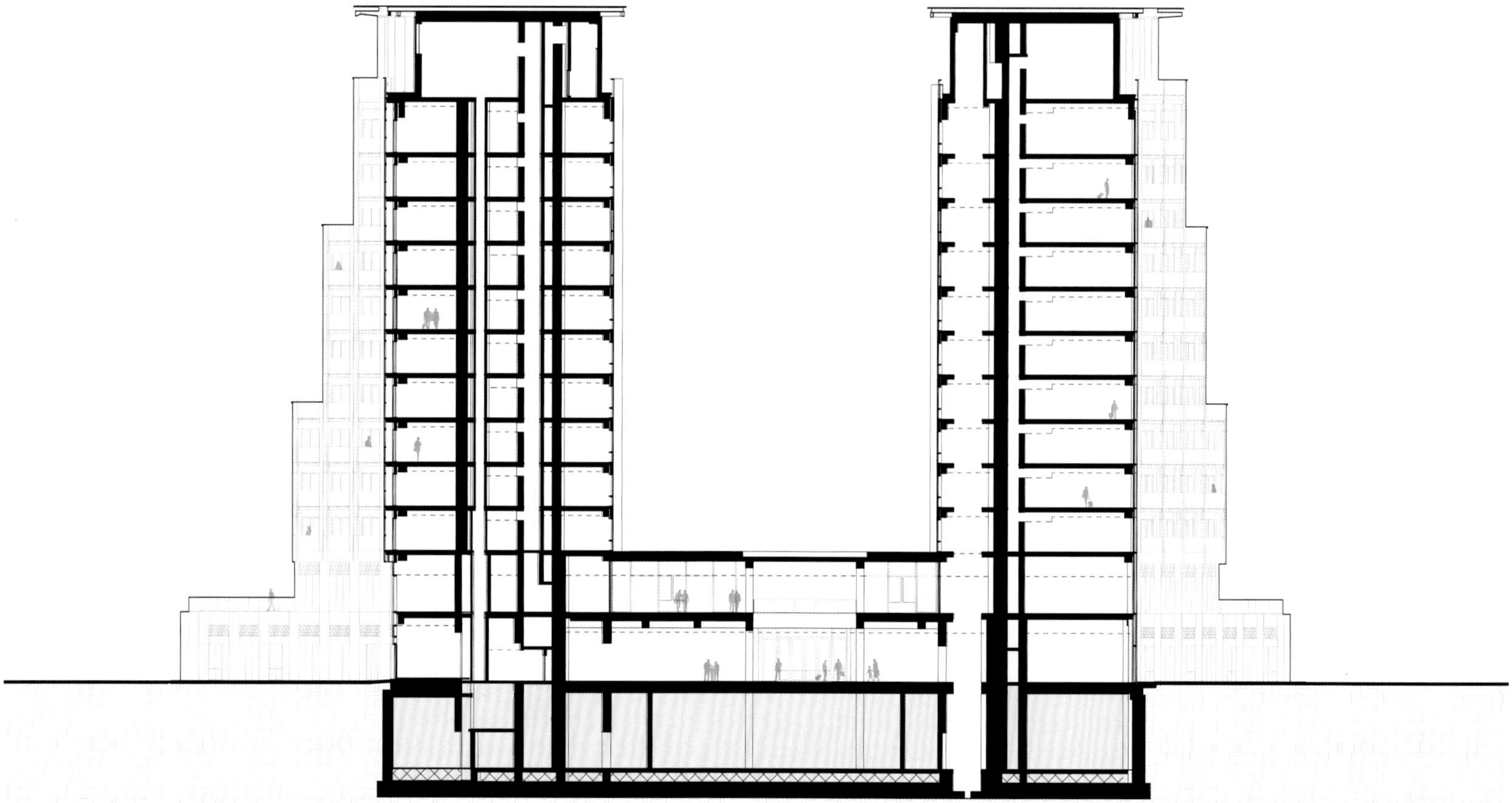

HOTEL ELEVATION

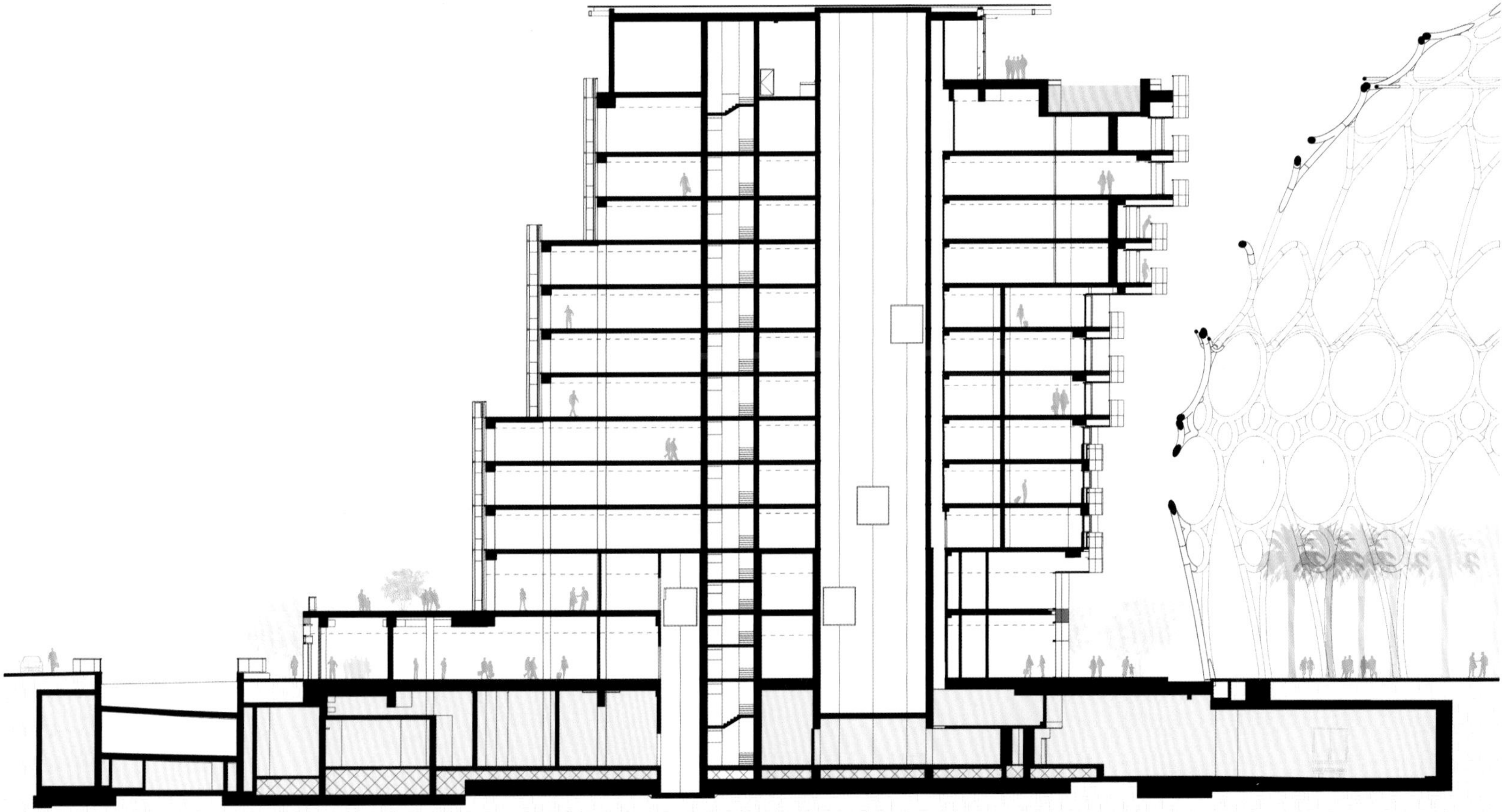

HOTEL SECTION

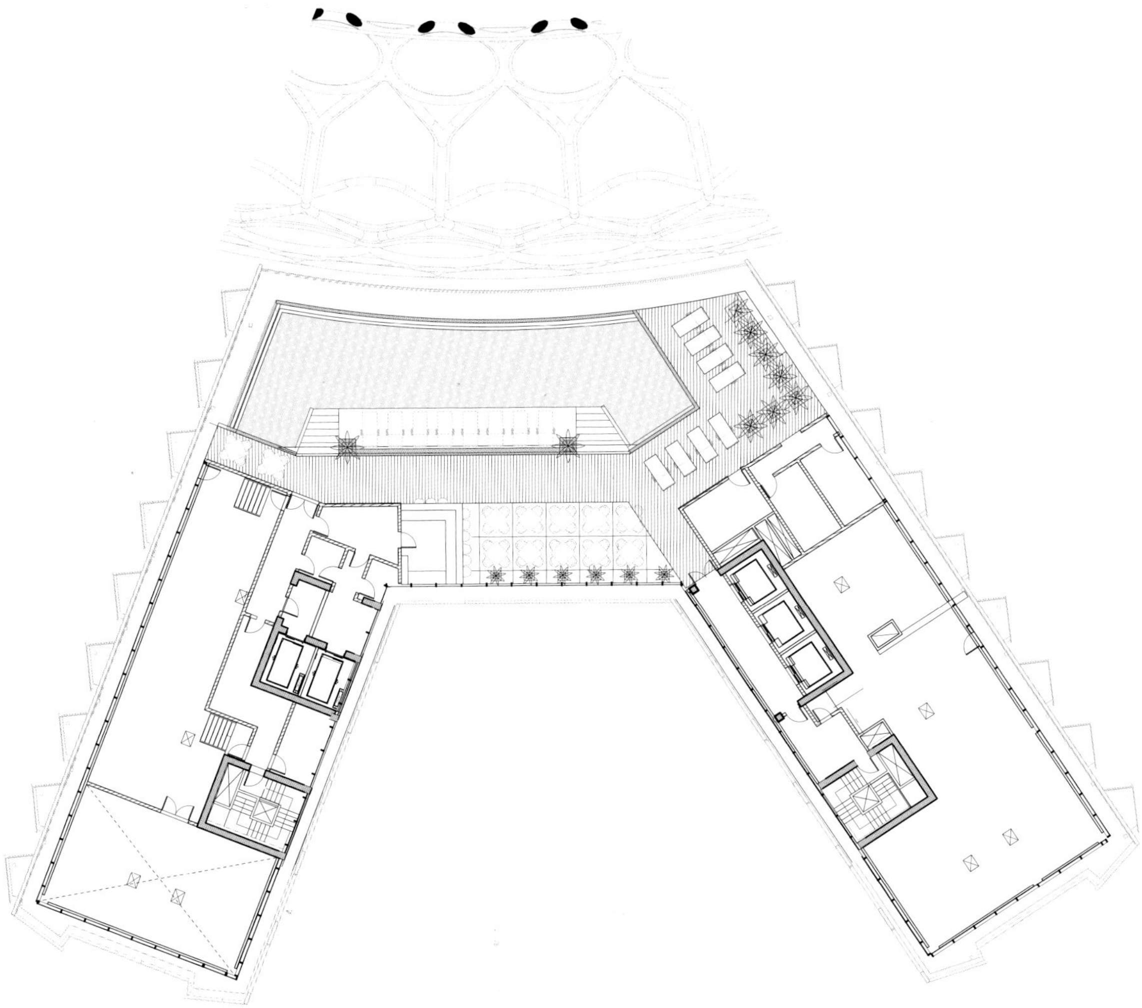

HOTEL ROOFTOP

With the highest occupiable rooftops in the district, the hotels have a premium vantage point of Al Wasl Plaza and the surrounding district. The trellis rises over the edge of the roof creating the irreplaceable experience of perching atop the grand dome. With outstanding views, the serviced outdoor lounge areas are premium amenities within the district. An infinity pool cascades over the edge toward the trellis, reflecting the bold geometry during the day and the dynamic movement of projection at night. Imagine a projection of the moon or earth sweeping over the trellis, transporting the viewer into space. Each vantage point on Al Wasl is unique. The view from this rooftop to the center of the plaza is distant, but the vibrant garden and activity below remain visible through the fabric. This experience is particularly unique as the viewers can participate in the immersive experience from the highest point looking down. A canopy of photovoltaic panels shades a portion of the roof deck and provides renewable solar energy to the buildings.

مركز الزوار 9
Visitor Centre 9

ROVE
مركز الزوار 8

LEADERSHIP PAVILION

The Leadership Pavilion is a "Majlis of the Union," a place for the leaders of the UAE and Expo 2020 to convene for meetings and events. In this context, a majlis is an intimate gathering focused on conversation. It is hosted by senior leaders on specific topics in this space, a platform for diverse dialogue on national and international cultural relations, innovation, and more. These leadership functions occupy the north hotel building and a one-story addition during the six-month expo event.

The approach for the architectural expression was to celebrate the culture and vibrancy of the young nation with simple bold forms to accommodate the distinguished meeting spaces. The complex is organized around three majlis volumes. Each of these spaces required a solid form for privacy thus the design strategy was focused on creating clerestory windows and skylight to bring daylight into the interior.

The three masses are expressed individually, creating a hierarchy of volumes. The main exterior wall system is clad with bright energetic sculptural diamond GRFC panels. A curvilinear fritted glass wall connects the hotel building with the Leadership Pavilion, allowing diffused light into the interior while maintaining privacy. The support and circulation spaces, which connect the main halls, and are clad with neutral white panels and glass to recede their appearance.

LEADERSHIP PAVILION DESIGN

The Leadership Pavilion project was introduced to AS+GG in December 2017 after the legacy hotel design was substantially complete and construction was starting on the foundation. At the request of the client, the hotel did not include ballrooms or meeting spaces to reduce investment costs for future hotel operators. Therefore, when the requirement for an Expo 2020 leadership meeting space was introduced, an addition was added behind the north hotel building. The project scope required the design team to work within the constraints of the existing building design and construction schedule with completely new spatial requirements. Structural modifications were minimized to maintain the fast-track schedule to achieve opening day and to minimize the legacy conversion by a hotel operator.

The goal for the complex was to provide the emirate leaders with inspirational architecture to welcome and entertain world leaders. The design aesthetic is a contemporary expression of local UAE culture, a celebration of the past and the future of the emirates. A high level of security and an intimate arrival experience are required for public figures. In response, the building has a framed arrival court for entry to the main hotel building on one side and the leadership pavilion. By design, privacy from the concourse street was achieved by placing a gallery connection from the main building to the pavilion along the public realm. As a result, the addition blocked the original vehicular drop-off access and parking ramp, so a new path was provided from the north creating an arrival into the framed drop-off courtyard.

The three large meeting spaces, the Royal Majlis, the Royal Dining, and VIP Dining are expressed as rectangular volumes with bold, yet solid exterior walls for privacy. Barrel vault roofs with clerestory windows over each of the three volumes diffuse natural light into the meeting spaces below. Neutral white glass reveals between the volumes provide daylight into circulation spaces and delineate the larger volumes. The interior design was directly commissioned to KCA International by the client. AS+GG coordinated and integrated KCA's interior design into the architectural enclosure.

Hundreds of temporary pavilions are designed and erected by participating countries for World Expos, Dubai Expo 2020 included. Therefore, the idea of a temporary VIP meeting pavilion is commonplace for the nature of the event. In the original design brief provided to AS+GG, the Leadership Pavilion was designated as temporary. The design, material selection, logistics, and delivery were optimized for the fast-track schedule to complete the project by expo opening day. From the onset of the project, there were clear sustainable and economic reasons to extend the life of this pavilion beyond Expo 2020 and adjustments were accommodated in the design to make the legacy use feasible.

Stakeholders including the hotel operator will determine whether the Leadership Pavilion will be maintained as an asset for the legacy hotel. The history of the pavilion having hosted world leaders for important idea exchange and decision-making during Expo 2020 is a significant draw. The pavilion can also be adapted for permanent use if desired through adjustments to the mechanical systems.

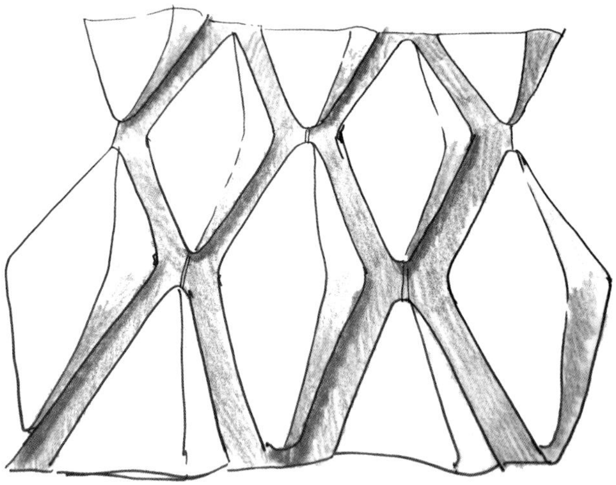

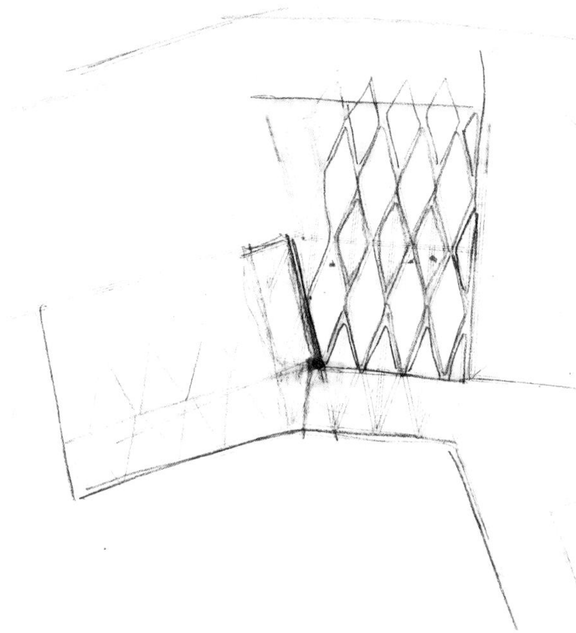

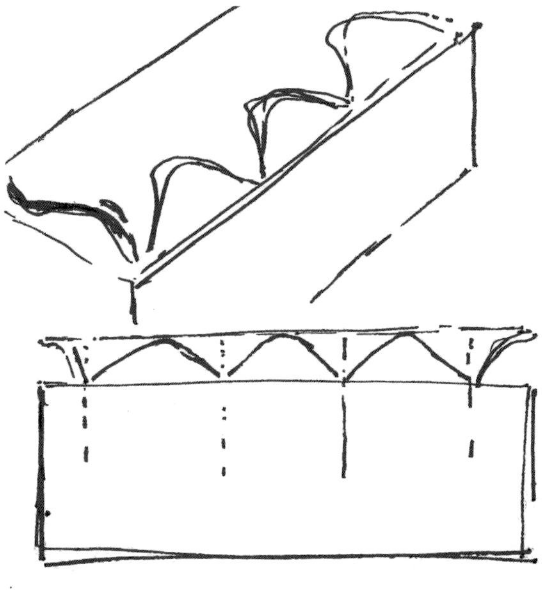

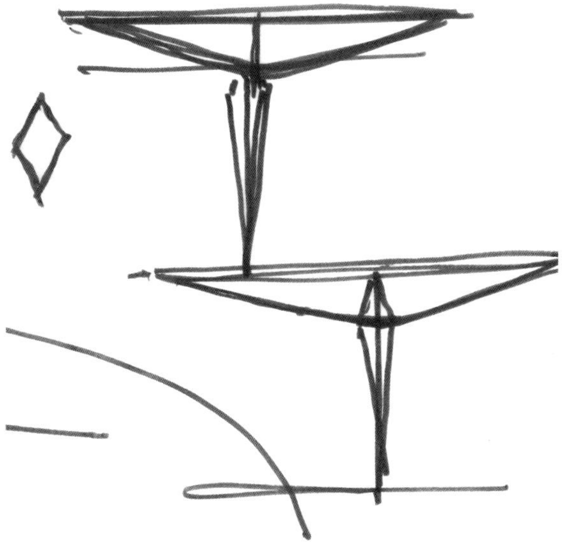

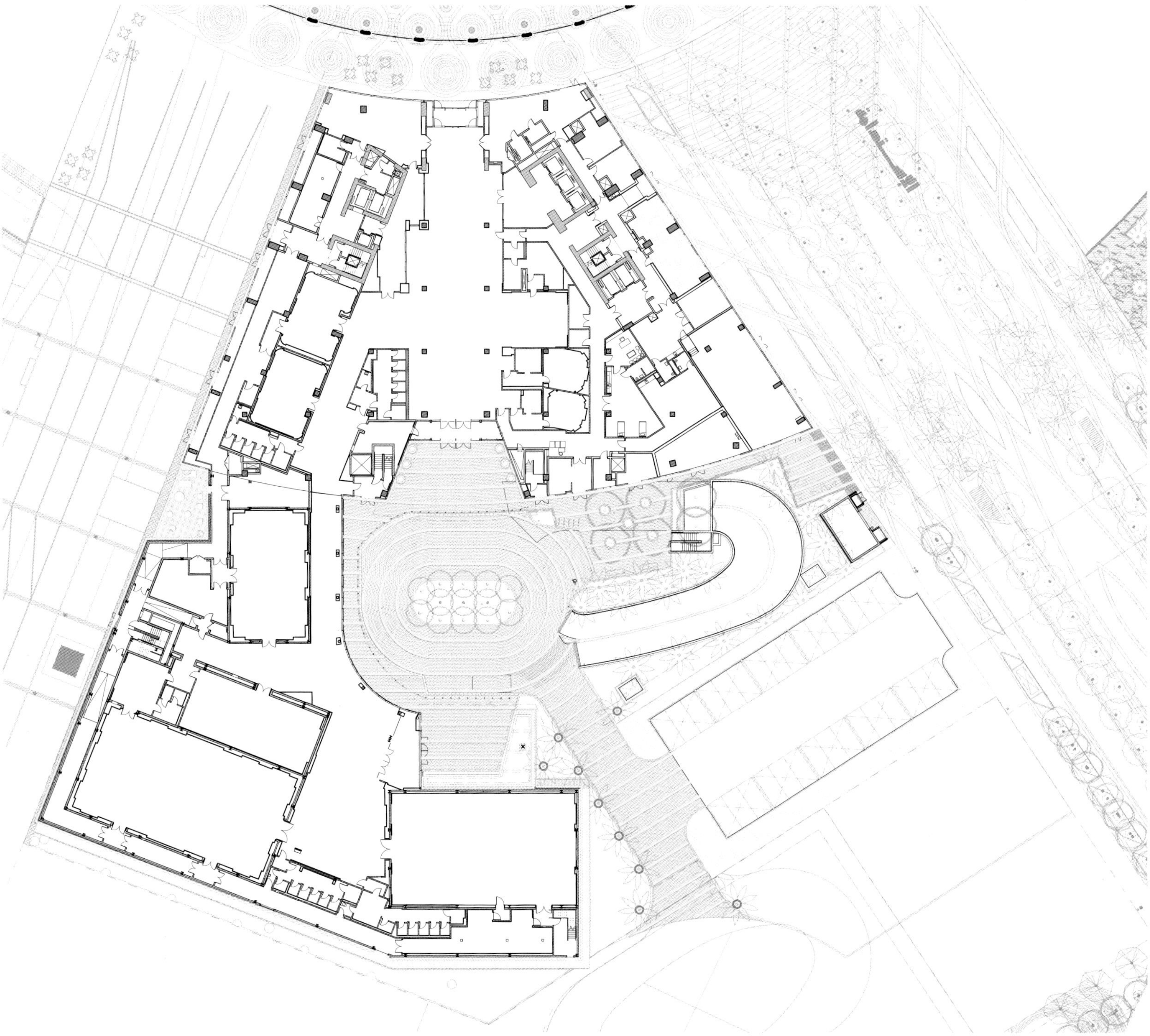

LEADERSHIP PAVILION GROUND LEVEL

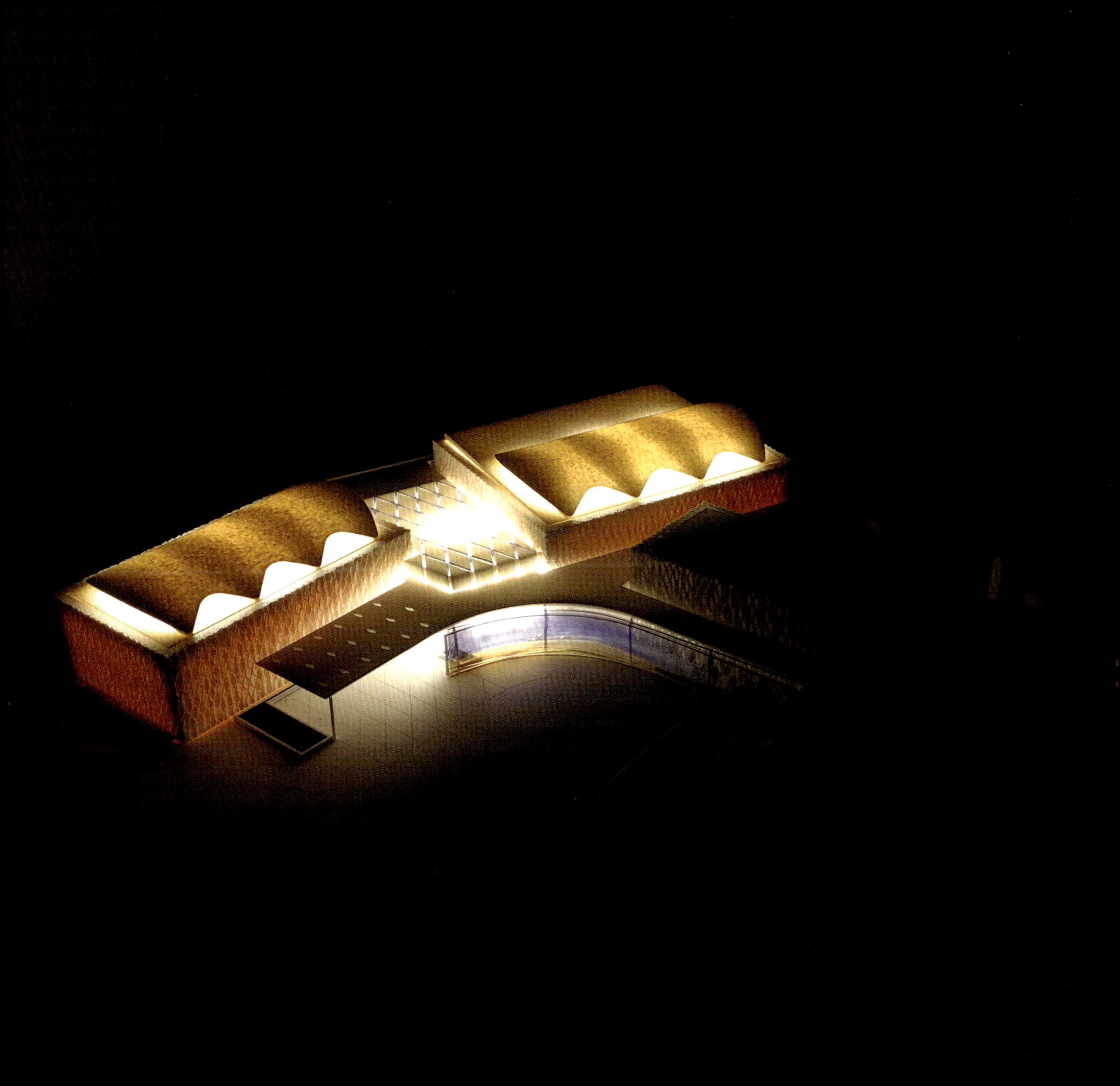

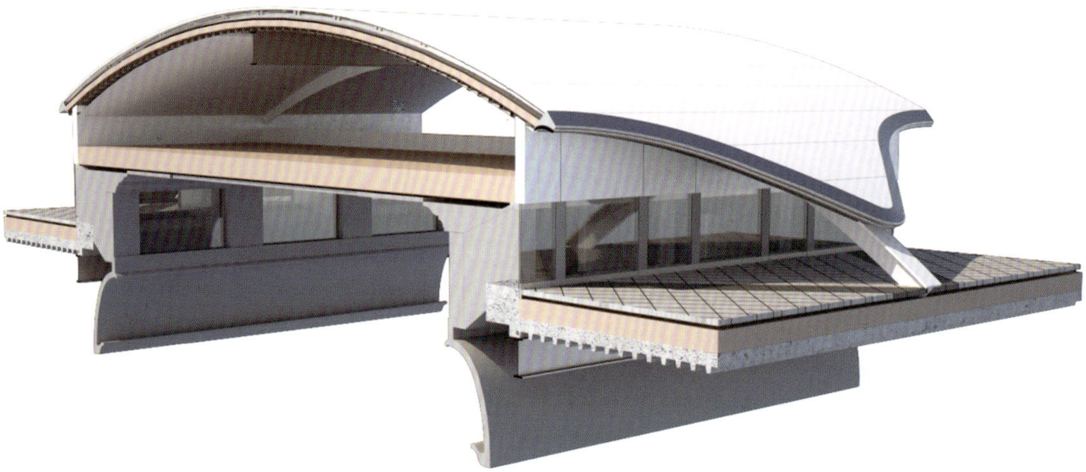

LEADERSHIP PAVILION VIGNETTE

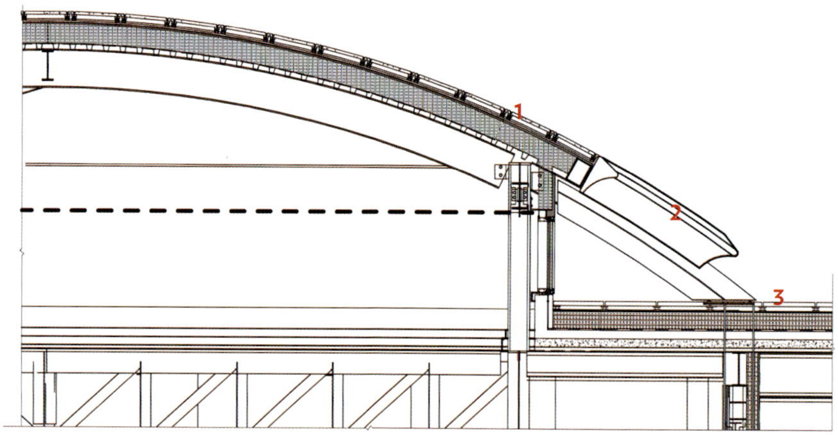

1 GFRC ROOF PANELS
2 FORMED METAL TRIM
3 ROOF PAVER

LEADERSHIP PAVILION ENLARGED SECTION

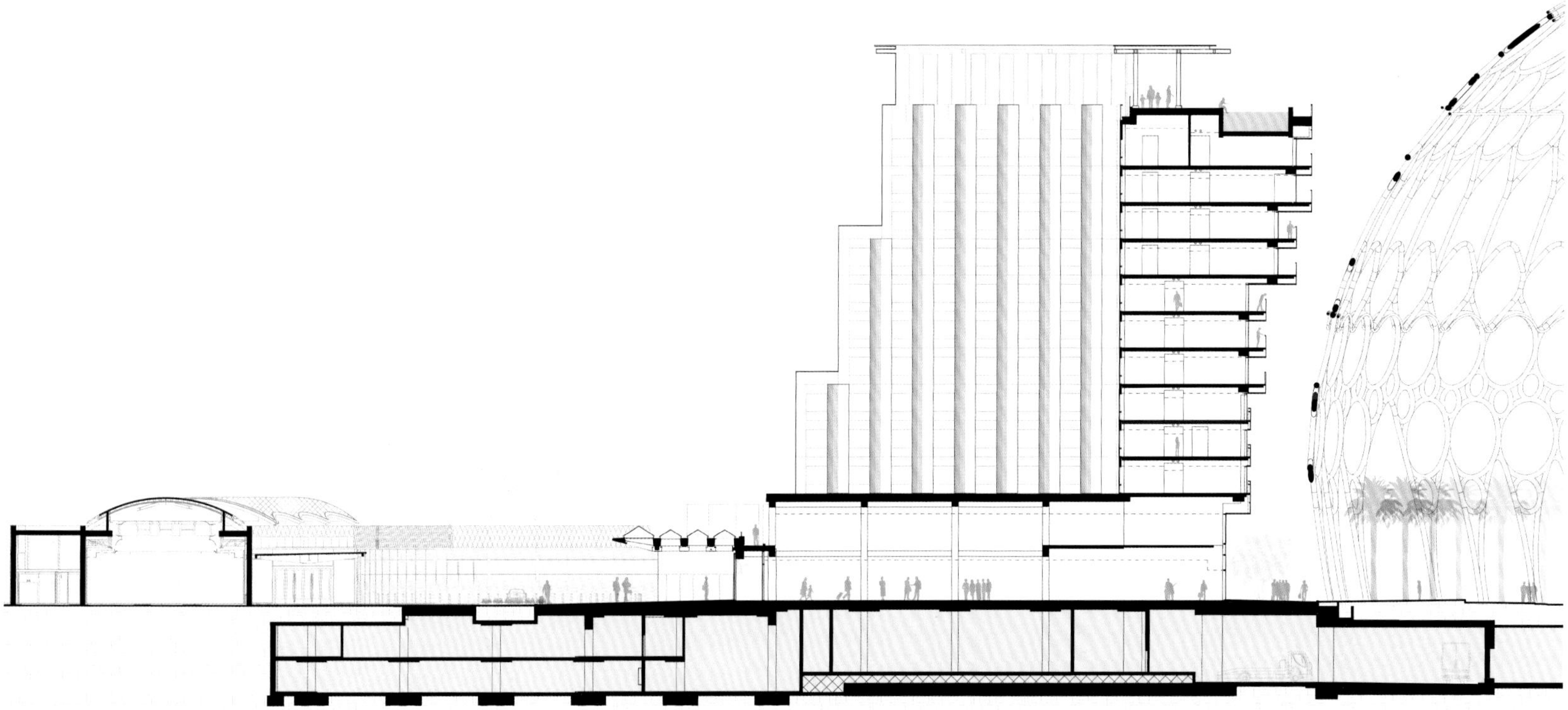

LEADERSHIP PAVILION SECTION

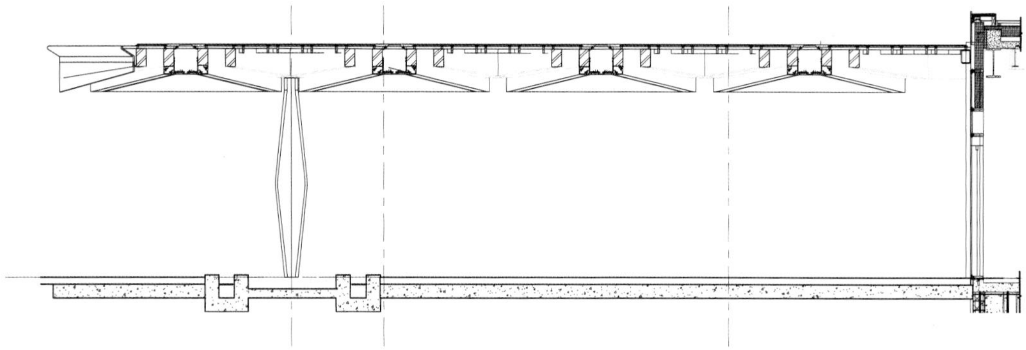

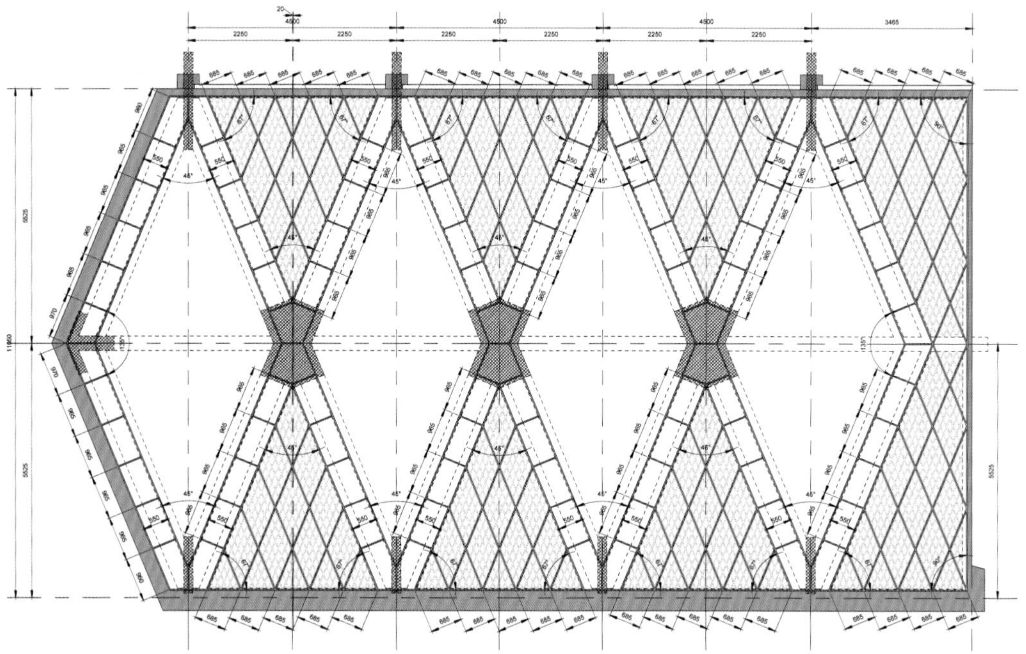

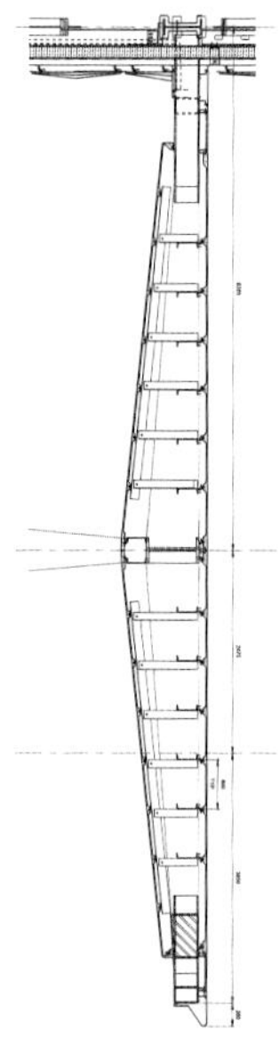

LEADERSHIP PAVILION ENTRANCE

The entrance to the Leadership Pavilion was designed as a peaceful respite within Expo 2020 to welcome UAE leadership and their guests from around the world. A delicate canopy marks the entry in contrast to the scale and solidity of the building, providing shade and diffused light to the arrival. The canopy is made up of a series of four three-dimensional diamond sculpted GFRC panels. The triangular space between the solid diamonds is infilled with fritted triangular glass panels. The structure touches down with a sculptural clad steel column only within a reflection pool. Sunlight filtering through the canopy and bouncing off the faceted glazed exterior wall creates a play of highlight and reflection in the water to achieve a restful atmosphere. Although visually lightweight, this steel canopy is not without support. It ties into the steel structure of the building at the four diamond points.

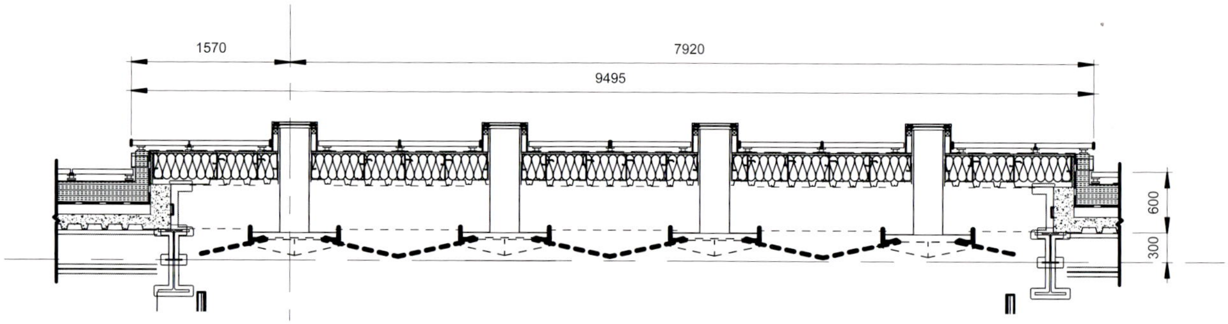

LEADERSHIP PAVILION LOBBY

Expo 2020 is a once in a lifetime celebration and the first expo hosted in the Middle East. During the lively six-month event, UAE leadership and their guests convene at the Leadership Pavilion in the Royal Majlis and dining rooms for conversation and fellowship. To meet the standard of this grand occasion, the central entrance lobby pre-function space, from which guests enter the Royal Majlis and Royal Dining halls, required an elevated design. The lobby features a unique skylight designed to allow indirect, dappled sunlight into the space, creating a dynamic energy on the interior. It is a rectangular structure infilled with sculptural diamond GFRC panels. Insulated laminated translucent glass strips between the solid forms creates an engineered pattern of light that changes the experience of the lobby based on the solar condition. The space transforms throughout the day as the sun moves through the sky.

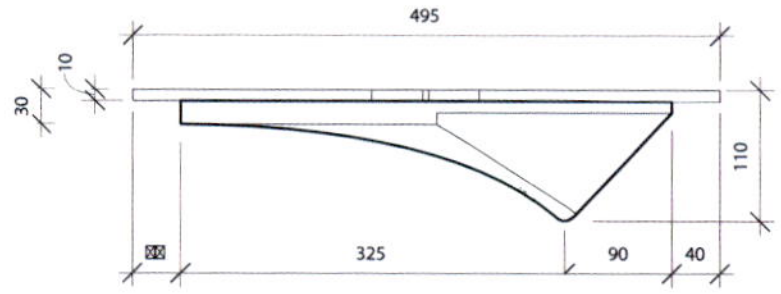

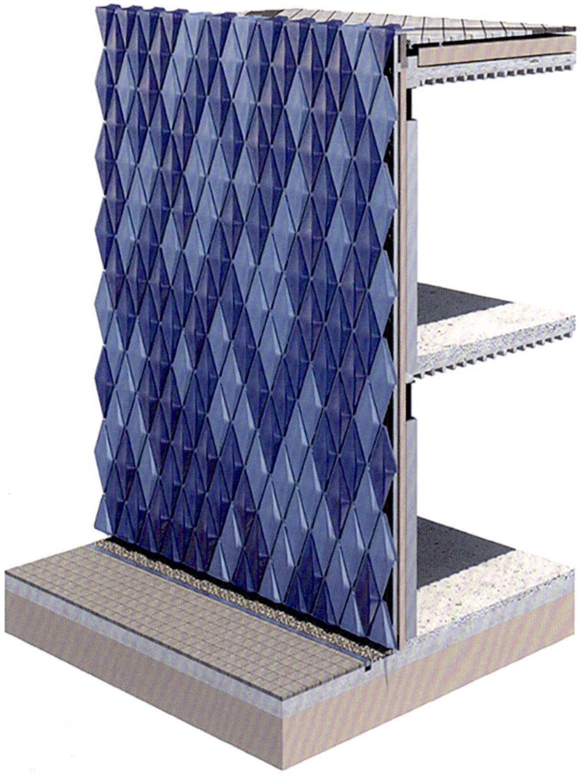

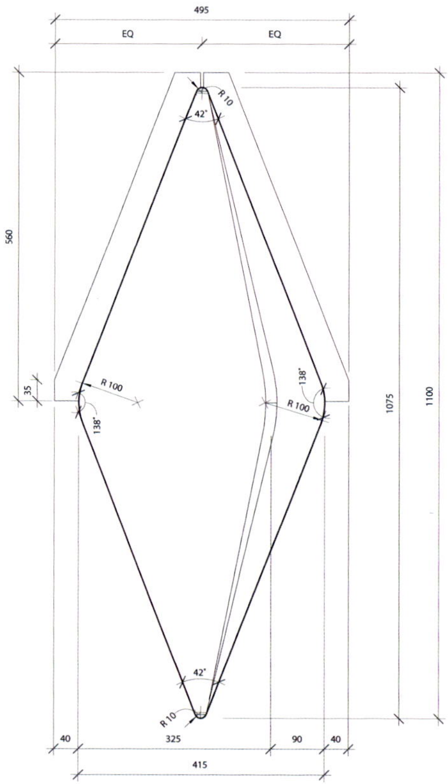

LEADERSHIP PAVILION EXTERIOR WALL

The three leadership meeting volumes are clad with a bold blue sculptural exterior wall. The three blue tones are a nod to local UAE culture and the Godolphin blue silks carried on some of the most famous thoroughbred racehorses in worldwide racing history. A three-dimensional diamond form, specifically rhomboidal panels, were designed to reflect sunlight at the varying angles. The glossy finish and soft folds in the exterior wall produce changing tones of color throughout the day. Each diamond-shaped panel is approximately 400mm wide by 1000 mm tall with a double-curvature form. The panels were originally envisioned in terracotta, however availability by local suppliers shifted the system to a glass fiber reinforced concrete (GFRC) rainscreen wall system. The panels were individually cast in Dubai. The local fabricator was integrated in the final procurement process to optimize the system, maximize geometric repetition, and minimize unique formwork, while also managing cost, schedule and maintaining the architectural expression.

ARRIVAL PLAZA

The experience of world events and iconic architecture is elevated by meaningful urban settings. A prominent arrival sequence sets the framework and creates an orienting sense of place for visitors. The arrival to the six-month Expo 2020 event and the legacy District 2020 deserves extraordinary care to welcome the world. The Arrivals Plaza serves as one of four visitor entrances to Dubai Expo 2020 and the only connection to Route 2020, part of the Dubai Metro system capable of transporting up to 36,000 passengers per hour. It is a vibrant, central axis connecting this busy transit station, Dubai Exhibition Center (DEC), and Al Wasl Plaza.

During Expo 2020, this pedestrian corridor functions to welcome and accommodate a large flow of visitors; it also provides egress after major events in the district to the transit station and serves as an emergency exit. At the close of the event, the plaza requires minimal construction to accommodate legacy functions and will enhance the experience of locals and visitors walking between Al Wasl Plaza, the hotels, the DEC, and the Dubai Metro. Due to its nature as a connector, the design had to manage the scale and configuration of the space to allow free flowing pedestrian movement.

The Arrivals Plaza design focused on enhancing the arrival experience and maximizing the urban impact of Al Wasl Plaza. Distant views of the trellis are framed between the tall hotel buildings. Site-specific landscape and hardscape enrich the path towards the new Dubai icon providing wayfinding and a pleasant, shaded experience for visitors.

The space is designed to welcome and introduce visitors to Expo 2020, framing a memorable journey along the gateway to Al Wasl Plaza. It is required to accommodate a large crowd flow of visitors during the event and remain vibrant as the pedestrian connection between Al Wasl Plaza, the hotels, and the DEC in legacy. The positioning of the Arrivals Plaza is prominent as the DEC leverages its geographic location adjacent Dubai World Center, Al Maktoum International Airport, and the legacy of staging Expo 2020. This large complex is integral in supporting Dubai's status as a world leading destination for major exhibitions, conferences, conventions, trade shows, and events. The visitors for these events will traverse the plaza.

Mobility District
منطقة التنقل
EXPO
2020
DUBAI
UAE

Mobility District
منطقة التنقل
EXPO
2020
DUBAI
UAE

PUBLIC REALM DESIGN

During Expo 2020, visitors from the northwest arrive at a grand circular plaza surrounded by a double allée of palm trees and a ring of 210 flagpoles that represent each of the Expo 2020 participants. The circle relates to Al Wasl Plaza and trellis by tying the arrival experience to the center of the master plan. Flanking the two sides of the circular plaza, rings of trees and plantings direct visitor movement to the People Mover stations and the Dubai Exhibition Center (DEC). Each of the groves are unique with varying tree species, understory planting, lighting, benches, and shade conditions. The circles are walkable, open spaces that are paved with decomposed granite that was designed without obstruction for the large crowds arriving and exiting Expo 2020.

The main promenade is also shaded by trees lining the walkway. Guest service buildings containing amenities such as toilets and lockers for visitors edge the parcel. The trees provide shade and a definition of space similar to a streetscape without blocking views of the amenities. A water feature and a palm tree garden frame the view towards the trellis at the intersection of the hotel plots. At the outer edge of the adjacent hotel parcels, a fountain plaza connects the intersection of the drop-off and arrival areas. Palm trees elevate the scale of planting in this area and the interactive fountain was designed flush with the pavers so it can be turned on or off depending on crowd flow.

Colorful paving was designed to delineate the space and create bold memorable patterns. Curvilinear lines of paving extend from the bold concentric circular pattern at the perimeter of Al Wasl Plaza and run the length of the Arrivals Plaza. The pattern extends over 230 meters with weaving bands of paving that lead to the DEC. Embedded lighting highlights nodes along the route and variations in color respond to the programs within the site.

The site is covered in precast concrete pavers, sourced locally, with the exception of a granite stone water feature. At the connection to Al Wasl Plaza, the paving bands and trees widen to allow expansive views of the trellis. Because the trellis was designed for viewing projection from both sides, this location is a spectacular viewing space for immersive events. The interior of the trellis is visible through the large archways and the exterior of the trellis is in the foreground.

Universal design was a driving factor for the public realm. To the greatest extent possible, all areas of hardscape, urban furniture and structures were designed in an equitable and dignified manner that allows use by all people. Custom benches throughout the site provide varying features to accommodate diverse users. The flush design of the water feature also provides no obstructions to people walking or with mobility assistance.

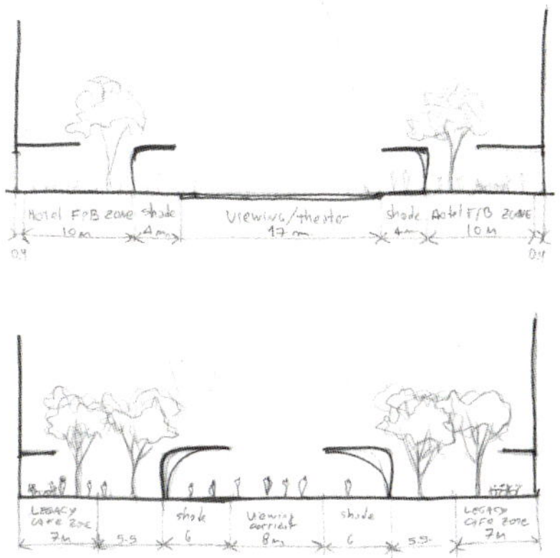

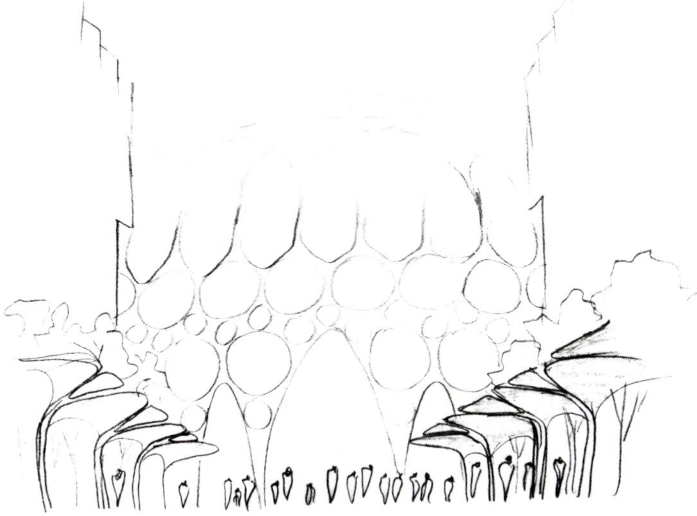

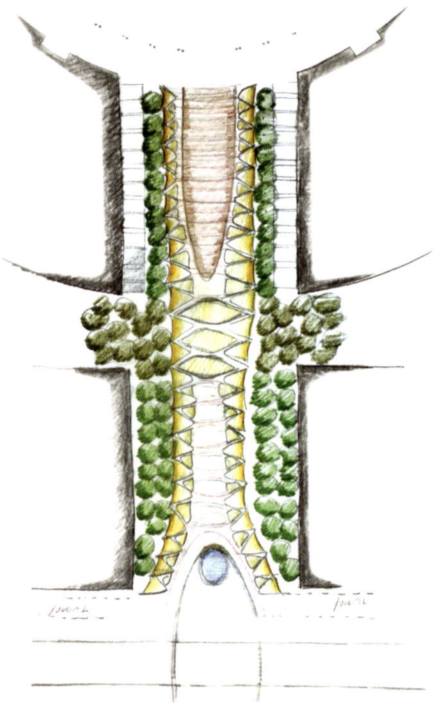

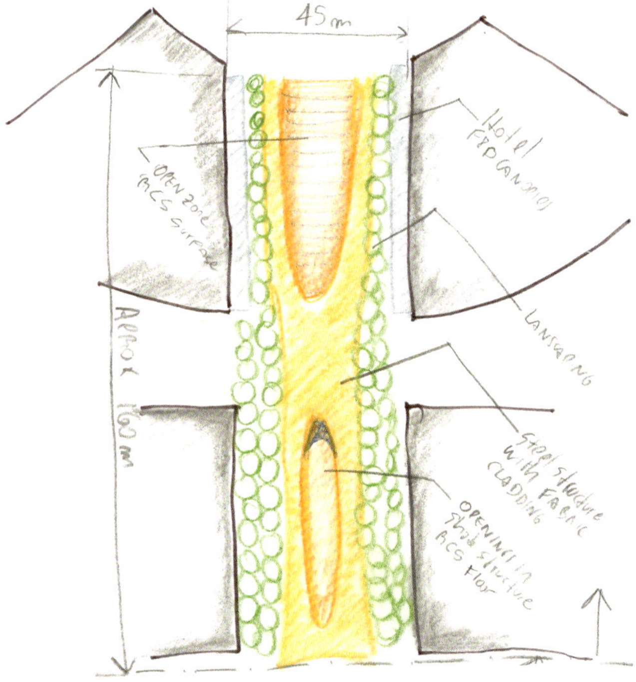
45 m

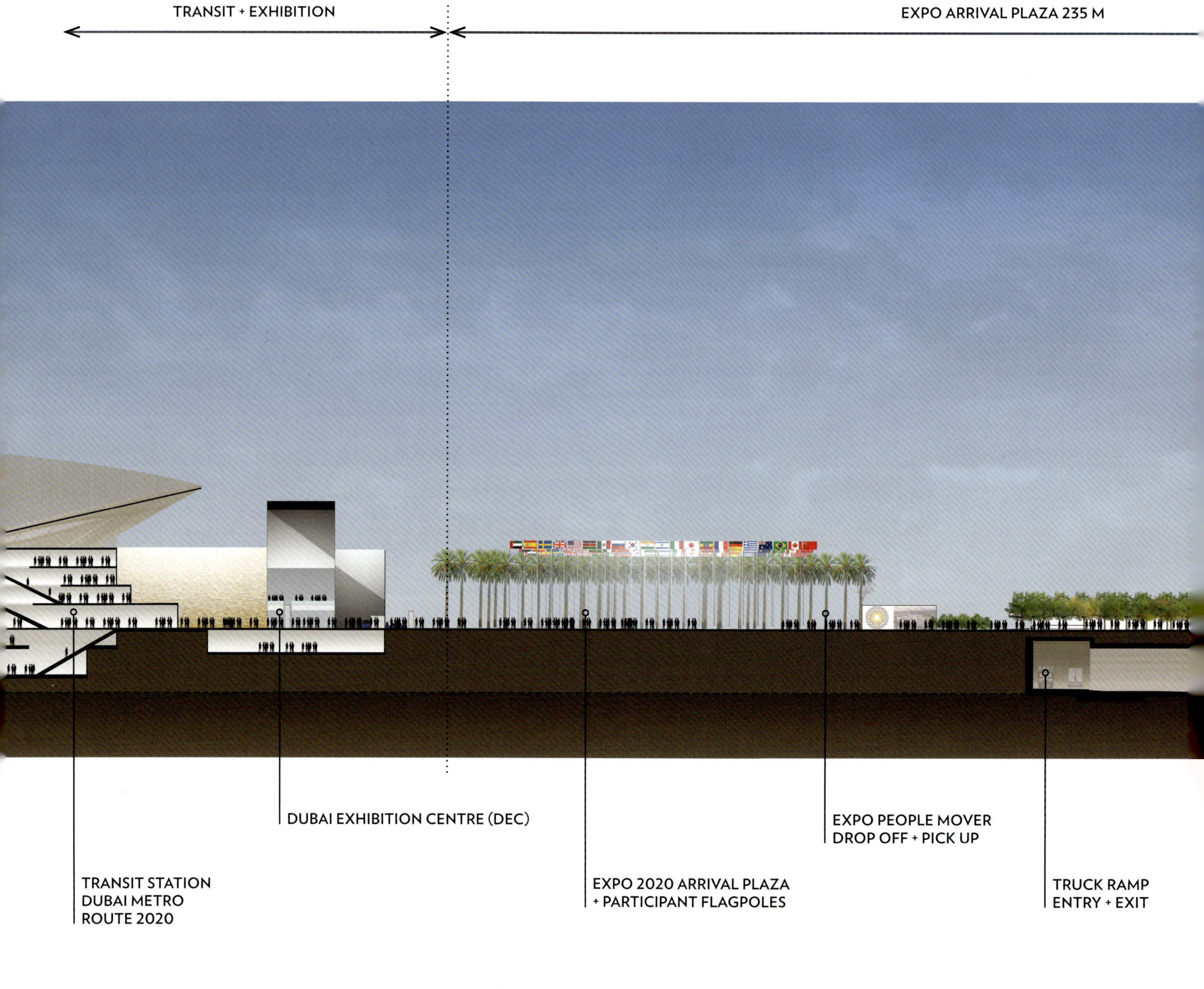

TRANSIT + EXHIBITION
EXPO ARRIVAL PLAZA 235 M
DUBAI EXHIBITION CENTRE (DEC)
EXPO PEOPLE MOVER
DROP OFF + PICK UP
TRANSIT STATION
DUBAI METRO
ROUTE 2020
EXPO 2020 ARRIVAL PLAZA
+ PARTICIPANT FLAGPOLES
TRUCK RAMP
ENTRY + EXIT

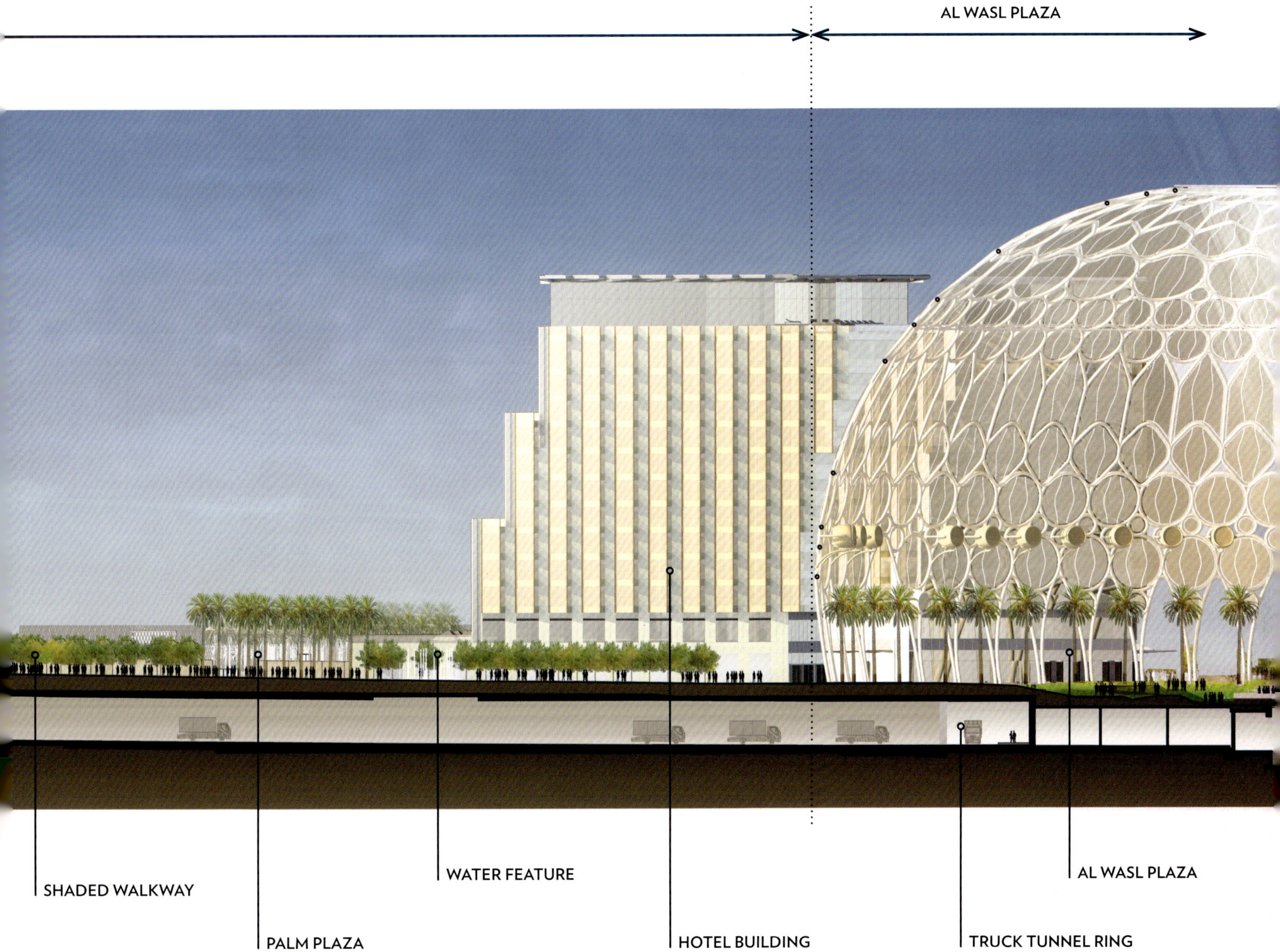
AL WASL PLAZA
SHADED WALKWAY
PALM PLAZA
WATER FEATURE
HOTEL BUILDING
TRUCK TUNNEL RING
AL WASL PLAZA

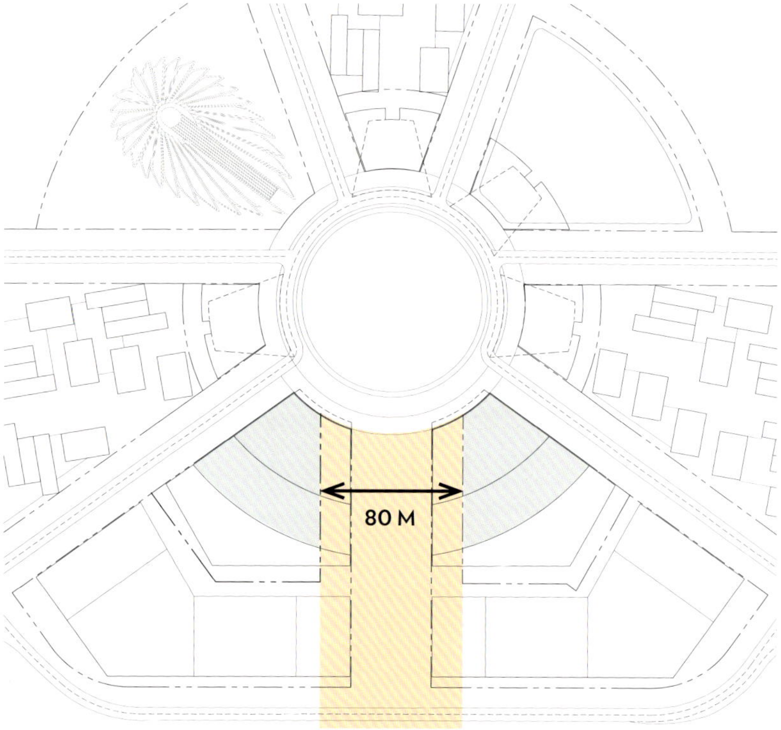

ORIGINAL MASTER PLAN ARRIVALS PLAZA

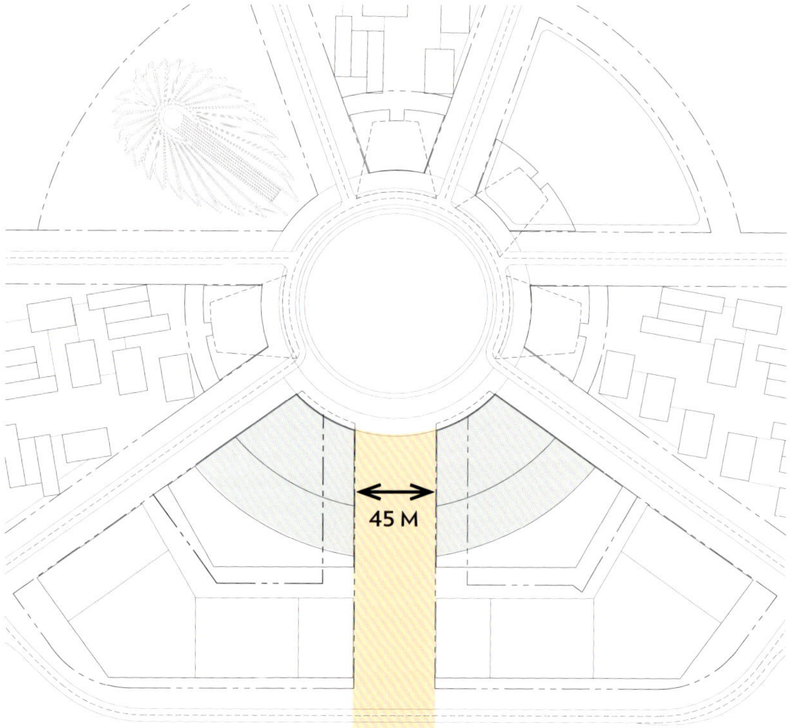

REVISED ARRIVALS PLAZA BY AS+GG

EXPO 2020 ENTRANCES

While reviewing the original Expo 2020 master plan, AS+GG noted that the width of the Arrivals Plaza was exceptionally wide at 80 meters. For comparison, it left only 20 meters of building frontage for the hotels on Al Wasl Plaza. This scale was not proportional to the hotel plots and the enclosure of the proposed plaza. Such a large adjacent public corridor was thought unnecessary and would have reduced the quality of Al Wasl Plaza. Therefore, AS+GG proposed narrowing the Arrivals Plaza width to 45 meters, allowing the hotel plots to expand 17.5 meters each. The shift would allow for greater design flexibility within the larger parcels, maximize the value of the hotels adjacent Al Wasl Plaza and create the desired enclosure around the trellis. Meanwhile, the western portion of the site was undergoing change as Expo 2020 was working with transport planners on the design of the expo bus network to move visitors around the site. The boundary of the plaza adjusted several times to finalize the intersection between these important, heavily trafficked nodes.

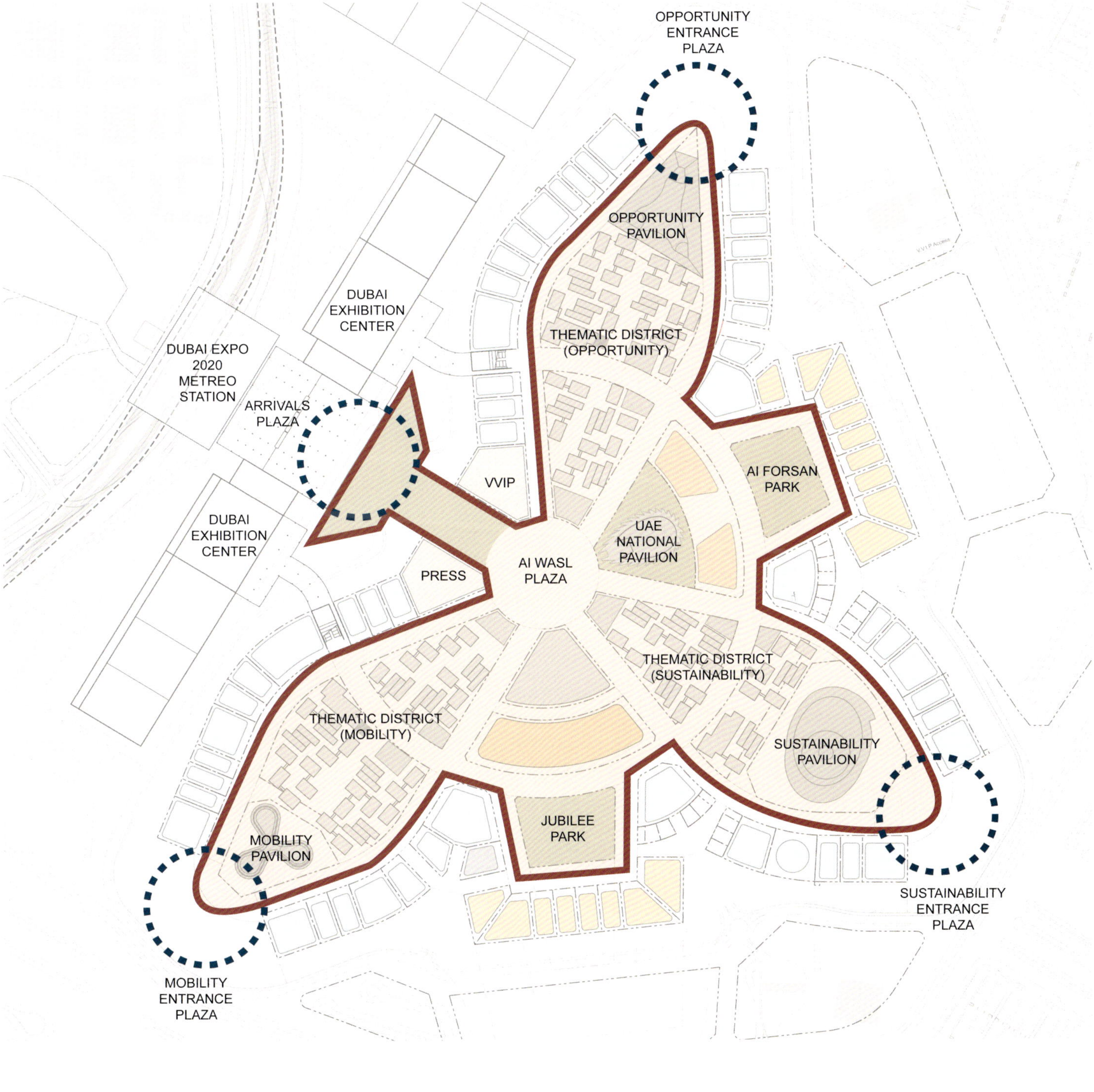
OPPORTUNITY
ENTRANCE
PLAZA
OPPORTUNITY
PAVILION
DUBAI
EXHIBITION
CENTER
THEMATIC DISTRICT
(OPPORTUNITY)
DUBAI EXPO
2020
METREO
STATION
ARRIVALS
PLAZA
AI FORSAN
PARK
VVIP
DUBAI
EXHIBITION
CENTER
UAE
NATIONAL
PAVILION
AI WASL
PLAZA
PRESS
THEMATIC DISTRICT
(SUSTAINABILITY)
THEMATIC DISTRICT
(MOBILITY)
SUSTAINABILITY
PAVILION
JUBILEE
PARK
MOBILITY
PAVILION
SUSTAINABILITY
ENTRANCE
PLAZA
MOBILITY
ENTRANCE
PLAZA

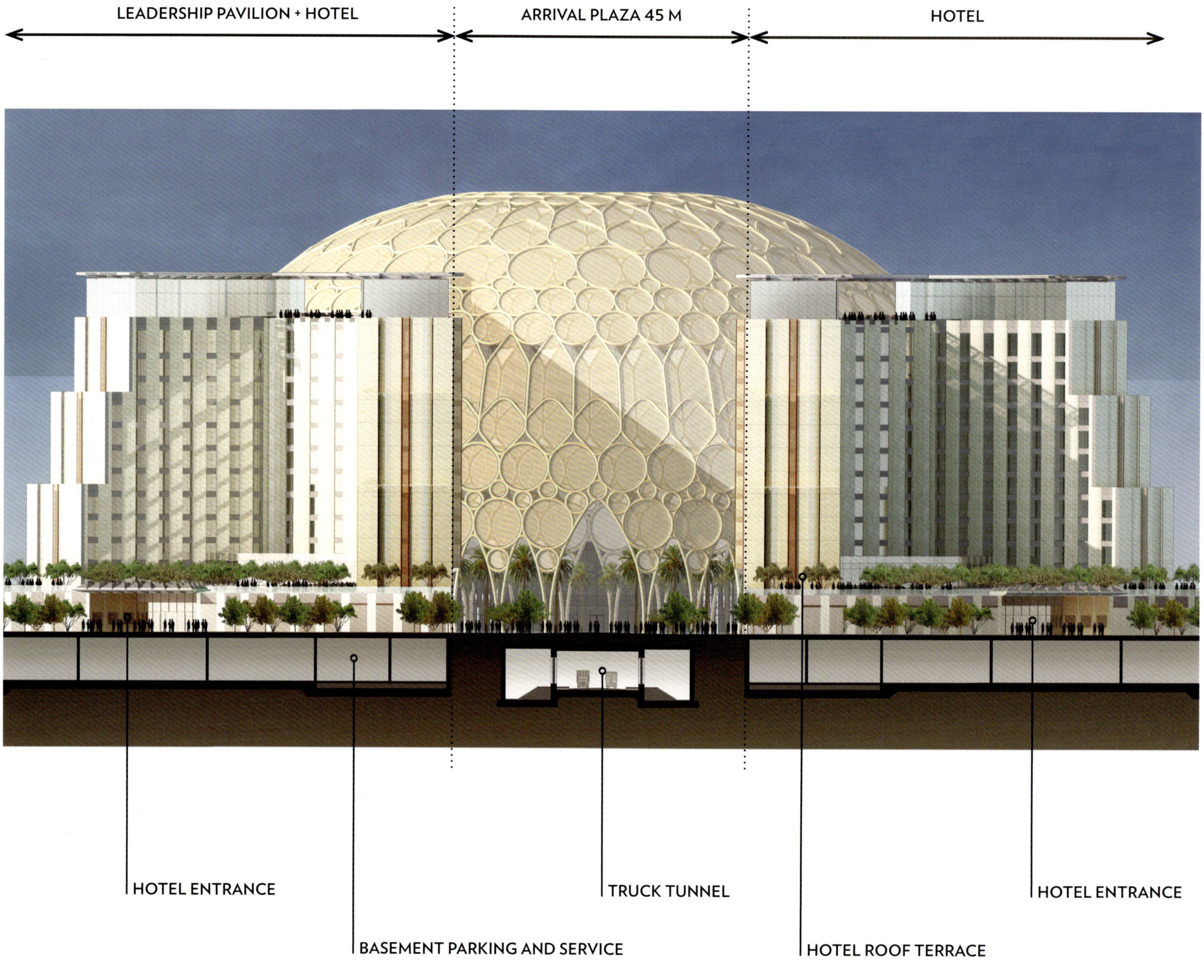
LEADERSHIP PAVILION + HOTEL
ARRIVAL PLAZA 45 M
HOTEL
HOTEL ENTRANCE
TRUCK TUNNEL
HOTEL ENTRANCE
BASEMENT PARKING AND SERVICE
HOTEL ROOF TERRACE

EXPO
TOTAL AREA: 20,567 SM

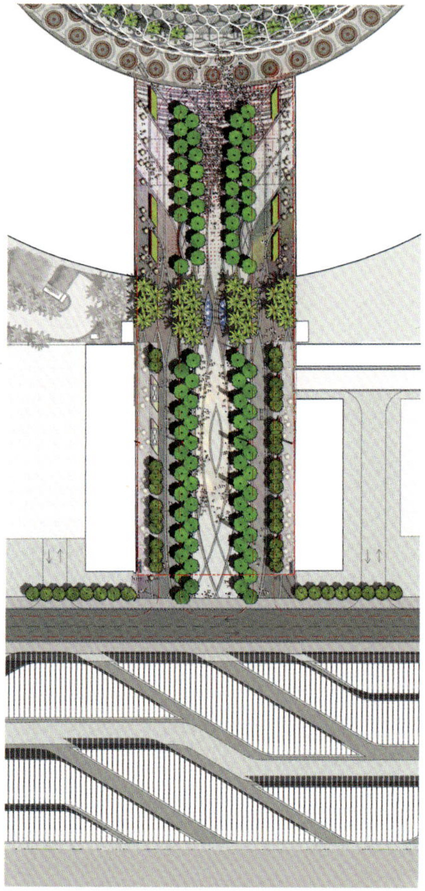

LEGACY
TOTAL AREA: 6,455 SM

ARRIVALS PLAZA EXPO TO LEGACY TRANSITION

At the close of Expo 2020, the western portion of the site will become an outdoor exhibition plaza for the DEC. The materials, construction methods and products for this temporary Expo 2020 entrance area have been designed with re-use and sustainability as primary considerations. Trees are planted in boxes with the intent of relocation and the paving is set in sand so it can be reused. The legacy portion of the Arrivals Plaza was designed for longevity and requires minimal construction for transition. Planters, which were not installed for Expo 2020 to maintain easy crowd flow, will be installed to enhance the quality of the space in legacy. The ground level of the hotel buildings, open for pedestrian circulation during the expo, will be occupied by food and beverage outlets with café tables extending into the terrace of the Arrivals Plaza. Newly installed planters will provide separation between the cafes and the pedestrian boulevard to create a more private and controlled outdoor experience next to a circulation zone.

ROVE

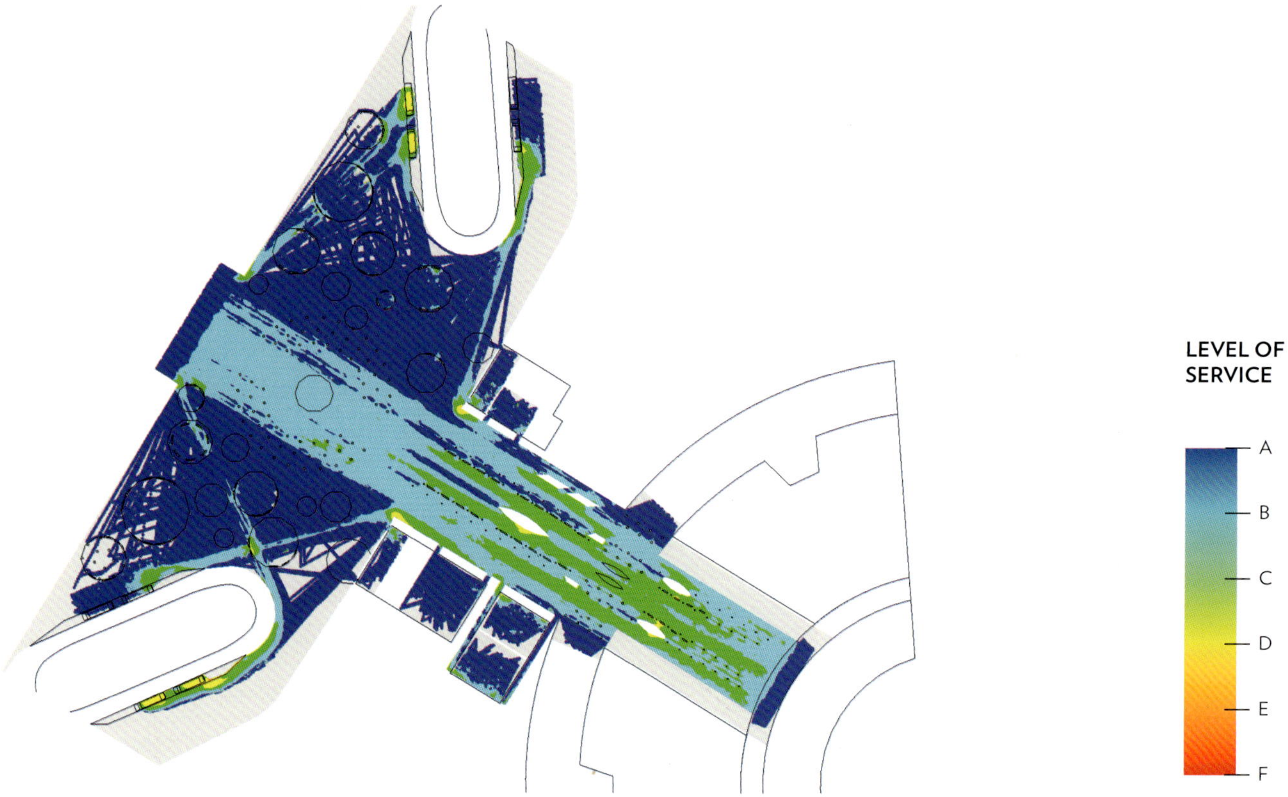

CROWD MICROSIMULATION

AS+GG engaged Mobility in Chain (MIC), an international transport planning firm headquartered in Milan, to run crowd microsimulations to confirm that the proposed 45-meter-wide Arrivals Plaza could sufficiently accommodate the expected visitors during Expo 2020. MIC input data for estimated peak arrival and departures from Al Wasl Plaza, the transit center and the adjacent Expo 2020 People Mover bus stations into sophisticated modeling and simulation software. The software simulates urban mobility flows with a Level of Service (LOS) scale from A (blue) to F (red); A identifying free-flowing crowd and F, the opposite end of the spectrum with no movement. The analysis accounted for real-time decisions as visitors stop and interact with attractions such as digital signage or may navigate around people or obstructions such as trees and water features. To design a quality expo event entrance and public corridor, the requirements are well beyond aesthetics. An effective public corridor must account for estimated peak flow to design a safe and comfortable user experience. This analysis confirmed the proposed 45-meter width to be sufficient, allowing the design to advance.

BASEMENT INFRASTRUCTURE

Often in architecture, a high level of human experience is achieved by means of sophisticated planning and execution not visible to the majority. These efforts are often underappreciated but are critical to the success of the visible architecture. The Arrivals Plaza is above the infrastructural lifeline of the district. A truck tunnel below grade allows back of house logistics to proceed throughout the district while vibrant activity takes place at the ground level.

The tunnel was engineered by the California-based Parsons Corporation, a global leader in transportation engineering. The entrance and exit are located off the sides of the western portion of the site, and the tunnel ramp descends below the public corridor for a length of 150 meters to a junction with the truck tunnel loop that surrounds the Al Wasl Plaza basement. From the loop, the tunnel branches through the adjacent Al Wasl parcel basements connecting to the thematic souk districts.

This network allows deliveries, maintenance, waste management, and other functions to operate without influence on the public experience above. This is particularly important as Al Wasl Plaza and surrounding buildings were designed with no back or service facade to integrate into the pedestrian oriented development. The sides facing Al Wasl may be the front, yet the opposite sides are the front as well with vehicle drop-offs and entrance lobbies for the offices and hotels. Therefore, this infrastructural connection below grade allows the activity above to operate efficiently and improves the architectural and pedestrian experience. The platform reinforces Dubai's position as a global leader in logistics, allowing the expo to run efficiently and to stimulate investment in the legacy.

Below the Arrivals Plaza, the tunnel is lined with 1,840 sm of support rooms for the technical aspects of the public realm and the truck tunnel itself. There is minimal architecture above grade in the Arrivals Plaza. The site can be understood as a delicate layer of landscape and public amenity atop a hidden sub-grade fortress of structure and networks to actualize the enjoyable quality of space visitors experience in the public areas above. On average, there is 1.7 meters of space between the plaza surface and the architecture below, a slim area to route a plethora of services with complex requirements. As a result of this restricted space, and the fast-track schedule, the project became a challenging puzzle to route the required power, water, data, and other conduits.

AS+GG developed the layout of the architecture adjacent to the truck tunnel in coordination with Parsons. The spaces are dedicated to mechanical chillers, fan rooms, power transformers, communications, water feature equipment tank rooms, maintenance, and other support space.

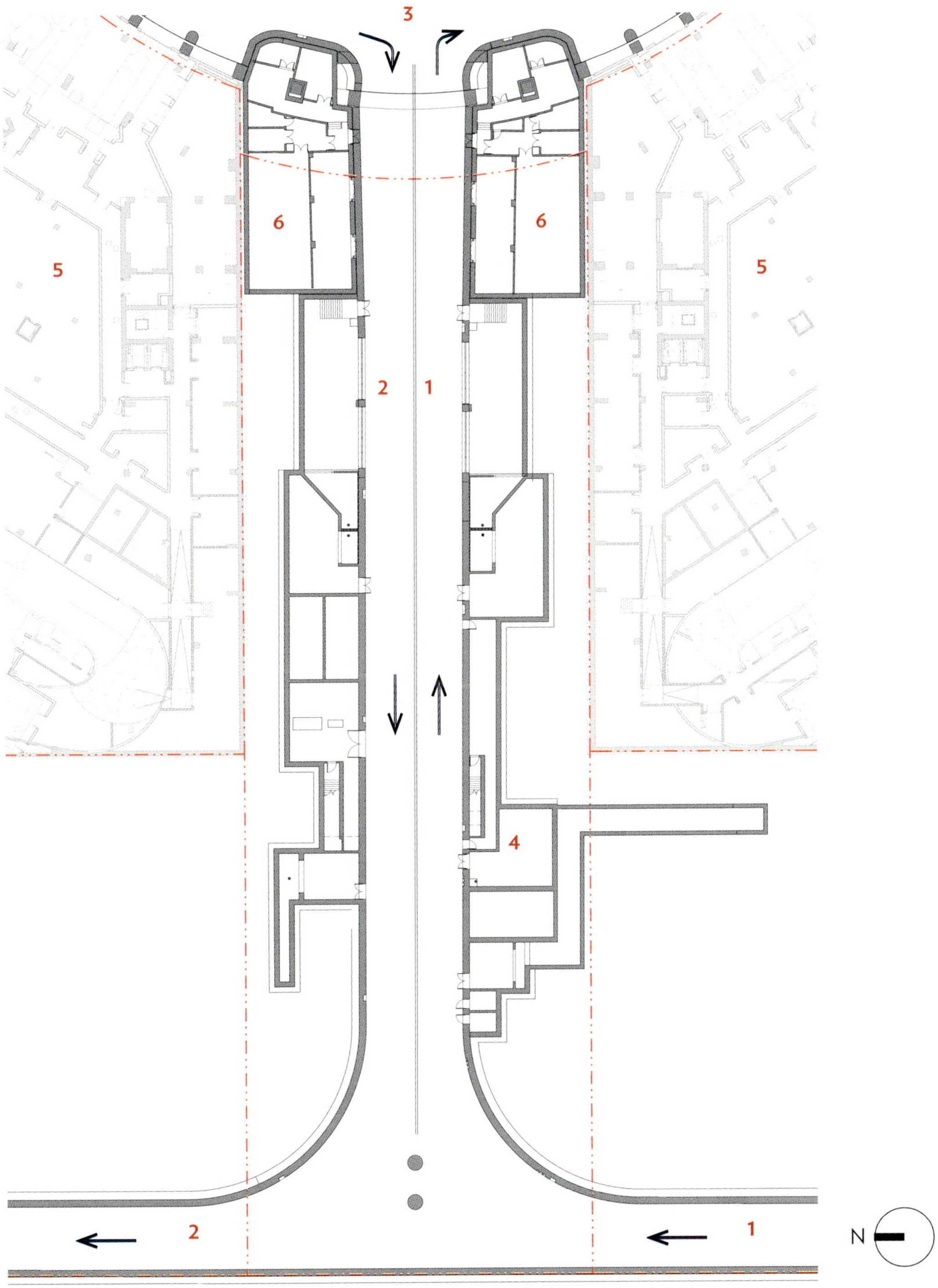

TRUCK TUNNEL HAMMERHEAD

1 RAMP DOWN TO BASEMENT
2 RAMP UP FROM BASEMENT
3 RING ROAD BELOW AL WASL PLAZA
4 WATER FEATURE EQUIPMENT ROOM
5 HOTEL BASEMENT
6 CEREMONIES POWER SUPPORT

CONSTRUCTION

Global events such as the Olympics, World Cups, and World Expos are a significant challenge to achieve as opening day is set years in advance and an enormous amount of work must be accomplished before welcoming the world. In great anticipation, the execution of the entire project becomes a several yearlong sprint towards the event. To complete Expo 2020 on schedule, a demanding and strenuous design, fabrication, and construction schedule was required. Al Wasl Plaza was one of the last major projects, apart from the national pavilions, to be awarded by the client. This significantly reduced the amount of time AS+GG had to design, obtain authority approvals, and construct the project in comparison to other major permanent structures at Expo 2020.

Due to the constrained timeline, Al Wasl was a fast-track project, meaning construction commences before the design is complete, shortening the overall project completion time. At the heart of the district, the construction of Al Wasl occurred simultaneous to the construction of the surrounding district infrastructure and architecture. At its height, over 32,000 workers were involved in the construction on the 1083-acre Expo site. Effective coordination with an immense variety of collaborators, authorities, and a highly involved client are necessary attributes required for a project like this to succeed. Success extends beyond timely completion to include cost and quality control and integration within the overall context of Expo 2020 Dubai.

Technologically advanced and an engineering feat, the construction of Al Wasl Plaza demonstrates Dubai's commitment to creating a memorable and transformative event with a legacy project to showcase the UAE's diversity, culture, and economy. Al Wasl Plaza is positioned above a complex basement and tunnel network. The construction of the trellis foundation and basements occurred while the trellis was still being engineered. The surrounding five buildings were under construction while the trellis was being erected and the plaza was constructed following the substantial completion of the trellis and surrounding buildings.

ACCESS HIRE

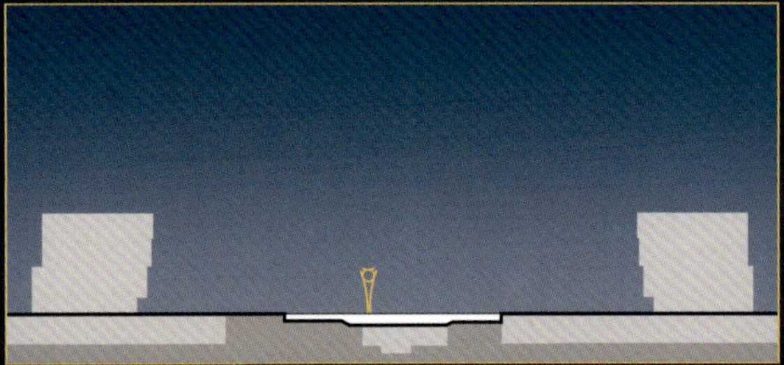

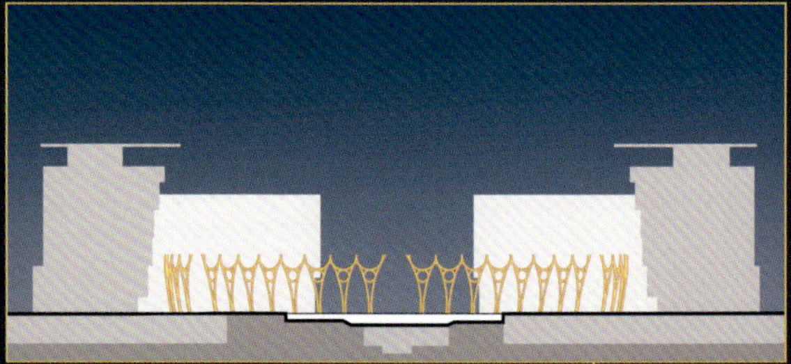

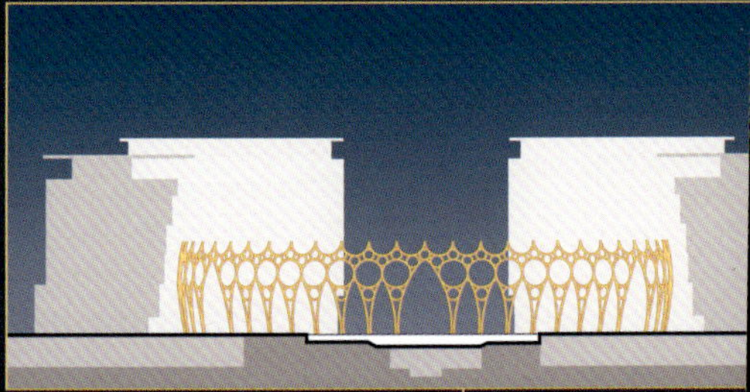

2016.08
Concept Design

2017.08
Ground Breaking

2018.02
Trellis Fabrication Start

2018.08
Trellis Outer Ring Installation Start

2018.11
Office Topping Out

2019.01
Hotel Topping Out

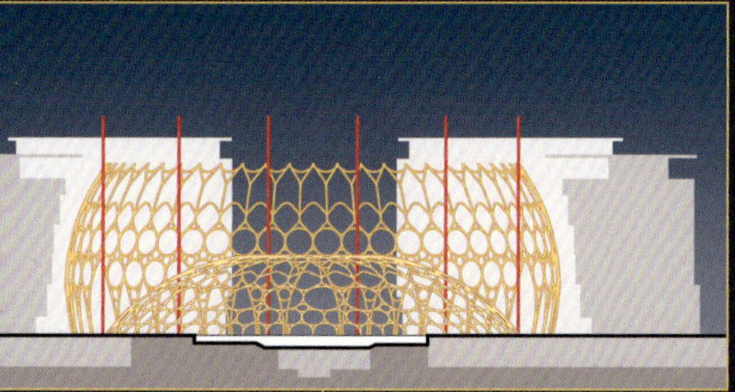

2019.04
Trellis Inner Ring Installation Start

2019.09
Crowning the Trellis

2019.12
Trellis Pod Installation Complete

2020.01
Trellis Fabric Installation Complete

2020.07
Plaza Complete

2020.10
EXPO 2020 Scheduled Opening

Postponed due to global COVID-19 pandemic

2021.10
EXPO 2020 Opening

2022.03
EXPO 2020 Closing

Legacy Garden Construction

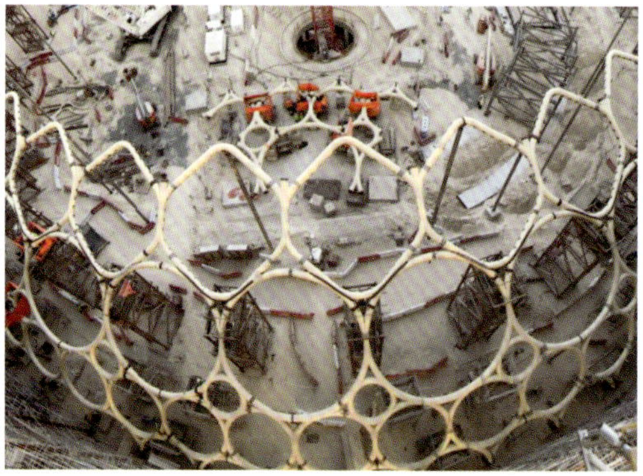

CONSTRUCTION COORDINATION OF AL WASL PARCELS

The sequencing of the construction of the Al Wasl parcels was a significant challenge due to the complex geometry, scale, and proximity to the buildings to Al Wasl trellis. Each piece depends on the other. All seven AS+GG parcels lean toward the trellis. The basements intertwine and connect to the truck tunnel by others. The garden parcel overlaps the hotel and office basements as well as the truck tunnel. A portion of the architecture below the Arrivals Plaza provides infrastructure for the garden, another portion for the hotels. The mechanical and service spaces for the trellis and truck tunnel are located below the plaza. Above grade, the union is more obvious as the office and hotel buildings follow the curvature of the trellis, cantilevering over the public realm. These connections blur the boundaries of each parcel. While the resultant is a highly sophisticated campus, the coordination to realize the project required an extraordinary effort.

The scale of the development and the variety of typologies required specialized contractors for the Al Wasl parcels. While CRME oversaw the trellis fabrication and erection, Al Futtaim Carillion (AFC) oversaw the office, and Laing O'Rourke (LOR) the hotels, Leadership Pavilion, Al Wasl Plaza and basement and the Arrivals Plaza public realm. The documentation for and schedules of these contractors were organized and sequenced with an overall logistics strategy. Hundreds of specialty sub-contractors had to be coordinated. The project could not have been achieved by simultaneously constructing the parcels in isolation from one another. Precise organization and delivery of the construction documents to the applicable contractors who were working closely with similar delivery dates yet bound by separate contracts was critical. The intertwined boundaries of the parcels create unique conditions of scope for project management. It also required coordination with contractors and designers of adjacent parcels outside of AS+GG scope of work.

Not only did constant collaboration between the contractors and site team occur, coordination was also required between the contractors and the design team to prepare for the site constraints. The construction sequence and site accessibility had a direct impact on the design detailing. For instance, the exterior wall systems facing Al Wasl Plaza were installed from inside the buildings. This impacted the facade detailing and is atypical to conventional construction methods. Installation of photovoltaic panels on the office roofs cantilever over the trellis and were installed in sequence with the trellis installation schedule.

TRELLIS CONSTRUCTION

The construction documents for the trellis foundation were issued in August 2017 and construction commenced; approximately six months before the completion of the trellis design and award of the trellis contract. The trellis foundation system consists of a continuous, reinforced concrete, two-meter wide by 1.5-meter-deep ring beam. The ring beam is supported on 47, 1.5-meter square piers, on a continuous, two-meter wide by 1.5-meter-deep footing.

Steel and elastomeric pot bearing assemblies (more properly called confined elastomeric bearings) are anchored to the top of the ring beam, spaced approximately 7.55-meters apart, coinciding with the foot of each leg of the trellis. They are in concrete pockets, approximately 1.3-meters below ground level. The pot bearings are required to support the trellis, while allowing small amounts of movement at the base of each leg, when the trellis moves due to wind loads or due to changes in temperature.

From a shortlist of three specialist structural steel fabricator tender finalists; Cimolai Rimond Middle East (CRME) was selected for their experience on complex projects, understanding of the aesthetic, technical and logistical aspects of this project, including the fabrication, delivery, assembly, and erection of the trellis structure on site. As previously described in the Trellis chapter, segments of the steel frame were prefabricated in Italy before transportation by ship and arrival to a pre-assembly facility near to the Expo site. The individual segments were welded together into sub-assemblies and then transported to site for installation.

The final on-site assembly sequence and erection procedures were carefully studied, and several options were investigated and rejected before the final methodology agreed and implemented. The trellis was divided into thirds over its height. The lowest third was identified as lower ring 1, the next upper ring 1 and the top or crown as ring 2. The sub-assemblies that made up lower and upper ring 1 were assembled from the ground, held in place by 18 temporary props and welded together. While ring 1 was being completed, the sub-assemblies that made up ring 2 were also assembled on the ground. While Ring 2 was being completed, strand jacks were installed at each of the 18 vertical props and their cables attached to the perimeter of ring 2. The jacking lift took place over a 36-hour period. During this period, strict location controls were in place and wind speeds were constantly monitored. If the wind velocity exceeded 33.75 meters per second, the lift would stop, and a safety blocking system would be activated by remote control to temporarily stabilize the yet to be complete structure. The lift was successfully completed on September 14, 2019. Once positioned, the ring 2 crown was welded into place, a process that took 25 days to complete.

Following completion of the trellis structure, a significant amount of work continued on-site. Not only did the structure itself require the welds to be ground down and prepared for finish painting, but installation commenced on the fabric panels, LED lights, projector pods, access gantries and associated control and power cabling infrastructure.

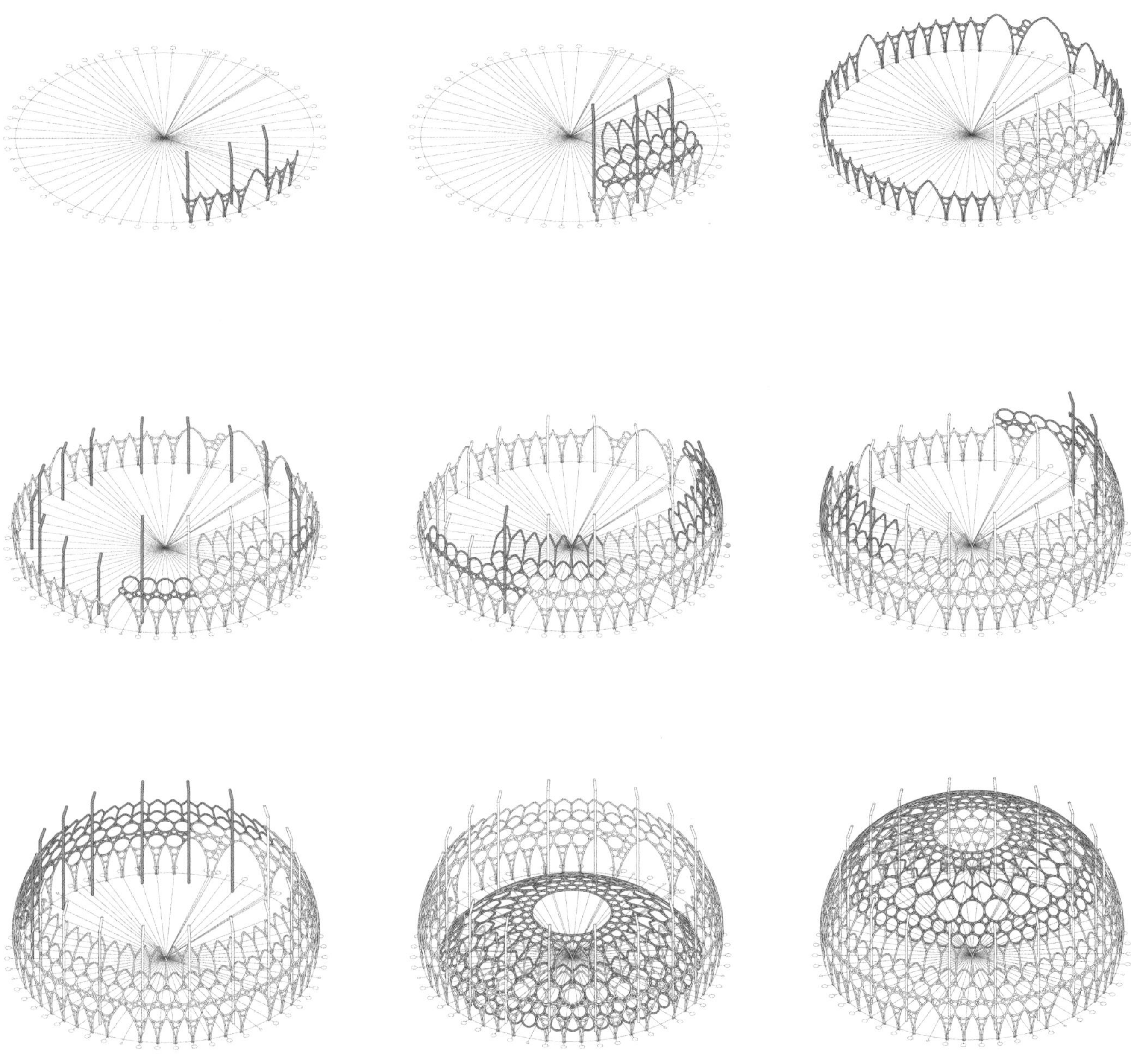

"Crowning Al Wasl Dome was both incredibly exciting and one of the most challenging engineering operations in the world. Lifting such a large and heavy structure involved a huge number of variables. Something as simple as a shift in direction of the wind or change in air temperature could have had a big impact on our calculations, so constant monitoring and reassessment was essential throughout the process."

- AHMED AL KHATIB

Expo 2020 Chief Development and Delivery Officer

PROJECTOR ENCLOSURE FABRICATION

The design of these nacelle-like enclosures includes a variety of highly customized components from very large to small scale. An international and interdisciplinary team was necessary to conceptualize and solve the mechanical, electrical, structural, and aesthetic components supported by specialized software for design, calculation, and parametrization. Special procurement and production processes were developed having to find materials and methods in different parts of the world. Methods and technologies from leading aeronautical, automotive, metal-mechanic, and electronics industries had to be adopted.

To meet the accelerated schedule a transversal and parallel production lines were installed processing materials and generating the necessary assemblies. As final products, such large and complex elements would typically be transported by sea. Given the project needs, however, air freight was necessary using the one of the world's largest cargo aircrafts the ANTONOV An–124.

The enclosure design allows for the accommodation of six super-high-definition projectors. Each projector weighting 140kg is mounted on a racking system that is secondary to the primary structure designed to support the weight of the projectors and MEP units. The rack system is made of aluminum, integrating sliding trays with heavy-duty stainless-steel sliders that hold the projectors in place. The tray movement is controlled by a DC Motor allowing smooth movement of the tray even with a full load while an inductive sensor system feedbacks the main control digital interface to limit the extension and retraction of the trays.

The IGU doors are composed of low iron ultra-clear glass. Anti-reflective on all 4 surfaces to prevent any double imaging and a hydrophobic coating for the exterior face. The glass is installed as a sealed unit with custom made profiles and gaskets. The AC System was designed using CFD analysis to maintain the airflow and inside temperature optimal for projectors functionality.

The exterior shell is a monocoque structural system utilizing aluminum as the primary construction element. A waffle ribbed structure comprising of 150mm deep aluminum plate ribs running perpendicular to each other and clad with a hydroformed double curved aluminum sheet skin on both interior and exterior with insulation them between completes the primary structure. The front and rear leading edges are radiused and constructed of spun aluminum. All exterior aluminum is finished with a high-performance coating. The enclosures are structurally hung from the trellis superstructure by three AESS support arms that serve as containment for all A/V and MEP service lines feeding into the enclosures. Each enclosure has its own orientation, pitch, and yaw angles that are defined to cover all the dome surface area.

These first of their kind systems provide an architectural and technical solution to Al Wasl envisioned unique experience. They also represent a concept-to-fabrication success opening a new horizon of ingenious capabilities to solve complex fabrication problems in the architecture and construction industry.

©800MANLIFT
©800MANLIFT
kinetica

PROSPAC
RENTALS

Genie GS-3246

kinetica
kinetica

KUKA

EXPO
2020
DUBAI
UAE
kinetica

VOLGA DNEPR
kinetica
kinetica
kinetica
EXPO
2020
DUBAI
UAE
ZOVALO

A BLEND OF LOCAL AND GLOBAL EXPERTISE

A combined effort of local specialists in the UAE and experts from around the world were involved in the design, engineering, material supply, fabrication, and installation of Al Wasl. The goal was to execute the architectural vision in the most efficient manner possible regarding cost, energy, and carbon reduction. Whenever possible, local materials and fabrication were prioritized. This is a priority in AS+GG work, and a tenet of the Bureau International des Expositions (BIE), the intergovernmental organization in charge of overseeing and regulating World Expos since 1931; who have stated that World Expos "are laboratories for an urban future anchored in a commitment to sustainability. To create an enduring legacy, Expos must limit their impact on the environment, promote responsible sourcing, benefit the whole community, and encourage more sustainable behavior."

To achieve novel details and systems in Al Wasl Plaza, world leaders in dozens of fields from audiovisual to structural engineering were engaged to provide expertise on state-of-the-art systems and technologies. Innovation often results from the synthesis of diverse disciplines around the world. The diversity of the collaboration on Al Wasl elevated the project to achieve several blended systems that had not previously been tested. For example, the immersive experience technology, including projectors and LED lights, were manufactured in Canada, the audio speakers in France, and the projector pods were engineered and fabricated in Mexico. Companies from Italy, Czech Republic, and Poland participated in the development and fabrication of the trellis structure. Furthermore, the fabric panels on the trellis were sourced from the USA then shipped to China where a Japanese team lead the fabrication.

Global collaboration elevates local industry expertise while local engagement increases the project exposure, streamlines the process from a knowledge and local approvals standpoint, and boosts the economy. The global intellectual investment in Al Wasl made a significant impact on the local architecture, engineering, and construction industries in Dubai. Local engagement in areas of fabrication, labor, project management, document control and authority approvals root the project delivery in the UAE culture and elevate the associated industries to the world stage through the expo event. Building an icon with local involvement increases pride and appreciation for the building, especially for a public space. The impact of the global knowledge share, as well as the energy and inspiration infused by this large technological endeavor, has raised the bar not only in the UAE but globally for this new typology. Dubai is a leader in architectural firsts, and industry leaders involved in the novel process of creating Al Wasl Plaza and the entirety of the Dubai Expo 2020 development will inspire further innovation launching from the high standards that were achieved in this remarkable project.

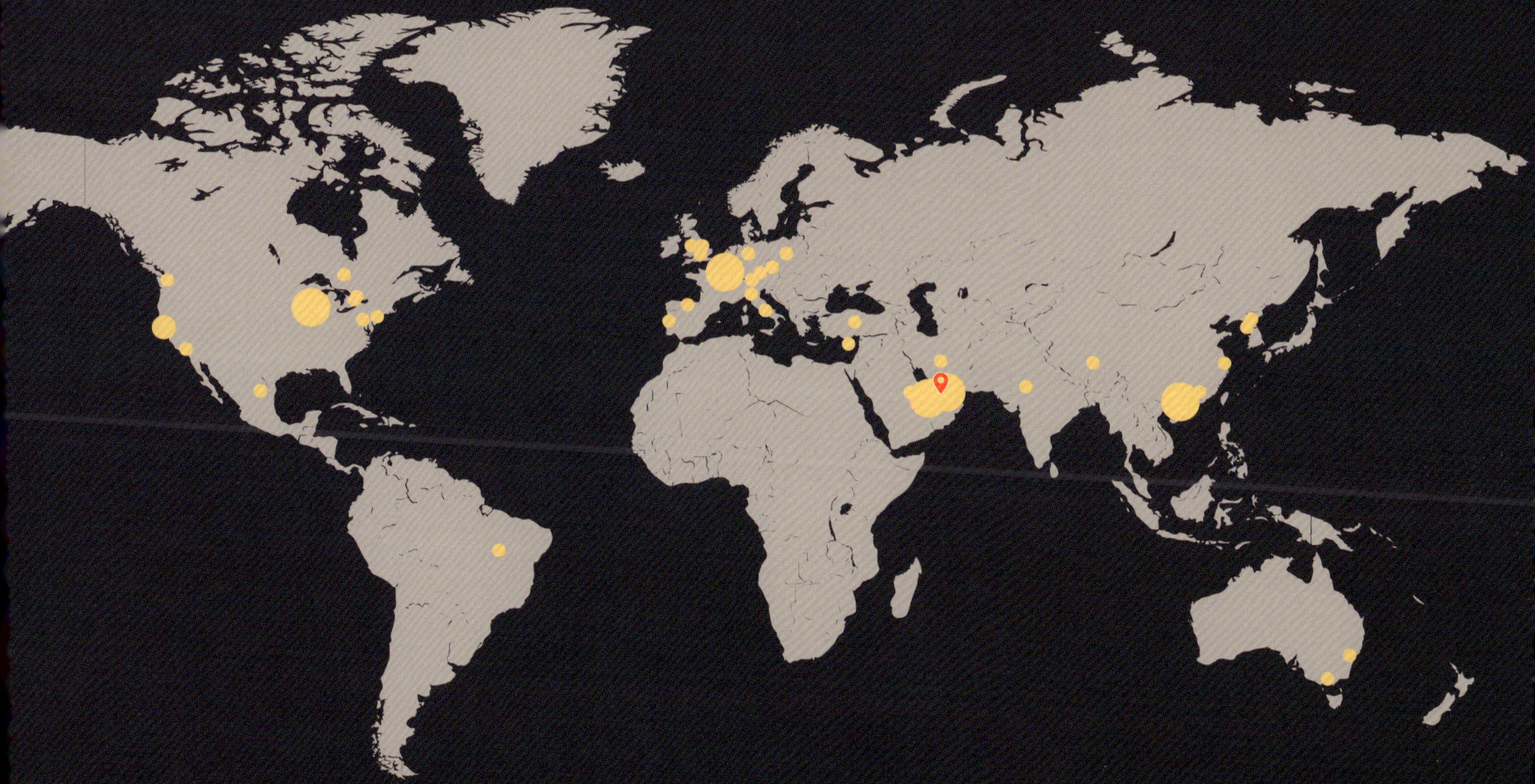

SUSTAINABILITY

Expo 2020's vision is to "host an inspirational, safe, and inclusive Expo event that leaves a sustainable legacy for Dubai and the UAE." Sustainability is not only integral to the event vision but it is highlighted as one of the three sub-themes of the Expo, along with Mobility and Opportunity. Expo 2020 developed this mission in line with the Dubai Government and Bureau International des Expositions (BIE) General Assembly whose overarching vision is to ensure the event respects environment and civil city on environmental issues.

This high expectation of sustainable excellence attracted AS+GG, whose foundation is based on the design of efficient high-performance architecture that shapes civic life. When approached by Expo 2020 in 2016, the opportunity to engage with an innovative client deeply focused on the creation of a sustainable World Expo and legacy district was an obvious opportunity to positively shape civic life for future generations.

To achieve this sustainability intent by project teams across the district, guidelines and measurable outcomes were set as Key Performance Indicators (KPIs) by Expo 2020 for the event. The client reviewed each project team's compliance through monitoring and reporting by the respective teams throughout the design and construction process.

At the onset of the Al Wasl project, AS+GG reviewed the Expo 2020 KPIs for implementation across the eight central parcels and identified additional measures to be implemented and identified legacy guidelines to prioritize the longevity of the development. Energy, water, materials, waste, emissions, transport, ecology, biodiversity, site, public realm, awareness and education, operations, and certification or value generation were key categories of the sustainability KPIs by Expo 2020. AS+GG built upon this platform and added four new themes for the legacy development: Live, Work, Mobility, and Wellness addressing sustainability in a broad sense beyond environmental for community and civic life in District 2020.

At the heart of the master plan, the concept for Al Wasl Plaza is rooted in balancing nature and humanity in a place of gathering. It was designed to encompass social, environmental, and economic sustainability. As a vibrant social environment embodying the Expo 2020 theme Connecting Minds, Creating the Future, the architecture must sustain for future generations.

SUSTAINABLE DESIGN

Environmentally, the self-shading architectural form uses high-performance design strategies, and the buildings themselves use energy efficient systems, potable water use reduction strategies and sustainable materials. Perhaps the most sustainable aspect of the Al Wasl development is the longevity of the project; designed originally as a legacy garden and public amenity for the community, the social and economic stability of the Expo centerpiece beyond the event was essential. By design, the plaza and surrounding buildings require minimal construction transition at the close of Expo 2020, thereby spurring growth in District 2020 and the greater Dubai South City region.

The high-performance design strategies are rooted in research in collaboration with expert consultants. Nature is central to the architectural and urban strategy for Al Wasl Plaza and the creation of a comfortable microclimate was paramount. AS+GG worked with Klimaat Consulting to simulate the thermal comfort within the plaza by simulating the Standard Effective Temperature (SET) throughout the space. SET is a temperature metric that factors in relative humidity, mean radiant temperature, and air velocity, while also considering the anticipated activity rate and clothing levels.

The modeling process accounts for the geometry of the space and adjacent buildings, the material surface properties, the localized climate, and physics such as wind flow or evaporative cooling. The designed comfort in the plaza includes trellis shade, tree canopies, utilizing planting to enhance transpiration, promotion of wind movement, water features promoting evaporative cooling and local heat absorption, light colored surfaces that reduce heat island effect, and the use of darker paving to activate thermal mass into the evenings at certain times of the year. As a result of these strategies and testing, the SET temperature is estimated to be lowered by 4–8 degrees Celsius throughout the year.

To achieve high performance, the architect must carefully consider the climate and site in its form and orientation integrating a blend of systems to support the building before additional environmental strategies or systems are deployed. The conceptual idea for the project must be rooted in sustainable principles to guide the project in a certain direction. In Al Wasl, the core detailing, optimizing systems and documenting the process for certifications are important steps towards the resulting sustainability achievements. It is in the inception, however, the root and core ideas of the project that must be organized with a sustainable directive.

The use of resources for multiple functions was a key feature of the project throughout. When the economic and embodied carbon impact of the built environment can serve multiple uses, more can be gained. The idea to extend the use of the shade structure beyond its daytime hours, met the intent to maximize every aspect of the project. The nighttime projection enabled the strategy to bring the community together during the night extending the impact of the public venue. Each of the sustainable strategies implemented in Al Wasl are intertwined with the original vision; the creation of community space, where nature and technology work together for the enjoyment of users and sustainable future of Expo 2020 Dubai and the legacy District 2020.

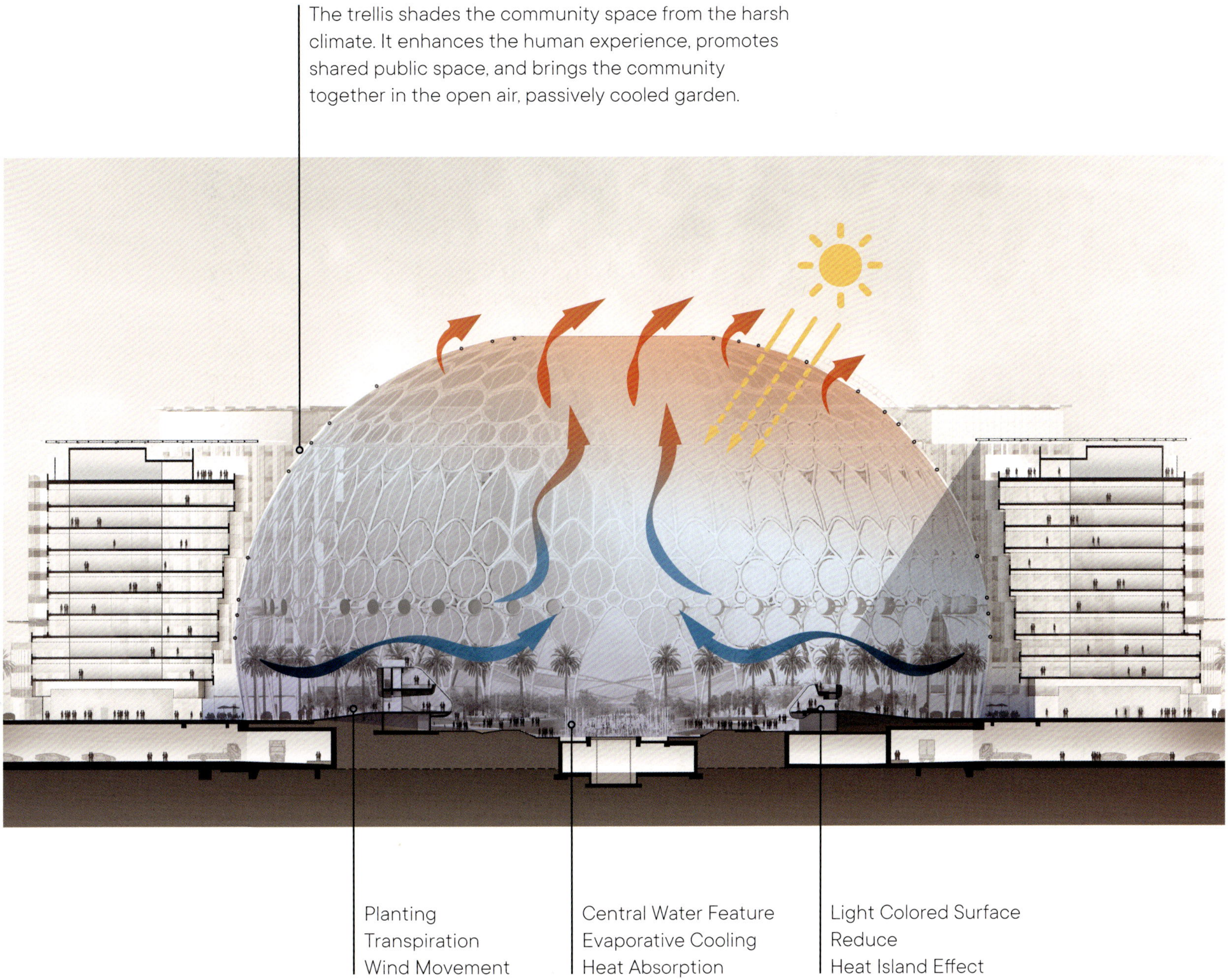
The trellis shades the community space from the harsh climate. It enhances the human experience, promotes shared public space, and brings the community together in the open air, passively cooled garden.
Planting
Transpiration
Wind Movement
Central Water Feature
Evaporative Cooling
Heat Absorption
Light Colored Surface
Reduce
Heat Island Effect

LEGACY SUSTAINABILITY VISION

Live

- Create a neighborhood with reliable access to educational and recreational facilities
- Support the development of an inclusive and diverse community
- Create a Smart living environment

Work

- Create a healthy working environment that enhances productivity and inspires creativity
- Create a Smart working environment

Mobility

- Provide access to low carbon mobility
- Support emerging low carbon mobility and logistics solutions
- Create Smart mobility

Wellness

- Access to healthy and organic food options
- Encourage Smart wellness

Energy

- Reduce energy consumption
- Reduce carbon emissions
- 100% Energy from renewable sources

Water

- Reduce water consumption
- Minimize potable water consumption through use of recycled water
- Manage and reuse stormwater on-site

Materials

- Minimize depletion of natural resources through designing for reuse and legacy
- Promote use of sustainable materials in terms of environmental, social and economic impact
- Reduce lifecycle carbon emissions

Waste

- Minimize quantity of waste to landfill
- Reduce solid waste generation
- Reduce emissions from waste management

Ecology + Environment

- Protect and enhance the ecological value of the site and promote the use of local plant species
- Create a community that is resilient to climate change

Public Realm

- Create people centric, accessible and comfortable spaces
- Create a pedestrian and cycling friendly environment

Awareness + Connectivity

- Enhance community sustainability awareness
- Embrace internet of things technologies to promote environmental awareness

Value

- Demonstrate added value through sustainability certification
- Create equal employment opportunities for men and women
- Develop home grown talent in the fields of logistics and mobility

Waste
Value
Energy
Live
LEGACY
A SUSTAINABLE
AND SMART
LIFESTYLE
Awareness +
Connectivity
Work
Mobility
Materials
Wellness
Public Realm
Water
Ecology +
Environment

SUSTAINABILITY ACHIEVEMENTS

SOLAR ENERGY

The PV arrays on the three office buildings produce 120% of their required electricity. They are the first commercial office buildings in Dubai to be electricity positive.

MATERIAL REUSE

Materials and construction CO2 emissions were reduced by 39% for Al Wasl Plaza and the Trellis by using high-recycled content steel manufactured using renewable energy and replacing cement with low embodied carbon alternatives.

WATER REUSE

Rainwater, condensate, grey water and treated waste water are used for all hotel and office non-potable water uses, meaning that no fresh water is used for toilet flushing or in the cooling towers. They are the first buildings of their kind in Dubai.

UNIVERSAL ACCESSIBILITY

Al Wasl Plaza is designed for inclusivity accommodating persons of all physical ability using the highest safety standards. Low sloped paths are provided through all public spaces, a variety of bench types are provided for rest along the way.

NATIVE PLANTS

Most of the landscape species were grown locally in Dubai and are adapted to the desert climate. Al Wasl Plaza is more shaded than a typical desert environment so adaptive plants that thrive in this hot environment with less sunlight were chosen.

SUSTAINABILITY CERTIFICATIONS

The two hotel buildings are certified LEED Gold and the three office buildings are certified LEED Platinum. The plaza achieved a CEEQUAL excellent rating for infrastructure and public realm projects.

TRELLIS SHADING

Lightweight UV resistant PTFE fabric in the Trellis canopy reduces solar heat gain by 50% and allows air flow for visitors and plants in the garden. This fabric doubles as the projection screen.

SELF SHADING

The buildings around the plaza provide shade to the adjacent pedestrian areas. The buildings were designed to step towards the Trellis and garden for enhanced views

EMBODIED CARBON

Embodied carbon was reduced by material efficiency in concrete and steel structures. The trellis fabric brackets were optimized to reduce the steel required by nearly 40% and post-tensioned concrete slabs in the buildings reduce material required.

ENHANCED MICRO-CLIMATE

The temperature in Al Wasl Plaza is reduced by up to 9 degrees Celsius due to the shading, planting, water features and the lowered garden landform.

HEAT ISLAND EFFECT REDUCTION

Over 70% of ground level and roof surfaces for the plaza and buildings use surfaces with minimum values of Solar Reflective Index (SRI) and Light Reflectance Value (LRV) in order to minimize heat in the environment.

ENERGY EFFICIENCY

The hotel and office buildings reduce energy use by up to 73% by implementing reduced window-wall ratios, external fins, thermally broken frames, high-performing certain walls and using active high performance mechanical systems.

DISTRICT 2020

The AS+GG legacy master plan for Expo 2020 Dubai established the long-term vision for the Expo site and investments in its infrastructure and buildings to advance long-term UAE objectives for economic and social advancement. Following the Expo, the entire site will transform into a mixed-use technology hub focused on global logistics to leverage its adjacency to new international airport and deep-sea port assets.

Rebranded District 2020, this urban innovation lab will contain 32 million sf at full buildout of mixed work-live-learn development with public transit, exhibition facilities and regional attractions. The 500–acre site is accessible via regional expressways and Dubai Metro commuter rail is under construction. Approximately 5.4 million sf of permanent buildings are being constructed for the Expo that will be converted into office, residential and educational facilities organized around small-scale blocks and neighborhood parks.

AS+GG performance specifications and guidelines were implemented to assure Expo 2020 is among the most sustainable global events on record with power to influence UAE development policy for decades to come.

LIVE-WORK COURTYARDS

Mixed-use highly amortized live-work cluster of corporate, SME, startup + educational typologies. Al Wasl will be the Center of the Regional Knowledge Economy. The Dubai Exhibition Centre will provide a platform for exhibition to the world.

COLLABORATION CORE

Larger sites for corporate offices + educational uses anchor urban neighborhoods with parks, schools + retail in walkable, pedestrian-oriented courtyard configurations.

R+D TESTBED

Research and development district for higher education, corporate and institutional collaboration. Mixed-use environment with integrated student and researcher housing. Adjacent, large-scale parcels enable outdoor production and testing facilities.

TESTBED + DEVELOPMENT DISTRICT
EXPO METRO STATION
COEX
CENTER OF AVIATION
COEX ENTRY PLAZA
AL WASL PLAZA
DISTRICT PARK
INNOVATION DISTRICT
R+D DISTRICT
THEATER CULTURE + EDUCATION
UAE PAVILION
MOBILITY INSTITUTE
SCIENCE EXPLORATORIUM
MIXED-USE DISTRICT
DISTRICT PARK
MIXED-USE DISTRICT
R+D DISTRICT
R+D DISTRICT
TESTBED + DEVELOPMENT DISTRICT
TESTBED + DEVELOPMENT DISTRICT

CREDITS

THANK YOU

Adrian Smith + Gordon Gill Architecture would like to thank His Highness Sheikh Khalifa bin Zayed Al Nahyan for sharing this unparalleled Expo 2020 with the world. Thank you to His Highness Sheikh Mohammed bin Rashid Al Maktoum for his vision and leadership of Dubai. A special thank you to Her Excellency Reem Al Hashimi for her commitment and vision of Expo 2020 and it's legacy plan. Lastly, a sincere appreciation to all who participated in making Expo 2020 one of the world's greatest events. May this legacy continue for generations to come.

Gordon Gill   Robert Forest   Adrian Smith

AL WASL PLAZA PROJECT CONTRIBUTORS

Adrian Smith + Gordon Gill Architecture

Design Partners:	Gordon Gill, Adrian Smith
Management Partner:	Robert Forest
Design Director:	Alejandro Stochetti
Technical Director:	Peter Weismantle
Sustainability Director:	Dr. Chris Drew
Urban Planning Director:	Richard Wilson
Al Wasl Plaza + Arrivals Plaza:	Allison Conley
Trellis:	Timothy Winstanley
Office:	Patrick Keeney
Hotel:	Michelle Swanson
Leadership:	Alyson Sternquist

Project Team

Narjes Abbasabadi, Tyler Austin, Alexander Bahr, Gregory Barber, Sara Beardsley, Nicholas Berchtold, Aaron Berman, Frederik Berte, Marc Cerone, Jennifer Cooper, Rebecca Cryder, Stephen Dinnen, Tobias Dold, Matthew Dumich, Kiel Fahnstrom, Kyle Faulkner, Sobieslaw Fedyk, Katrina Fernandez Nova, Gail Goldstead, Felix Griggs, Victoriano Hernandez, Theodore Hogan, Brian Jack, Lizhi Jiang, Joel Kerner, Changhoon Kim, Sunghak Ko, Ryan Kukuraitis, Inyong Lee, Soeun Lee, Yifei Li, Miaoqi Liu, Yuchen Liu, Yue Liu, Alvaro Luna, Melissa Marrero, Jose Marti, Cory Mollet, Dilip Muralidharan, Christian Newman, Loran Newman, Sae Hwang Oh, Hazem Owais, Luis Palacio, Jongpil Park, Griffin Pemberton, Jessica Pfeiffer, Natalia Quintanilla, Daniel Ramos, Mario Romero, Michael Sandrzyk, Thomas Schneider, Jeff Snodgrass, Donald Stark, Maria Sturchio, Jennie Tolfa, Eric Tomich, Pablo Velazquez, Ning Wang, Amber Watkins, Xi Yi, Yuxin Zheng, Ruoqi Zhong

Consultant Team

Architect of Record:	e.construct LLC/The Fraser Nag Partnership
Structural Engineering:	Thornton Tomasetti
Microclimate:	Klimaat
Civil Engineering:	Langan International
Landscape:	SWA Group
Immersive Experience:	Obscura Digital (MSG)
Lighting:	Office for Visual Interaction (OVI)
Water Features:	Crystal Fountains
Cost Consulting:	Rider Levett Bucknall
Wind Simulation:	RWDI
MEP Engineering:	Hoare Lea
Vertical Transportation:	FS2
Façade Access:	Altitude
Fire Life Safety:	Jensen Hughes Associates
Crowd Modeling:	Mobility in Chain (MIC)
Wayfinding/Signage:	Forcade
Wayfinding/Signage:	Space Agency
Acoustics/AV:	Threshold
Security and ICT:	Mediatech
Waste Management:	Tricon
General Contractor:	Laing O'Rourke
Steel Manufacturer:	Cimolai
Projection Pod Manufacturer:	Kinetica
AV Integrator:	Creative Technology
Projector Manufacturer:	Christie
Fabric Mesh Manufacturer	Taiyo

PHOTO CREDITS

Images © Adrian Smith + Gordon Gill Architecture pages 19, 20, 21, 22, 23, 24, 25, 26, 27, 28, 29, 31, 32, 33, 34, 35, 36–37, 40–41, 43, 44, 45, 46–47, 48–49, 51, 52–53, 54–55, 56, 57, 58–59, 60, 61, 62, 63, 64–65, 66, 67, 68–69, 71, 72, 73, 74, 75, 76, 77, 78, 79, 80, 81, 82–83, 85, 86, 87, 90–91, 94–95, 97, 98, 99, 100, 101, 102, 103, 104, 107, 108, 111, 112, 113, 115, 116, 117, 118, 120, 121, 122, 123, 124, 125, 129, 131, 132–133, 136–137, 138, 139, 140, 149, 150, 151, 154, 155, 157, 158, 160–161, 164–165, 167, 168, 170, 171, 174, 175, 176, 177, 178–179, 180, 181, 182, 183, 184, 185, 186, 187, 188, 189, 190–191, 193–194, 197, 198, 199, 200, 201, 202, 203, 204, 205, 206, 207, 208–209, 210, 211, 212, 213, 214, 215, 220–221, 223, 224, 225, 226, 227, 228, 229, 230, 231, 236–237, 239, 240–241, 242, 243, 244, 245, 246, 249, 251, 252–253, 258–259, 265, 277, 279, 280–281, 284, 285

Images © Expo 2020 Dubai LLC pages 6–7, 8, 10–11, 15, 32, 105, 106, 119, 127, 135, 142–143, 145, 146, 147, 148, 153, 169, 172–173, 216–217, 247, 256–257, 260, 261, 263, 266, 267, 269, 270, 271, 289

Images © Bureau International des Expositions (BIE) pages 14, 15

Images © SWA Group pages 88, 89

Images © Mobility in Chain (MIC) page 248

Image © Sandeep Revadigar page 253

BOOK CREDITS

Adrian Smith + Gordon Gill Architecture would like to thank His Highness Sheikh Khalifa bin Zayed Al Nahyan for sharing this unparalleled Expo 2020 with the world. Thank you to His Highness Sheikh Mohammed bin Rashid Al Maktoum for his vision and leadership of Dubai. A special thank you to Her Excellency Reem Al Hashimi for her commitment and vision of Expo 2020 and it's legacy plan. Lastly, a sincere appreciation to all who participated in making Expo 2020 one of the world's greatest events. May this legacy continue for generations to come.